MICROPROGRAMMING PRIMER

McGRAW-HILL
COMPUTER SCIENCE SERIES

RICHARD W. HAMMING
Bell Telephone Laboratories

EDWARD A. FEIGENBAUM
Stanford University

BELL and NEWELL Computer Structures: Readings and Examples
COLE Introduction to Computing
DONOVAN Systems Programming
GEAR Computer Organization and Programming
GIVONE Introduction to Switching Circuit Theory
GOODMAN and HEDETNIEMI Introduction to the Design and Analysis of Algorithms
HAMMING Computers and Society
HAMMING Introduction to Applied Numerical Analysis
HELLERMAN Digital Computer System Principles
HELLERMAN and CONROY Computer System Performance
KAIN Automata Theory: Machines and Languages
KATZAN Microprogramming Primer
KOHAVI Switching and Finite Automata Theory
LIU Elements of Discrete Mathematics
LIU Introduction to Combinatorial Mathematics
MADNICK and DONOVAN Operating Systems
MANNA Mathematical Theory of Computation
NEWMAN and SPROULL Principles of Interactive Computer Graphics
NILSSON Artificial Intelligence
RALSTON Introduction to Programming and Computer Science
ROSEN Programming Systems and Languages
SALTON Automatic Information Organization and Retrieval
STONE Introduction to Computer Organization and Data Structures
STONE and SIEWIOREK Introduction to Computer Organization and Data Structures: PDP-11 Edition
TONGE and FELDMAN Computing: An Introduction to Procedures and Procedure-Followers
TREMBLAY and MANOHAR Discrete Mathematical Structures with Applications to Computer Science
TREMBLAY and SORENSON An Introduction to Data Structures with Applications
TUCKER Programming Languages
WATSON Timesharing System Design Concepts
WEGNER Programming Languages, Information Structures, and Machine Organization
WIEDERHOLD Database Design
WINSTON The Psychology of Computer Vision

MICROPROGRAMMING PRIMER

Harry Katzan, Jr.
Chairman, Department of Computer Science
Pratt Institute

McGRAW-HILL BOOK COMPANY
New York St. Louis San Francisco Auckland Bogotá
Düsseldorf Johannesburg London Madrid Mexico Montreal
New Delhi Panama Paris São Paulo Singapore Sydney
Tokyo Toronto

MICROPROGRAMMING PRIMER

2 3 4 5 6 7 8 9 0 DODO 7 8 3 2 1 0 9 8 7

This book was set in Times Roman by Progressive Typographers. The editors were Peter D. Nalle and Annette Hall; the production supervisor was Dennis J. Conroy. The drawings were done by Fine Line Illustrations, Inc.
R. R. Donnelley & Sons Company was printer and binder.

Library of Congress Cataloging in Publication Data

Katzan, Harry.
Microprogramming primer.

(McGraw-Hill computer science series)
Bibliography: p.
Includes index.
1. Microprogramming. I. Title.
QA76.6.K367 001.6′42 76-25002
ISBN 0-07-033387-4

Contents

Preface

The objective of this book is to present an introduction to microprogramming and emulation, and to clarify the complex relationships among programs, computers, and modern methods of implementation. It is assumed that the basic notions of computers, of programming languages, of operating systems and language processors, and of programming are known to most readers either through an introductory computer science course or through practical experience. Also, most readers would benefit from a second computer science course on computer organization, although the latter is not an explicit requirement.

The book is designed to provide the reader with three kinds of knowledge: (1) an introduction to microprogramming concepts, (2) actual experience in writing microprograms, and (3) principles of emulation. The subject matter is presented through introductory textual material, through actual examples, and through translator and simulator systems that allow the student to write microprograms and to execute them on any computer system with FORTRAN language facilities.

The book is organized so that topics necessary for writing microprograms are presented in an orderly fashion, using good academic judgment and actual experience with the subject matter. The reader is presented first with microprogramming concepts and the relationship of those concepts to the organization of modern computer systems. Next, the concept of emulation, a microprogramming language, and a microprogrammable computer are presented so that the student possesses the tools for writing microprograms. Finally, the principles of emulation are stated so that the student can apply the concepts to design and development of practical systems.

The book utilizes a translator and simulator program written in standard FORTRAN IV. The programs can be implemented on any computer system with FORTRAN IV facilities in less than one day—by actual experience. The programs are contained in an Instructor's Manual that is available from McGraw-Hill.

It is a pleasure to acknowledge the contribution of E. W. Reigel, who introduced us to the D-machine, and the administrative support of J. T. Lynch—both of the Burroughs Corporation; the diligent effort on the translator and simulator by Sheldon Orloff and Myron Sagall, graduate assistants at Pratt Institute; the excellent cooperation and technical support of Hall Robins and P. S. Young III of Calldata Systems; and the assistance of my wife, Margaret, who helped throughout the entire project.

Harry Katzan, Jr.

Chapter 1

Introduction to Microprogramming Concepts

1.1 MODERN IMPLEMENTATION TECHNIQUES

Modern society is currently experiencing the electronics revolution, which affects practically all aspects of the computational, informational, and communication sciences, as well as many other areas of everyday life. Thus, for example, we have powerful hand calculators, sophisticated radio, television, and recording devices, surveillance and monitoring equipment, and a wide variety of communication and control devices. Electronic equipment is used in most areas of business, education, and government.

1.1.1 The Black Box Concept

As with many other devices or commodities, such as the automobile, one does not have to be knowledgeable in electronics to effectively utilize an electronic device, and this fact has led to the "black box" concept, in which the major concern is over the inputs, outputs, and functions performed by a system. Figuratively speaking, the components within the black box are beyond the reach of the system's designer, implementor, or analyst employing the black box concept.

1.1.2 Traditional Computer Design and Development

Computers are frequently regarded as black boxes by the people who use them. The reason is simple: Most computer users are not computer engineers or computer scientists, and they normally specialize in other areas. As a matter of fact, one of the most important factors contributing to the widespread use of computers is the fact that a person does not have to be an electronics expert to utilize a computer effectively.

As a result of the black box concept, a computer is normally described through its instruction set, its instruction and data formats, its data flow characteristics, and the overall system configuration. The traditional view of computers is that the architecture of the computer is established when the components of the computer are assembled. Most, if not all, first- and second-generation computers were synthesized in this fashion, and most modern micro-, mini-, and ultra-high-speed computers are also. To sum up, the functional structure of the computer is determined by hardware components that are connected when the computer is assembled, and these functions cannot be changed except through hardware modifications.

1.1.3 Modern Computer Design and Development

In the design of modern small-, medium-, and large-scale computers, more flexibility is needed than is ordinarily available with hard-wired hardware components. From both the computer manufacturer's and the computer user's point of view, it is economically and technically desirable to have families of computers with the same architecture to provide growth potential without reprogramming for a user installation. When it is necessary to change computer systems, it is desirable to have facilities that permit old programs to be run on new machines. This flexibility is achieved through microprogramming.

Thus, the major benefits of microprogramming are that it permits more than one model of computer per instruction set and more than one instruction set per computer. An example of the former benefit is the System 360/370 family of computers. An example of the latter benefit is the compatibility feature available on many modern computers. The benefits of microprogramming are expanded upon later in this chapter.

1.2 THE CONCEPT OF MICROPROGRAMMING

The processing unit of a computer system can be viewed as being composed of two kinds of circuits: data flow circuits and control circuits. Data flow circuits include the wires and storage elements through which flow the electrical pulses that represent data. Data are transformed as they pass through arithmetic and logical components. Control circuits interpret computer instructions and establish appropriate data paths among the network of data flow circuits.

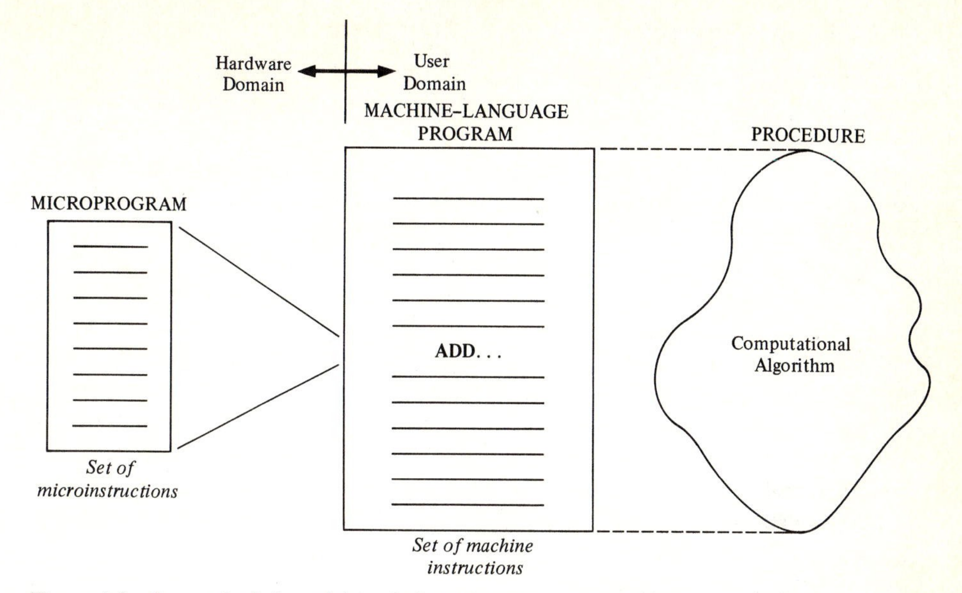

Figure 1.1 Conceptual view of the relationship between machine-language instructions and microinstructions.

1.2.1 Microprogram Control

The control circuits in the processing unit operate as a series of discrete steps, much like the instructions in an ordinary computer program. The process of programming the control unit of a computer system is termed *microprogramming*. There is an analogy between machine-language programming[1] and microprogramming and, accordingly, between a machine-language program and a microprogram. The relationship is depicted conceptually in Figure 1.1. A computational algorithm is represented as a source program in a procedure-oriented language or in assembler language, and that source program is translated into machine-language instructions by an assembler or a compiler. The execution of the machine instructions comprising the program is accomplished through a microprogram that performs the computational function specified by the instruction.

However, there is a limit to the analogy since a set of microinstructions does not exist for each instruction. In the translation of a statement in a procedure-oriented language to a set of machine instructions, instructions are generated on a statement-by-statement basis. At the microprogram level, the microprogram interpretively executes the machine instructions by decoding each instruction and then performing that function dynamically. Thus, a microprogram is similar in operation to a language interpreter.

[1] The terms *assembler language programming* and *machine-language programming* are frequently used interchangeably. Both terms relate to machine-level programs, so that assembler language is a symbolic form of machine language.

1.2.2 Microprogram Storage

During execution of a microprogram, it is held in a high-speed storage unit known as *control storage,* which usually exists in two forms: read-only and writable. Read-only storage, frequently referred to as ROS, is fixed for a given computer and cannot be modified under microprogram control. Changing the contents of read-only storage is tantamount to changing the computer, except that read-only storage is considerably easier to change than hard-wire components. The contents of writable control storage, known as WCS, are also fixed for a given computer, but can be modified under microprogram control. Thus, with writable control storage, the functional structure of a computer can be changed on a dynamic basis. Computers that operate under microprogram control frequently use a combination of read-only and writable control storage.

Normally, microprograms for a given computer system are established by the computer manufacturer, and they cannot be changed by the user. When writable control storage is designed into the computer system, it is used to enhance the functional capability of the system by allowing alternate modes of operation. The manufacturer-supplied microprograms give the computer its external appearance—through instruction and data formats and through the instruction set—from the user's viewpoint, and it is not considered to be a sound practice to allow users to actually modify the microprogram of a computer system that is used for general applications.

Computers in the marketplace that can be microprogrammed by users tend to be mini- or microcomputers that are microprogrammed for special applications or for educational purposes.

1.2.3 Basic Hardware Functions

A microprogrammable computer is synthesized from basic hardware components, such as switches, adders, registers, and control circuits. The purpose of a microprogram is to utilize these basic components to emulate conventional machine instructions. As a result, a typical microprogram would perform the following kinds of functions:

1 Clearing the adders
2 Moving the contents of the adders to the accumulator
3 Moving a word of data from a buffer register to the accumulator
4 Increasing the current-address register by a fixed value—usually 1

Each instruction performed by the computer requires a microprogram composed of microinstructions, such as those given above, to perform the required machine operation. For example, an *add* instruction would require microinstructions for performing the following steps:

1 Fetching the instruction (that is, the add instruction) from main storage
2 Decoding the instruction

3 Computing an effective address
4 Fetching the operands
5 Performing the add operation
6 Placing the result in the accumulator

Normally, a common microprogram routine is used for instruction fetching and effective-address generation, and a separate routine is used for each different computer operation.

1.2.4 Brief History of Microprogramming

Professor M. V. Wilkes of the Cambridge University Mathematical Laboratory recognized in the early 1950s that the control circuits of a computer system operate as a series of discrete steps, much like an ordinary computer program; and Wilkes proposed a concept, *microprogramming,* whereby the control unit of a computer could be programmed to use the other components in the system in a prescribed fashion. The concept was indeed revolutionary but not practical on a large-scale basis until the mid-1960s when read-only storage (ROS) became available for widespread use. Originally, the utilization of a microprogram only involved placing the microprogram in a form of ROS for use by the control unit of the computer. A loaded ROS, usually provided by the computer manufacturer, is not accessible to a computer program and is usually fixed for a given ROS unit. The subsequent development of *writable control storage* permitted a microprogram to be loaded from the computer console or from main storage by using a computer instruction.

In the traditional sense, a microprogram is neither hardware not software. The late Ascher Opler proposed the following:

> To better understand the nature of microprogramming . . . I believe it worthwhile to introduce a new word into our vocabulary: *firmware.* I use this term to designate microprograms resident in the computer's control memory, which specializes the logical design for a special purpose, e.g., the emulator of another computer. I project a tremendous expansion of firmware—obviously at the expense of hardware but also at the expense of software.[1]

The relationship between hardware, software, and firmware is further characterized by Opler in a quote from the same paper:

> Take floating-point addition as an example. In the first generation, it was performed with a normally-programmed subroutine. In the second generation, it was implemented in circuitry. In third-generation microprogrammed computers, the floating-point addition is performed using a microprogram stored in read-only memory.[2]

[1] A. Opler, "Fourth-Generation Software," *Datamation,* January 1967, p. 22.
[2] Ibid.

1.3 INTRODUCTORY EXAMPLE OF A MICROPROGRAMMED SYSTEM

Microprogramming is a complex process that requires knowledge of software programming and basic hardware functions. A hypothetical computer and sample microprogrammed operations are presented as a general introduction to the nature of microprogramming.

1.3.1 Hypothetical Machine

A hypothetical microprogrammed processing unit is given in Figure 1.2. It represents a one-address computer with one accumulator used for arithmetic operations. The functional components shown in Figure 1.2 are described as follows:

Instruction address register (IAR) holds address of the next instruction to be executed.

Storage address register (SAR) holds a storage address for use by main storage read or write functions.

Incrementor (I) used to increment the IAR by 1.

Adder performs addition.

Instruction register (IR) holds instruction during decoding.

Accumulator (AC) holds results during computation.

Storage buffer register (SBR) holds data during main storage read or write function.

Main storage (MS) main storage unit organized on a word basis.

Control (C) causes a microprogram branch to a specified microroutine.

The control, incrementor, and adder components perform special functions.

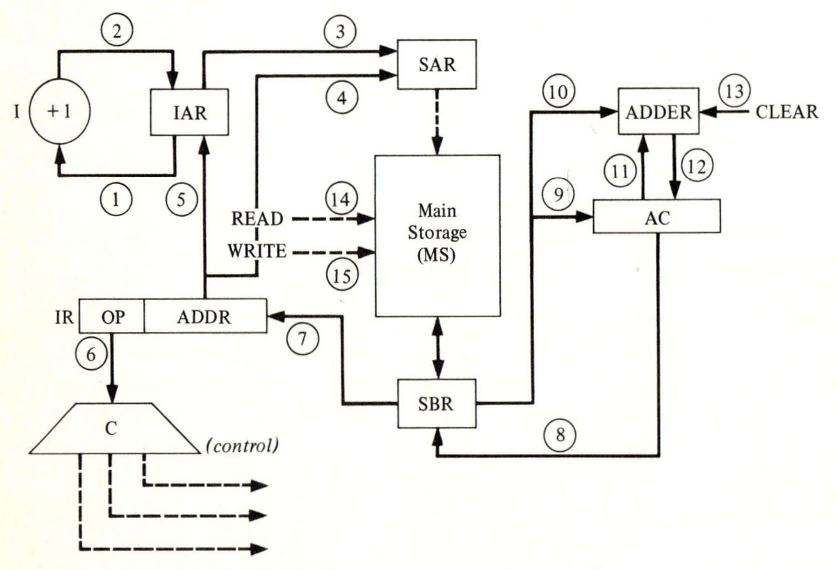

Figure 1.2 Hypothetical microprogrammed processing unit.

The *control* component causes a microprogram branch to an appropriate microroutine, when it is supplied with an operation code or a microprogram address. The implementation of the control component involves a transfer table held in control storage, or it is hard-wired into the circuitry of the computer. The movement of information from a component in the processing unit to either the incrementor or the adder causes the respective function to be executed. Thus, for example, the function AC→ADDER, which is described in the next section, causes the contents of the accumulator to be added to the adder component.

Thus, microprogramming essentially involves the specification of microinstructions that cause movement of data from one component to another.

1.3.2 Microprogram Functions

A *microprogram function* is a microprogram operation performed by the execution of a microinstruction. Sixteen microprogram functions are defined here that correspond by number to the data flow arrows in Figure 1.2:

(1) IAR→I
(2) I→IAR
(3) IAR→SAR
(4) IR(*addr*)→SAR
(5) IR(*addr*)→IAR
(6) IR(*op*)→C
(7) SBR→IR
(8) AC→SBR
(9) SBR→AC
(10) SBR→ADDER
(11) AC→ADDER
(12) ADDER→AC
(13) 0→ADDER
(14) Read[MS(SAR→SBR]
(15) Write[SBR→MS(SAR)]
(16) (Unconditional branch)→C

For example, the function IAR→SAR specifies a movement of data from the instruction address register (IAR) to the storage address register (SAR). Similarly, the function IR(*addr*)→SAR specifies a movement of the contents of the address field of the instruction register to the storage address register.

The *read* and *write* functions use the storage address register (SAR) and the storage buffer register (SBR). The read function causes the contents of the main storage location specified by the address in the SAR to be moved to the SBR. The write function causes the contents of the SBR to be placed in the main storage location specified by the address in the SAR.

1.3.3 Machine Operations

Each machine operation in an object computer must be implemented through microprogramming since the microprogram functions do not, in general, lend themselves to the representation of algorithmic processes and do not correspond to typical machine instructions. The microprogrammed implementation of four machine operations is given to demonstrate the manner in which the hypothetical computer can be microprogrammed.

1.3.3.1 Instruction Fetch The instruction fetch microroutine retrieves an instruction from main storage, moves it to the instruction register, increments the instruction address register, and sends the operation code to the control components, which branches to the appropriate microroutine to execute the operation specified by the operation code. An appropriate microroutine for FETCH is given as follows:

```
FETCH   IAR→SAR
        Read[MS(SAR)→SBR]
        SBR→IR
        IAR→I
        I→IAR
        IR(op)→C
```

1.3.3.2 Load Instruction The load microroutine causes the contents of the main storage location specified in the instruction address field to be moved to the storage buffer register and then to the accumulator. Control then is passed to the control component to execute the next instruction. An appropriate microroutine for LOAD is given as follows:

```
LOAD    IR(addr)→SAR
        Read[MS(SAR)→SBR]
        SBR→AC
        (FETCH)→C
```

1.3.3.3 Add Instruction The add microroutine clears the adder, adds first the contents of the accumulator and then the contents of the main storage location (specified by the address field of the instruction) to it, moves the result to the accumulator, and passes control to the control component. An appropriate microroutine for ADD is given as follows:

```
ADD     IR(addr)→SAR
        Read[MS(SAR)→SBR]
        0→ADDER
        AC→ADDER
        SBR→ADDER
        ADDER→AC
        (FETCH)→C
```

1.3.3.4 Store Instruction The store microroutine places the contents of the accumulator into the main storage location specified by the address field of the instruction. An appropriate microroutine for STORE is given as follows:

```
STORE    IR(addr)→SAR
         AC→SBR
         Write[SBR→MS(SAR)]
         (FETCH)→C
```

1.3.4 Final Remark

It should be noted that the examples of microroutines given above are overly simplified, as is the hypothetical computer. Nevertheless, it is possible to grasp the concept of microprogramming: Every computer instruction is "broken down" into primitive microfunctions, such as those given above, and the level of detail is one step lower than conventional machine language.

1.4 APPLICATIONS OF MICROPROGRAMMING

The applications of microprogramming fall into three general categories: (1) design and implementation of general-purpose computers; (2) development of control devices, and (3) special-purpose computer applications. Most applications involve similar concepts—as far as microprogramming is concerned—but the end result differs markedly.

1.4.1 General-Purpose Computers

A computer system that employs the microprogramming concept would necessarily include the following:

1 Microprogrammed processing unit
2 Main storage unit
3 Control storage
4 Set of microroutines
5 Peripheral devices

The microprogram plus the other components establishes the architecture of the computer.

1.4.1.1 Microprogrammed Implementation The key to microprogrammed implementation is that all computers are interpreters. What this means is that the processing unit is designed to interpret the operation specified by a machine instruction and then to execute that operation using the given operands. The major benefits of this concept are twofold:

1 More than one model of computer per instruction set
2 More than one instruction set per computer

In the first case, it is feasible to develop a series of computers, differing in computing power, but with the same instruction set, so that the instruction set is independent of the engineering design of the computer. Thus, the user is provided a growth path without reprogramming, and programs may be exchanged among a range of models. An example of more than one computer per instruction set is the System/370 family of computers. There are nine models in the System/370 family, and each model represents a distinct design. However, there is no hard-wired System/370 computer. All that exists is a definition of the System/370 architecture, and each of the nine models is microprogrammed to operate as a System/370.

1.4.1.2 Emulation The second benefit of microprogramming is that it facilitates conversion by allowing programs from earlier computers to be run on a new computer[1] without modification. The process, termed *emulation,* requires a set of microroutines to perform the instructions of the emulated computer.

1.4.1.3 Instruction Simulation The efficiency of emulation is dependent upon the relative compatibility of the foreign and host computers. When the two computers are relatively incompatible, the microcode frequently requires the use of software subroutines to implement functions that are impossible or inefficient in microcode. In other words, microprogramming is used as much as possible, and for operations that cannot be emulated, instruction simulation by software is used.

1.4.1.4 Compatibility and Integrated Emulation A *compatibility* feature is the capability of running the programs of a foreign computer on a host computer; it is frequently achieved through microprogramming and special hardware features.

When control storage is exclusively read-only, compatibility is an all-or-none proposition. The transfer between the normal mode and the compatibility mode is achieved by suspending the operation of the computer and setting a switch. Thus, the computer can run in either mode, but manual intervention is required to change the mode.

When control storage is completely or partly writable—that is, writable control storage (WCS)—then the mode can be changed dynamically through a computer instruction without operator intervention. This capability is termed *integrated emulation,* and it permits normal-mode jobs and compatibility-mode jobs to be mixed in the input job stream. The user indicates, either explicitly or implicitly, the desired mode with control cards, and the operating system reads the appropriate microprogram into writable control storage.

1.4.1.5 Variable Micrologic It is a known fact that programs from a given programming language operate more efficiently on a particular computer than

[1] The computer on which a program is run is accurately labeled a *host computer*.

programs from another language, due to the machine-language structure. Thus, a computer that runs FORTRAN programs efficiently may not run COBOL programs efficiently. An alternative in this case is to develop an efficient machine language for each programming language, and to have the language compilers translate source programs into the respective machine language. When an object program is loaded into main storage for execution, the operating system reads the microprogram developed to interpret that machine language into writable control storage. The technique is known as *variable micrologic,* and it provides relatively efficient execution over a range of programming language.

1.4.2 Control Devices

Several devices in a computer system essentially function as small hard-wired computers. Typical examples are the data channel and the device control unit. More specifically, a device of this type is a special-purpose processing unit with a limited amount of register storage and without main storage. In modern computer systems, control devices are frequently implemented as small processing units microprogrammed to operate as a control device. This technique permits a great deal of flexibility in the design and development of control devices.

1.4.3 Special-Purpose Applications

In many technological systems, minicomputers are used to control a physical process, to monitor the operation of a device, and to collect experimental or laboratory data. In most applications of this type, programming is done in machine language, and the programs are complicated because machine-language instructions are not functionally related to the processes involved. A recently developed technique with applications of this type is to use microprocessors that are microprogrammed to perform a limited set of functions—precisely those required by the application. The practice of using microprogramming in this way is less expensive as far as the computer equipment is concerned and provides a more operationally efficient system design.

VOCABULARY

The reader should be familiar with the following terms in the context in which they were used in the chapter:

Black box concept
Control circuits
Data flow circuits
Microprogramming
Control storage
Machine language
Microprogram
Read-only storage (ROS)
Writable control storage (WCS)
Firmware
Microprogram function
Interpreter
Microprogrammed implementation
Family of computers
Emulation
Instruction simulation
Host computer
Compatibility feature
Integrated emulation
Variable micrologic

QUESTION SET

The following questions are intended to test your comprehension of the subject matter. All questions can be answered from the text directly or possibly through a logical extension of the subjects presented. Some questions would be suitable for discussion sessions.

1 Attempt to name a half-dozen or so devices from everyday life that are customarily regarded as black boxes.
2 In light of the fact that with modern microminiaturized circuitry complete processors can be placed on a single chip, does the concept of microprogramming seem to make sense at all?
3 In what way is microprogramming similar to machine-language programming?
4 In the traditional view of computers, is control storage part of the processing unit or part of the main storage unit? A good way to start answering this question is to consider the manner in which control storage and main storage are implemented in modern computers. Afterward, you may want to consider some modern computers as a model. (Your professor can help with this question.)
5 In what way is a microprogram similar to a language interpreter?
6 "Changing the contents of read-only storage is tantamount to changing the computer." How can this be?
7 Suppose that a computer installation had a general-purpose computer, such as the System/370, but ran only FORTRAN programs for numerical applications. Do you think it would be possible to re-microprogram the system so that the job mix could execute more quickly on the same hardware? (*Hint:* Ask your professor about *tuning*.)
8 Try to rationalize the need for and the use of the term *firmware*.
9 In the hypothetical computer discussed in the chapter, several components and functions have been omitted to make the model easier to understand. Name as many obvious omissions as you can.
10 Peripheral devices are an important part of a computer system and are used to store data, source programs, and object programs. Is it feasible to think of a peripheral device for microprograms? If so, how would it be used and for what purpose?
11 Is there a similarity in concept between integrated emulation and variable micrologic?
12 In a microprogrammed computer, language translators translate a source program to an object program, and a microprogram interprets the machine language after the object program has been loaded for execution. An interesting question is: Why don't language translators translate directly into microcode? Using ordinary common sense and your knowledge of basic computer fundamentals, give advantages and disadvantages of the proposition.

EXERCISES

1 The branch instruction is implemented in computer circuitry by placing the branch address in the instruction address register and by continuing instruction execution from that address. Write a microroutine to implement the branch instruction using the hypothetical microprogrammed computer given in the chapter.

2 Assume you are going to do a microprogramming project and select one of the following topics:

a Search a linked list for a given symbol
b Internal sort routine
c Dynamic address translation for a virtual memory system
d Associative memory search
e Pattern matching and replacement in string manipulation
f Square root function

Develop a short flow diagram of the process. Next, write typical machine-language instructions to program the function. Lastly, assuming you are going to design a single machine instruction for the function, develop sample microcode for the instruction and compare the two as far as efficiency is concerned. The basic idea here is to think about microprogramming and what it can do; so do not be overly concerned with accuracy: deal in concepts and orders of magnitude. Your professor can help and may want to add topics to the list.

Chapter 2

Computer Fundamentals

2.1 SYSTEM STRUCTURE

While most readers of this book are familiar with basic computing concepts, the widespread and rapid growth of computers has created a situation in which all readers may not be familiar with precisely the same thing. For example, general notions, such as the fact that the computer can extend our intellectual capability in a manner analogous to the way in which the tool can extend our physical capability, and the fact that a computer is an automaton that must be controlled in all its operations by a computer program, are reasonably well known. On the other hand, the subject of computer organization may have been introduced to the reader from either a hardware or an algorithmic point of view. It is important, therefore, to guarantee "that we are all talking about the same thing," by presenting a brief overview of those aspects of computer organization that pertain to microprogramming.

2.1.1 Computer Organization versus Computer Architecture

The terms *computer organization* and *computer architecture* are frequently used interchangeably and carelessly. The reason is quite obvious: they are rarely defined but often used. Also, there is little need to distinguish between the two in conventional subjects because computer structures are introduced at a topical level and it is convenient to emphasize other topics. However, the fact that computers actually function in the real world means that someone has to "tie down" the basic concepts, so that the machines can be synthesized from hardware components and established through firmware.

Computer organization refers to the physical organization of the components in a computer system, and to the characteristics of those components. Thus, when one deals with computer organization, reference is usually, but not always, made to "large" components, such as processing units, storage units, and devices. In a general sense, the attributes of the components explicitly govern how the system can be organized and implicitly determine the functional constraints on the system. Computer organization tends to reflect physical rather than logical phenomena.

Computer architecture refers to the logical organization of a computer system with an emphasis on internal properties of that system. Thus, an internal entity, such as a general-purpose or index register, may not actually exist. It may be a logical concept for which a word of the main storage unit is used to hold the corresponding data item. Thus, the architecture of a computer may exist as a set of hardware components, which are microprogrammed to have a particular logical structure, or more specifically, as a combination of hardware components and microprogrammed structure. When a computer system is completely hard-wired, computer organization and computer architecture are the same—except for the difference in emphasis.

When the user conceptualizes a computer system, computer architecture is visualized. With the System/370 family of computers, for example, it is possible to refer to and develop programs for a computer with System/370 architecture without regard to the specific engineering model under consideration. Therefore, the organization of a computer system that supports the architecture can be developed with proper consideration to economic and performance factors.

2.1.2 Overview of a Computer System

A *system* is defined as a set of objects with relationships between the objects. The objects are the components of the system, and the relationships connect the components so that they can be regarded as a single entity. In this case, the single entity is the computer system, or, in a more concise form, the computer.

The components in a computer system are (1) the processing unit, (2) the main storage unit, and (3) the input/output subsystem. The relationships enable the components to function collectively and take the form of control signals and data. The structure of a computer system is given in Figure 2.1.

The *processing unit* controls the operation of the computer system and is composed of a control component and an arithmetic/logic component. The *control component* allows the computer to operate automatically by reading an instruction from the main storage unit, by decoding that instruction, and by sending the control signals for having that instruction executed. When the exe-

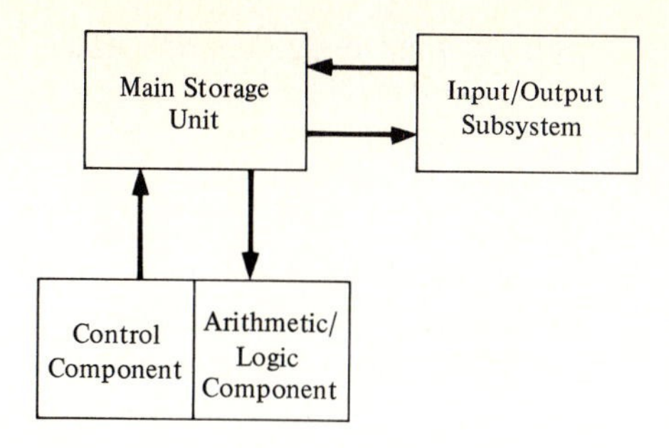

Figure 2.1 Overview of a computer system.

cution of an instruction has been completed, the control component reads the next instruction and the process is repeated. The *arithmetic/logic component* contains the circuitry necessary for performing the arithmetic and logical operations of the computer, as well as those operations that sustain arithmetic and logical operations. The *main storage unit* is a high-speed storage unit that is used to hold programs and data during the operation of the processing unit. In other words, the instructions that comprise an executable program must be read into the main storage unit before they can be executed, and operational data also must be read into the main storage unit before they can be referenced by a program. The main storage unit also is used to hold intermediate values during computation. Clearly, the main storage unit is not used for the long-term storage of either programs or data.

The *input/output subsystem* is composed of devices for data input, data output, remote access, and mass storage of high-volume information, along with associated support equipment. Input and output devices are necessarily related to a type of recording medium, such as punched cards, punched or magnetic tape, printed information, or direct-access storage. Although the input/output subsystem is an important set of components in a computer system, an extensive presentation of the subject is beyond the scope of this primer. It is important to note, however, that many input and output components are in fact microprogrammed. The reader is directed to the Selected Readings at the end of the text for additional information on this subject.

2.1.3 Data Representation

The computer is effectively a symbol processor, which simply means that a symbolic representation of a number, a truth value, an expression or string of characters, or an event is manipulated by the computer, so that an efficient and economical means of internal representation is important. It has been shown that the binary symbols are the most efficient means of recording an amount of information, in terms of the binary symbols required, and binary devices are cost effective and relatively easy to implement.

A single binary device can be in one of two possible states and is capable of representing two symbols. Therefore, several binary devices must be used in combination to represent a larger number of symbols. For example, two binary devices can be used combinatorially to represent four distinct symbols as follows:

Symbol	State of first device	State of second device	
1	0	0	Symbol represented by 00
2	0	1	Symbol represented by 01
3	1	0	Symbol represented by 10
4	1	1	Symbol represented by 11

where, in this case, the binary digit 1 denotes an on condition and the binary digit 0 denotes an off condition. Each single binary digit, that is, either a 0 or a 1, is known as a *bit*. It follows that with n bits, 2^n distinct symbols can be represented.

Because of the relative simplicity of engineering an on/off device, all modern computers use binary representation. Moreover, computers that can be viewed as nonbinary machines at the architectural level are actually binary machines at the hardware (or organization) level.

2.1.4 Words versus Bytes

The main storage is used to hold instructions and data for use by the processing unit, and the means of accessing an item of information is through its address. Thus, the main storage unit is composed of locations (sometimes referred to as *storage cells*), and each of these locations is assigned a numerical address through which the contents of a location can be referenced.

A key question in computer design is, How much information should a location hold? The question can be answered from the viewpoint of computer organization and from the viewpoint of computer architecture.

In the realm of computer organization, that is, the computer hardware, a location can hold from 8 to 60 bits. Micro- or minicomputers frequently have a word size of 8, 16, or 24 bits. This is the case because computers in this class are frequently used for control applications in which high-precision data values are not customarily needed. Small, medium, large, and super computers usually have a word size that ranges from 24 to 60 bits, with the choice of word size being based on performance and cost considerations. The word size is usually fixed for a given computer, so that whenever main storage is referenced, a word's worth of information is accessed. For example, assume a computer has a word size of 32 bits (which is equivalent to 4 bytes for byte-oriented people). If the processing unit needs 64 bits (or 8 bytes), then two storage references are needed to obtain the required information. Similarly, if the processing needs 16 bits (or 2 bytes), then one storage reference of 32 bits is made and the processing unit must select the exact 16 bits that it requires.

In the realm of computer architecture, a storage location can be conceptualized to contain any reasonable number of bits to meet the design objectives of the computer. Two schools of thought exist. In a word-oriented computer, a location contains a large number of bits, such as 36, and is known as a *word*. In a byte-oriented computer, a location contains a relatively small number of bits, such as 8, and is known as *byte*. It follows that in a word-oriented computer, a single word location can hold an instruction, a numeric data item, or several characters of information; in a byte-oriented computer, a single byte location can hold a single character of information, and successive byte locations are used to store instructions or numeric data items.

When microprogramming is employed as an implementation technique, either a word-oriented computer architecture or a byte-oriented computer architecture can be defined over a given computer organization. As a result, microprogrammable computers usually contain a minimal set of operational instructions and registers, but they operate at very high internal speeds. For example, a typical "basic" microprogrammable computer may contain only a fixed-point add instruction, so that the remaining fixed-point arithmetic instructions and all floating-point instructions would be implemented through microprogramming. Because the basic machine operates at very high speeds, however, the time necessary to execute a given instruction would not be greater than with hard-wired components, and implementation costs would be less, taking into consideration large-scale integration techniques and modern methods of fabrication.

2.1.5 Character, Logical, and Numeric Values

In a computer system, information is stored and interpreted according to a convention established when the computer is designed. The precise interpretation of an item of information is also dependent upon how and when it is used during the execution of a program. Four separate interpretations are generally possible for the meaning of an item of information:

1. It is character data.
2. It is a truth (that is, logical) value.
3. It is numeric data.
4. It is an instruction.

Character, truth, and numeric values are covered briefly in this section; instructions are covered in the next section.

2.1.5.1 Character Data The meaning of a character datum is dependent upon a coding structure, wherein each character in a usable alphabet is represented by a string of bits of predetermined length. The established meaning of each set of bits is considered in the design of peripheral devices and in the development of computer software and application programs. Figure 2.2 gives examples of character data stored with 6- and 8-bit codes, for word- and byte-oriented computers, respectively. A representative set of 6- and 8-bit codes can be found in most introductory books on computers or data processing. A coding structure of the kind given here is frequently referred to as *binary coded decimal* (BCD).

2.1.5.2 Logical Data Truth values are usually represented by the presence or absence of 1 or more data bits. Two familiar modes of representation are given as follows:

Word *n*

100100	011001	010011	101001	100110	100111
M	I	C	R	O	P

Word *n*+1

101001	100110	010111	101001	010001	100100
R	O	G	R	A	M

Word *n*+2

100100	011001	100101	010111	110000	110000
M	I	N	G	b̸	b̸

a Six-bit characters in a word-oriented computer.

Byte *n*	Byte *n*+1	Byte *n*+2	Byte *n*+3	Byte *n*+4	Byte *n*+5	Byte *n*+6
11010100	11001001	11000011	11011001	11010110	11010111	11011001
M	I	C	R	O	P	R

Byte *n*+7	Byte *n*+8	Byte *n*+9	Byte *n*+10	Byte *n*+11	Byte *n*+12	Byte *n*+13
11010110	1100111	11011001	11000001	11010100	11010100	11001001
O	G	R	A	M	M	I

Byte *n*+14	Byte *n*+15
11010101	11000111
N	G

b Eight-bit characters in a byte-oriented computer.

Figure 2.2 Six- and eight-bit character representation.

Condition	**One bit representation**	**Byte representation**
True (on)	1	00001101 (at least 1 bit set)
False (off)	0	00000000 (all bits 0)

The concept is extended systematically to computer words, and in general, the representation of logical values is independent of the coding structure of the computer.

2.1.5.3 Numeric Data Numeric data are stored using a positional number system in one of two bases: binary form or a binary coded form. For example, the number 123 to the base 10 is evaluated as

$$1 \times 10^2 + 2 \times 10^1 + 3 \times 10^0$$

In the binary number system, $(123)_{10}$ is equivalent to $(1111011)_2$, which is evaluated as

$$1 \times 2^6 + 1 \times 2^5 + 1 \times 2^4 + 1 \times 2^3 + 0 \times 2^2 + 1 \times 2^1 + 1 \times 2^0$$

Binary is the primary base to which numeric data are stored in computers. The alternate form is binary coded decimal, which exists in two forms: (1) numeric character, or (2) packed decimal. With *numeric character* data, numeric information is stored in BCD form and can be displayed; that is, it can be printed, without output conversion. In most computers, however, numeric character data cannot be used in arithmetic operations without conversion to either binary or packed decimal form. It should be clear by now that a special class of operations, such as arithmetic operations defined on numeric character data, could be implemented through microprogramming if the computer architect had designed that feature into the computer. With *packed decimal* data, each decimal digit is represented by 4 bits. This form is equivalent to numeric character data with the zone bits stripped off. Table 2.1 gives a set of 4-bit codes for the digits 0 through 9, so the decimal number 6,183 would be represented as:

0110	0001	1000	0011

Table 2.1 Four-Bit Packed Decimal Codes

Digit	Code
0	0000
1	0001
2	0010
3	0011
4	0100
5	0101
6	0110
7	0111
8	1000
9	1001

Packed decimal representation is "halfway" between binary and numeric character, figuratively speaking, and arithmetic operations defined on packed decimal operands are frequently implemented through microprogramming.

Another consideration with regard to numeric data concerns the scale of the operands, and generally includes three types:

1 Fixed-point operands
2 Floating point operands
3 Variable-length operands

The operational details of each type are presented later as an instance of microprogrammed implementation. Fixed- and floating-point operations are defined on fixed-length binary operands—usually computer words or registers. The only class of arithmetic operations that generally permit variable-length operands is packed decimal operations that utilize operands held in main storage.

The base to which a numeric operand is stored is independent of whether a byte- or word-oriented computer architecture is used. As mentioned previously, words are synthesized from bytes in byte-oriented computers, and several characters are stored in a single word in word-oriented computers, so that the mode of doing arithmetic is dependent upon the microprogram and in some cases the hard-wired components and not the method of representation.

2.1.6 Computer Instructions

The representation of a computer instruction is conceptually identical to a character, logical, or numeric data item; it exists as a set of binary digits. It is important, therefore, that the processing unit is directed to an actual instruction during the instruction fetch cycle and is directed to the correct type of data item during the operand fetch cycle. (The various types of cycles are covered later.) In general, the utilization of the appropriate information at the appropriate time is an important aspect of programming.

The various fields in a computer instruction reflect the basic architecture of the computer system. If the processing unit, for example, contains multiple accumulators, then a field must exist in the instruction format in order to specify the register that should participate in the execution of the instruction. A hypothetical computer instruction is given in Figure 2.3. The major fields in an instruction are listed as follows:

1 Operation code
2 Operand registers
3 Index registers
4 The address field

The primary function of each of the fields is given in Figure 2.3. However, each of the fields, except perhaps the operation code, can serve an auxiliary function

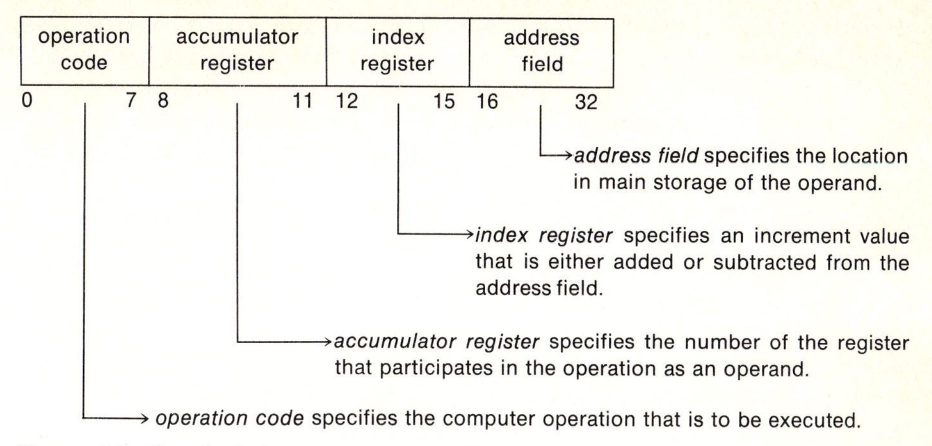

Figure 2.3 Hypothetical computer instruction.

for a particular operation, such as to specify the number of places in a shift operation or the device address in an input/output operation.

The size of each of the fields in an instruction also places practical limitations on the computer architecture. If the operation code field, for example, contains n bits, then 2^n different operation codes are possible. Similarly, if the index register field is 3 bits wide, then one of eight distinct index registers may be specified in an instruction. Of the practical limitations, the size of the address field is probably the most significant, since an address field of k bits permits 2^k storage locations to be addressed. With byte addressing, the addresses run up quickly, so that less physical storage can be referenced than with word addressing. Base registers are used in the architecture of some computers to alleviate this problem. The base register is set to point to a segment of the program, and the address field gives the displacement of the operand from the base address. The manner in which base addressing works is also covered later.

In the study of computer architecture, it is interesting to note the mutual influence of the various concepts. For example, byte-oriented storage usually requires some type of base/displacement addressing, which in turn requires multiple general-purpose accumulator registers, which then requires that a field exists in the instruction to specify the accumulator register that participates in the execution of the instruction. The benefit of microprogrammed implementation is that the design of computer architecture need not be constrained by hardware and that computer architecture can be adjusted more easily during the development of the computer.

2.2 PROCESSING UNIT

The primary objective of the processing unit is to fetch, decode, and execute instructions that reside in the main storage unit. The manner in which this is done varies widely between computers. Some computers, for example, prefetch instructions and operands; other computers contain multiple arithmetic/logic components that can operate in parallel. In most computers, however, instructions are executed sequentially, and instructions and operands are referenced in a normal order. Correspondingly, a straightforward approach is taken here.

2.2.1 Registers

A *register* is a high-speed storage area used by the processing unit during the execution of a program. An example of a register might be an accumulator, index register, general-purpose register, or the current-address register. Some registers, such as a general purpose register, can be explicitly addressed by an executing program. Other registers, such as a current-address register, cannot be explicitly addressed by an executing program and are used by the processing unit to sustain its operation.

Registers used by the control component of the processing unit are not addressed by an executing program; two major registers exist: the instruction register and the current-address register. Registers used by the arithmetic/logic unit can be addressed by an executing program; three major types of registers exist: arithmetic/logic registers, index registers, and addressing registers.

2.2.1.1 Instruction Register The *instruction register* is used by the control component of the processing unit to decode and interpret an instruction. After an instruction is fetched from the main storage unit, it is routed to the instruction register where the operation code, register, and address fields are isolated and used during the execution of the instruction.

2.2.1.2 Current-Address Register The *current-address register* is used by the control component of the processing unit to keep track of the main storage address of the current instruction. When the control component needs to fetch an instruction, it goes to the current-address register to determine its location.

After an instruction is executed by the processing unit, the current-address register is incremented by the length attribute of the current instruction so that the following instruction is executed next. This fact explains, to a limited extent, why instructions are placed sequentially in main storage.

2.2.1.3 Arithmetic/Logic Registers With regard to *arithmetic/logic registers,* one of two philosophies is generally adopted: a single accumulator register or multiple arithmetic registers.

When a single accumulator register is used for arithmetic/logic operations, both fixed- and floating-point operations, in addition to logical operations, are performed in that register. Use of a single accumulator necessitates the frequent storing of intermediate values, as in the following example:

Higher-level language	**Assembler language**
A=(B+C)*(D−E)	LOAD B ADD C STORE TEMP LOAD D SUB E MULT TEMP STORE A

A single accumulator is not realistically sufficient since fixed-point multiplication operations generate a double-length product and fixed-point division operations use a double-length dividend. Therefore, single accumulator systems employ an extension to the accumulator, as follows:

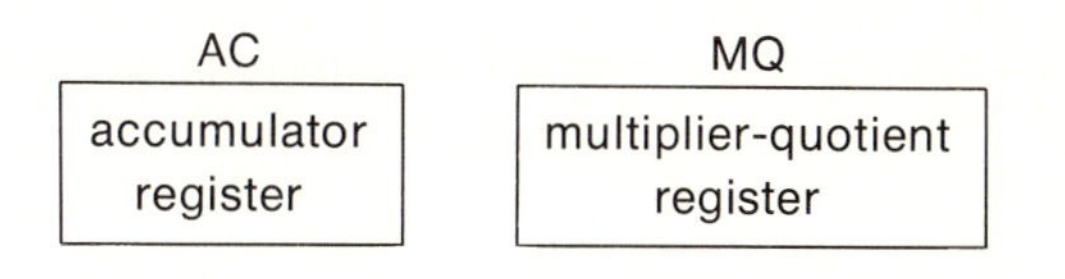

or alternately as:

A-register B-register

In systems with multiple arithmetic registers, a distinction is frequently made between fixed-point registers (or "general-purpose registers" as they are usually called) and floating-point registers. The advantages of the distinction are that general-purpose registers are then free for auxiliary use as index or base registers and that floating-point registers can then have a larger width for added precision. The use of multiple accumulators requires less temporary stores to main storage than with a single accumulator, as demonstrated in the following example:

Higher-level language	**Assembler language**
A=(B+C)*(D−E)	LE 2,B AE 2,C LE 4,D SE 4,E MER 2,4 STE 2,A

The design of accumulators in a general-purpose computer is essentially an engineering tradeoff between cost, efficiency, and flexibility.

2.2.1.4 Index Registers In performing computational operations on array data, it is necessary to effectively modify the address portion of an instruction without actually changing it in the actual instruction. This facility permits the same instruction to be used on different elements of the array.

In higher-level languages, an element of an array is denoted with a subscript, as in X(I). Suppose, for example, that the contents of X(I) were to be loaded into the accumulator—in a one-accumulator computer—and the computer had the following instruction format:

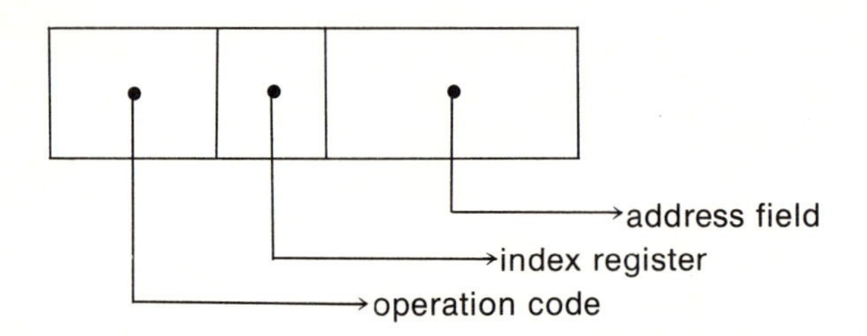

If 1-origin indexing were used with the language and the array were stored consecutively in locations beginning with location 4567, then the following computer instructions would be appropriate:

Assembler language (symbolic operands)	Assembler language (numeric operands)
LDX 3,I	LDX 3,6669
LOAD X − 1,3	LOAD 4566,3

assuming that I were stored at location 6669 and index register 3 contains the subscript. The LDX instruction loads index register 3 with the indexing value, and the LOAD instruction loads the required operand into the accumulator. Indexing is achieved by virtue of the fact that the processing unit computes the address to be loaded by adding the contents of the specified index register and the address field in the instruction, as depicted conceptually in Figure 2.4. In the figure, index register 3 contains the value 4, specifying the fourth element of the array X.

In a computer with multiple accumulators, one or more of the general-purpose registers are normally used for indexing, and separate index registers are not needed.

2.2.1.5 Addressing Registers Registers that are used for addressing normally compensate for a relatively small instruction address field used with byte-oriented computers. One of the general-purpose registers serves as a base register that points to a segment of the program when it is loaded in main storage; the instruction address then serves as a displacement from the base address. The use of an addressing (base) register, which is covered again later, is suggested in Figure 2.5.

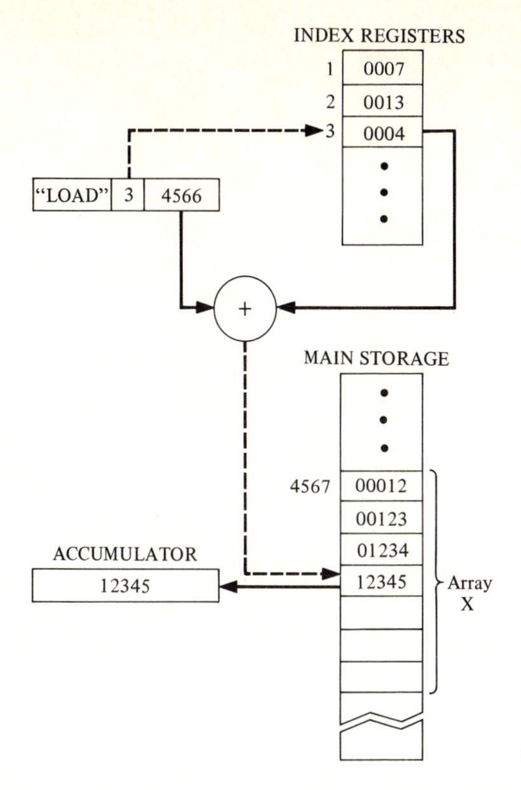

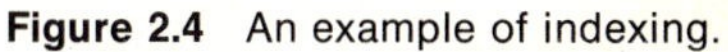
Figure 2.4 An example of indexing.

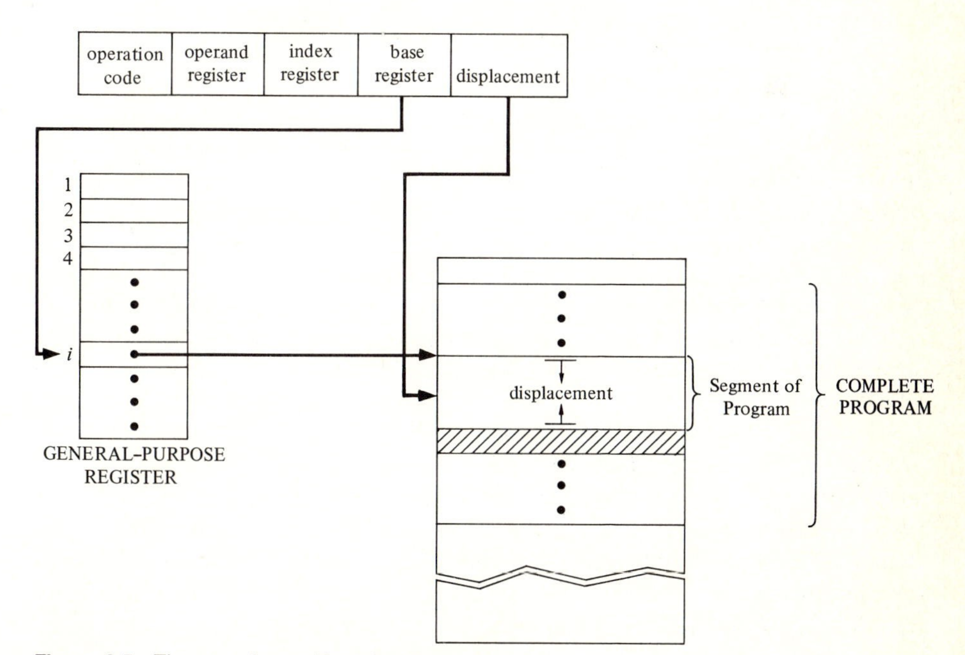

Figure 2.5 The use of an addressing (base) register.

2.2.2 Implementation of Machine Registers

Regardless of whether a computer system is hard-wired or microprogrammed, a design decision must be made about how the registers should be implemented. It should be emphasized that register design relates to computer architecture and not computer organization, so that a register need not necessarily exist as a separate entity in the processing unit.

Three options for the implementation of registers usually exist:

1 Use a unique register that is specifically designed into the processing unit.
2 Use a nonunique register of the processing unit on either a permanent or a temporary basis.
3 Use the main storage unit of the computer system to store the register.

Registers used by the control component of the processing unit, that is, the current-address and instruction registers, are normally implemented in hardware employing either option 1 or 2. Registers used by the arithmetic/logic component of the processing unit, that is, the accumulator, index, and addressing registers, normally use hardware registers on hard-wired computers and either hardware registers or main storage on microprogrammed computers. The main storage unit is used as a place to store registers in order to reduce hardware costs. Use of this technique, however, results in slower operational times.

All microprogrammed processing units include internal registers to sustain normal processing; however, in most cases these registers do not match those of the computer architecture. Therefore, one of the following options must be selected for each register assignment:

1 The computer architecture register is assigned to an internal register of the microprogrammed processing unit; the internal register is used solely for the purpose.
2 The hardware of the microprogrammed processing unit is modified (or designed) to include the needed register of the computer architecture. This is the case of specially developed machine registers.
3 An internal register of the microprogrammed processing unit is used to hold the architecture register on a temporary basis while that architecture register is in use. When the architecture register is not being used, it is held in main storage.

The disadvantage of using the main storage unit to store architecture registers is obvious. Whenever the contents of the register are needed, they must be brought in from the main unit, which takes processing unit time. Similarly, the information must be subsequently stored in the main storage unit, which also takes processing unit time.

Neither of the approaches to the implementation of computer architecture registers is necessarily superior to either of the other options, so that design decisions are made to satisfy economic and performance constraints.

2.2.3 Effective Address

An important aspect of the operational characteristics of the processing unit is the computation of the address used to access an operand from the main storage unit. This address is called the *effective address,* and the concept of an effective address is used with all computers. The significance of the effective-address concept is inherent in the fact that it must be calculated by the processing unit and, in the case of microprogrammed implementation, that it requires microinstructions to perform the calculations.

An effective address is computed by adding the contents of index and/or base registers to the value of the instruction address field to form a main storage address. One example of effective-address calculation was given in Figure 2.4 with relation to indexing. Figure 2.6 demonstrates effective-address generation for a byte-oriented computer with index/base/displacement addressing.

The effective address is computed by the processing unit after the instruction is fetched and decoded by the control component and before the operand(s) is used by the arithmetic/logic component.

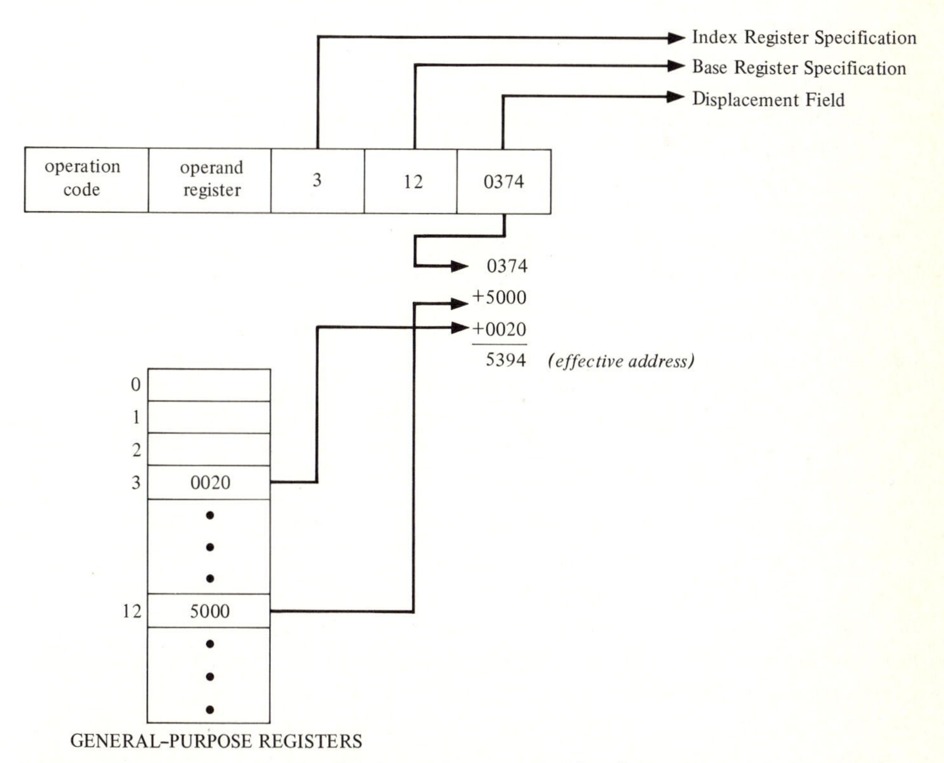

Figure 2.6 An example of effective-address generation in a computer that employs index/base/displacement addressing.

2.2.4 Operation of the Processing Unit

All internal computer operations take place in fixed intervals of time, governed by pulses emitted from an electronic clock as high as 1 billion per second. A fixed number of pulses is termed a *machine cycle*. In a machine cycle, the computer can perform one or more specific microoperations, which are combined with other microoperations for executing a computer instruction. The exact number of microoperations in an instruction is variable and depends on the particular instruction and the attributes of the operands. The processing unit operates in a prescribed sequence to perform the fetch, interpretation, and execution of an instruction. Two major cycles are identified: the instruction cycle and the execution cycle. These major cycles collectively establish the operation of the processing unit.

2.2.4.1 Instruction Cycle The first cycle in instruction processing is the *instruction cycle,* frequently referred to as the "I-cycle." During the I-cycle, the following functions are performed by the control component of the processing unit:

1 The address of the next instruction is obtained from the current-address register.
2 The instruction is fetched from main storage and moved to the instruction register.
3 The operation code field is inspected to determine the internal functions to be performed.
4 Base, index, and/or operand registers are identified.
5 The effective address is computed.
6 The current-address register is incremented by the length attribute of the instruction being processed (that is, by one word or a given number of bytes) so that it points to the next sequential instruction.

The I-cycle is conceptually summarized in Figure 2.7. The numerical value of the operation code is used by a control routine to transfer microprogram control to the appropriate microroutine for executing the instruction currently being processed. The effective address is normally placed in an internal register (frequently called an *address register*) for use by some microroutine as an operand address or as an instruction modifier—such as a shift value or an input/output address.

While different computers vary slightly in this regard, the instruction cycle usually takes a fixed length of time measured in internal machine cycles. This is the case because the same fetch, decode, and effective-address generation routines are used for all instructions during the I-cycle. In fact, the distinction between instructions is not generally recognized or needed by the control component.

2.2.4.2 Execution Cycle The instruction cycle is always followed by an execution cycle (referred to as the "E-cycle") during which time the specified

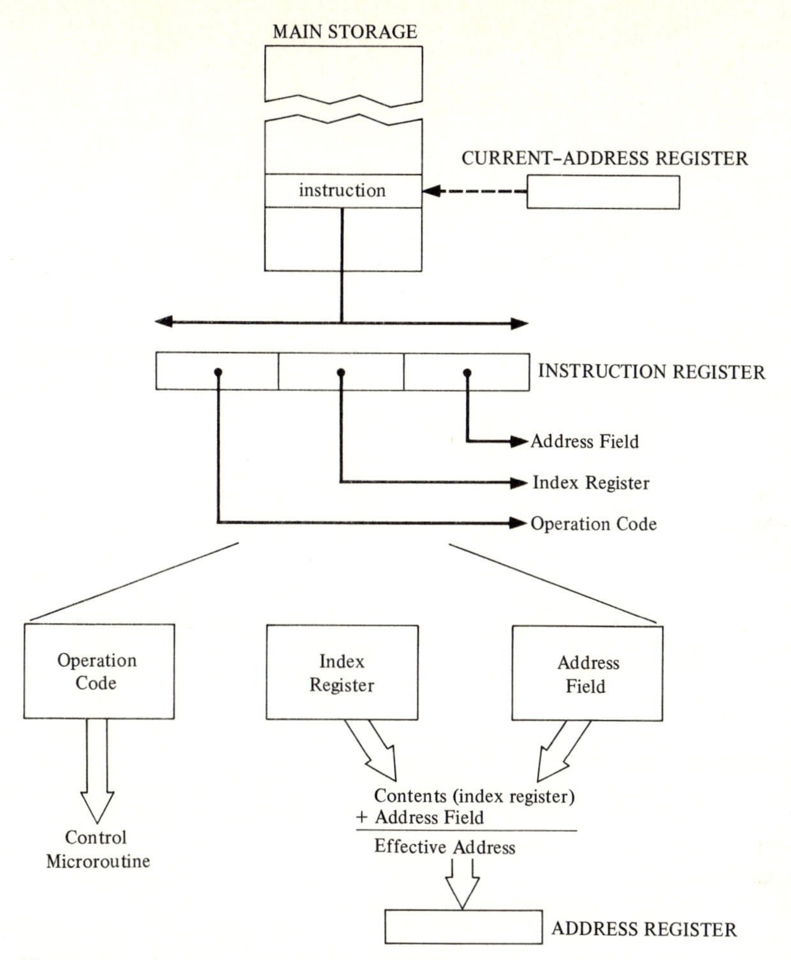

Figure 2.7 Conceptual view of the I-cycle for a computer employing index/address addressing.

operation is executed using internal hardware components. The effective address, as mentioned above, is used in the following ways:

1 As an operand address, for example, a load or add instruction
2 As a store address, for example, a store instruction
3 As the address of the next instruction, for example, a branch instruction
4 As an instruction modifier, for example, the length of a shift operation or the input/output address of an input/output operation

Clearly, operations vary in the characteristics of the computations performed and in the number of machine cycles necessary to perform the computations. Execution times can vary from a few machine cycles for a branch instruction to many machine cycles for a floating-point multiply operation.

The size of E-cycle microroutines also varies considerably, depending upon the operation performed. Microprogramming, in this regard, is very similar to conventional computer programming in the sense that microprograms are frequently structured on a modular basis to conserve the use of control storage. The "time and space" problem normally associated with conventional computer programming also applies to microprogramming.

2.3 RELEVANT NOTATION AND TERMINOLOGY

Because basic machine concepts are cumbersome and inefficient to describe and work with, descriptive notation and relevant terminology are used to facilitate the communication process. The notation and terminology enable us to deal with the underlying concepts in a more precise manner.

2.3.1 Descriptive Notation

In dealing with locations in the main storage unit, we are normally interested in two things:

1. The address of the location
2. The contents of the location

Locations are identified by a numerical address in machine language and by a symbolic address in assembler language, such as in the following sample instructions:

```
LOAD 321
STORE RES
```

We are frequently concerned with the contents of a storage location, identified numerically or symbolically, and those contents are specified by enclosing the address in parentheses. For example, the contents of location 456 are denoted by (456), and the contents of symbolic location MARK are denoted by (MARK). The notation also applies to registers, so that (reg#2) denotes the contents of register 2.

The standard reference is to a computer word on the computer being described. If reference is made to another unit of storage, that reference is denoted by a prescript as covered below.

A portion of a word, such as the address and operation code fields of an instruction or the exponent field of a floating-point number, is denoted by a subscript. Thus, for example, $(\text{IR})_{\text{addr}}$ denotes the address field of the contents of the instruction register. Similarly, $(\text{SAREA})_{0-7}$ denotes bits 0 through 7 of the contents of storage location SAREA, and $(9989)_{12-15}$ denotes bits 12 through 15 of the contents of storage location 9989. Parentheses can be nested to specify multiple levels of addressing. If bits 12 through 15 of the instruction register indicate a base register, then $((\text{IR})_{12-15})$ denotes the contents of that base register.

The expression is interpreted as follows:

1 The computer instruction is denoted by (IR).
2 The base register field is denoted by $(IR)_{12-15}$.
3 The contents of the base register are denoted by $((IR)_{12-15})$.

Arithmetic and logical operations are specified in the usual manner, except that *parentheses may not be used for grouping*. For example, the expression

(MARK) − (reg # 2)

denotes the contents of MARK *minus* the contents of register number 2, whereas the expression

(SAREA) + 4

means the contents of symbolic location SAREA *plus* the value 4. The right arrow (→) indicates replacement, so that

0→(MARK)

means that the value 0 replaces the contents of location MARK. Expressions are executed from left to right, so that

(reg # 3) + 1→(reg # 2)

means "The contents of register number 3 *plus* 1 replace the contents of register number 2." Other examples are given in Table 2.2.

Table 2.2 Examples of Descriptive Notation

Expression	Meaning
KTABLE→(reg#12)	The address of KTABLE replaces the contents of register number 12.
(A)* (B)→(C)	The contents of A *times* the contents of B replaces the contents of C.
(reg#7)+4→(reg#7)	The contents of register number 7 *plus* 4 replace the original contents of register number 7.
(reg#1)+(FACT)→(reg#1)	The contents of register number 1 *plus* the contents of FACT replace the previous contents of register number 1.
(VAL1)→(reg#3)	The contents of VAL1 replace the contents of register number 3.
(reg#3)→(VAL2)	The contents of register number 3 replace the contents of VAL2.

To demonstrate the manner in which descriptive notation can be used to describe machine instructions, consider the following instruction:

ADD 3,INCRE

The intended interpretation is, "Add the contents of symbolic location INCRE to the contents of accumulator register number 3." In descriptive notation the instruction is described as follows:

(reg #3) + (INCRE) → (reg #3)

Similarly, the instructions

LOAD 6,BIG

and

STORE 6,LITTLE

are described symbolically as

(BIG) → (reg #6)

and

(reg #6) → (LITTLE)

respectively.

The use of descriptive notation is a convenient method for presenting the calculation of effective addresses. With index/address addressing, for example, the effective address is computed for each operand in the following manner:

(index) + address = *effective address*

Similarly, the effective-address calculation for base/index/displacement addressing is described symbolically as follows:

(base) + (index) + displacement = *effective address*

The most frequent use of descriptive notation is to describe computer instructions in a precise and convenient form.

2.3.2 Microprogramming Terminology

When one introduces microprogramming concepts, confusion occasionally arises for several related reasons:

1 More than one programming language is involved.
2 More than one type of instruction is available.
3 More than one type of storage is used.

Therefore, it is necessary to know, for example, whether we are talking about main storage or control storage. The following terminology has been adopted in most of the microprogramming literature and is used in the remainder of the primer:

Term	Meaning
H-language	A higher-level language, such as ALGOL, COBOL, FORTRAN, or PL/I
S-language	Machine language as it exists in conventional computers (for example, binary 360/370 machine language, but *not* assembler language)
S-instruction	An individual machine instruction in S-language
S-program	A program composed of S-instructions
S-memory	The main storage unit in which S-instructions are held during execution
M-language	Microprogram machine language, which usually exists in binary form
M-instruction	An individual microinstruction
M-program	A microprogram composed of M-instructions
M-memory	Control storage in which microprograms are held during execution

The terminology is related in the following manner. The programmer writes a program in an H-language, such as FORTRAN or COBOL. It is compiled into an S-program composed of S-instructions and is loaded into S-memory for execution. Each S-instruction is interpreted and executed by the M-instructions of an M-program that resides in M-memory, or in common terminology control storage.

2.4 MAIN STORAGE UNIT

In a microprogrammed computer system, the main storage unit (that is, S-memory) is usually regarded as being outside the processing unit, which is microprogrammed to fetch S-instructions and data as they are needed to sustain operation of the system. When information is needed from the main storage unit, the processing unit must explicitly execute microinstructions (that is, M-instructions) to obtain that information. Similarly, the processing unit must also explicitly execute microinstructions to place information in the main storage unit when necessary for sustained operation of the processing unit or the computer program (that is, the S-program) being executed. The precise manner in which the main storage unit is accessed is dependent upon its operational characteristics.

For our purposes, the main storage unit and S-memory are the same thing. The term *main storage unit* is used whenever possible because it is the more common terminology and is used exclusively with systems that are not microprogrammed.

2.4.1 Access Width

Access width is the amount of information that is passed between the main storage unit and a component external to it with each main storage reference. Here, we are referring to computer organization, and the amount of data referenced is the same for each access. Components that typically access the main storage unit are the processing unit and the input/output subsystem.

One means of conceptualizing access width is to consider the number of information channels (that is, wires) running between the main storage unit and the processing unit. If the number of wires is large, for example, 32 or 64 lines, then bits can be transmitted in parallel so that the time necessary to move a given amount of information (for example, a 64-bit word) is relatively short. The computer operates quickly but costs more. If the number of wires is small, for example, 8 or 16 lines, then the amount of parallelism is reduced so that time necessary to move a given amount of information (for example, a 64-bit word) is relatively long. The computer operates more slowly but costs less. This concept explains to some extent why one computer with a fast machine cycle time effectively operates more slowly than another computer with the same cycle time.

Access width is transparent to the programmer, who utilizes the computer architecture as defined through microprogrammed implementation.

2.4.2 Operation of the Main Storage Unit

Normally, when a load instruction is executed in a program, the operation is viewed as the simple movement of data from a source (usually main storage or a register) to a destination (usually a register). The same thinking applies also to computer instructions that use an operand in the main storage unit and to the store instruction. However, the actual process of interacting with the main storage unit is not quite that simple, as was demonstrated in the introductory information on microprogram control given in Chapter 1.

The hardware operations necessary to access main storage are performed by a storage control unit, which is logically considered to be part of the main storage unit. The process of moving information from the main storage unit to the processing unit or the input/output subsystem operates as follows:

1 The address of the desired word of data is placed in a *storage address register* by the processing unit or the input/output subsystem. (It should be noted here that the desired data may be part of the data accessed or that the data accessed may be part of the data needed. The determination of the scope of needed data is the function of the microprogram.)

2 At this point, the storage control unit takes over, and the *fetch* operation is initiated.

3 The main storage unit is accessed, and the desired data are placed in a *storage buffer register* that can be referenced by either the processing unit or the input/output system.

The process of moving information from either the processing unit or the input/output system to the main storage unit is essentially the reverse of the above process and operates as follows:

1 The address of the data to be stored is placed in a storage address register.
2 The data to be stored are placed in a storage buffer register.
3 The storage control unit takes over, and a *write* operation is initiated to perform the store operation.

During the execution of an S-instruction, the total amount of data to be stored may be greater or less than an access width's worth of information. Moreover, many computers include variable-length S-instructions that effectively move information from one area of main storage to another, and the total length of the move may be considerably greater than an access width. The precise sequence of fetch and storage operations to successfully execute an S-instruction must be managed and controlled by the appropriate microroutine that is held in control storage for use by the microprogrammed processing unit.

2.4.3 Storage Mapping

One of the design problems in microprogrammed implementation is the mapping of S-memory as defined by the computer architecture to the physical main storage unit. The problem does not arise when the architecture uses a word size for instructions and data that are precisely the same size as the access width of the main storage unit. In this case, an S-program fetch or store corresponds exactly to a main storage fetch or store. Similarly, word-oriented computer architecture for which the word size is an integral multiple of the access width also is straightforward. If, for example, the S-memory word size is 32 bits and the main storage word size is 16 bits, then two fetches or stores are required for each S-program fetch or store, respectively. If the word addresses are assigned consecutively in both S-memory and main storage, then the following address mapping could be used:

first half-word: 2 × [S-memory-address] → [main-storage-address]
second half-word: 2 × [S-memory-address] + 1 → [main-storage-address]

It is necessary that the main storage address be computed by the fetch microroutine after the S-memory effective address has been computed. When the S-memory word size is smaller than the access width, then the address mapping involves a determination of the main storage word in which the needed word is contained. If, for example, the S-memory word size is 16 bits and the main storage word size is 48 bits, then the following address mapping, which uses an address mapping of three S-memory words to one main storage word, would be used:

S-memory word: FLOOR([S-memory-address] ÷ 3) → [main-storage-address]

where the FLOOR(X) function is defined as the largest integer not exceeding the argument X. Clearly, storage mapping may result in the inefficient use of main storage or in the need for additional storage references if S-memory and main storage are not compatible.

The storage mapping of S-memory bytes onto main storage words is a special case of the latter mapping technique, given directly above. With byte addressing, however, it is important to recognize that the length attribute must be known and generally is known by the microprogram, since instructions and operands frequently exceed the size of a main storage word. The length attribute of a data operand is usually inherent in the operation code of the S-instruction or is explicitly contained in the S-instruction as an operand length field. The length attribute of an S-instruction itself is usually inherent in the operation code field, so that additional fetches can be made if necessary. In the System 360/370 computer system, for example, the operation field of an instruction is 8 bits and is broken down as follows:

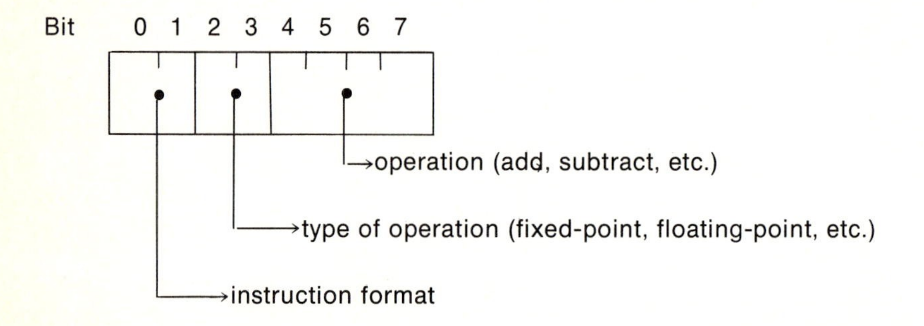

The instruction format field indicates the length and composition of an instruction word and is defined as follows:

Bits 0 and 1	Instruction format	Instruction length (in bytes)
00	Register to register	2
01	Register to indexed storage	4
10	Storage immediate	4
11	Storage to storage	6

A related technique, employed with some computers, is to use fixed-length instructions with a few well-defined exceptions. An exception occurs when the next sequential word following the current instruction is used to augment the instruction.

2.4.4 Boundary Alignment

A situation that can easily occur with byte-oriented computers is that an S-memory word, composed of perhaps 4 or 8 bytes, spans two or more main storage words due to the unfortunate arrangement of information in storage. When this occurs, extra storage references must be made to access the information over the optimum case. One means of alleviating this case is to require that fixed-length units, such as half-words, words, and double-words, be located on an integral boundary for that unit of information. An integral boundary for a given word of S-memory requires that its storage address be a multiple of the word length in bytes. For example, a 4-byte word is located so that its address is a multiple of the number 4. This method of locating information is known as *boundary alignment,* and it works with access width to minimize the number of required storage references.

An alternate to boundary alignment is *byte boundary alignment,* in which all fixed units of storage can be located on byte boundaries. Boundary alignment and byte boundary alignment are both used with microprogrammed computers.

VOCABULARY

The reader should be familiar with the following terms in the context in which they were used in the chapter:

Computer organization
Computer architecture
System
Main storage unit
Input/output subsystem
Control component
Arithmetic/logic component
Binary symbol
Bit
Word
Byte
Storage location
Binary coded decimal
Logical data
Numeric data
Packed decimal
Numeric character data
Character data
Byte addressing
Word addressing
Register
Current-address register
Instruction register
Index register
Arithmetic/logic register
Base register
Effective address
Machine cycle
Instruction cycle
I-cycle
Execution cycle
E-cycle
Descriptive notation
H-language
S-language
S-instruction
S-program
S-memory
M-language
M-instruction
M-program
M-memory
Access width
Storage address register
Storage buffer register
Storage mapping
Boundary alignment
Byte boundary alignment

QUESTION SET

The following questions are intended to test your comprehension of the subject matter. All questions can be answered from the text directly or possibly through a logical extension of the subjects presented. Some questions would be suitable for discussion sessions.

1 Investigate or simply think about the computer to which you have computing service. Is your conceptualization of the machine at the architecture level or at the organization level?
2 What are the major components of a computer system? Each major component is further structured into major subcomponents, etc. Continue one more level down and give the major subcomponents of the major components.
3 The term *bit* is an acronym for ______.
4 How much information should a location hold?
5 What is BCD?
6 What is the advantage of packed decimal?
7 When is a base register used?
8 What constraint does the width of the operation code field normally place on the architecture of the computer?
9 What is the difference between a register and a storage location?
10 Why is the current-address register important?
11 Is it possible to design a computer without arithmetic/logic registers? At what level—architecture or organization?
12 In what processing unit cycle is the effective address computed?
13 What function does the storage address register serve? The storage buffer register?
14 Why is byte boundary alignment inefficient?
15 Name at least three kinds of storage used in a microprogrammed computer.

EXERCISES

1 Thus far, we have conceptualized a computer as a collection of physical or logical components. However, we all know that many users view the whole process of computing from the viewpoint of a simple programming language. The exercise is to conceptualize the computer through a programming language of your choice.
2 Assume logical data of the form: true, false, and maybe. Develop a convention for storing it.
3 What is ASCII and how does it fit into the picture?
4 In what way is packed decimal inefficient? Be specific.
5 Describe how it would be possible to do without a current-address register.
6 Do some investigation and identify a computer that uses main storage to store registers.
7 Describe the following statement in symbolic descriptive notation:

A(I) = B(I + 1) + 4

Chapter 3

Organization of the Microprogrammed Computer

3.1 INTRODUCTION

The objective of this primer is to introduce microprogramming concepts and related techniques. Conceptually, microprogramming is analogous to conventional computer programming except that it is performed with different objects at a more basic machine level. The study of microprogramming, however, is not the study of microprogrammed computers. In this sense, it is also comparable to conventional computer programming. Information on the design of microprogrammed computers is available from engineering publications on computer design.

3.1.1 Implementation

In order to do microprogramming, a microprogrammed computer is needed, and this book utilizes a basic machine known as the D-machine. A complete bit-by-bit simulator is available for the D-machine, as is a translator for a suitable microprogramming language. The simulator and the translator, both written in standard FORTRAN IV, are available in an Instructor's Guide for this book.

Throughout the remainder of the book, the emphasis is on the process of doing microprogramming, which includes emulation techniques and the computer methodology necessary for supporting those techniques. The hardware is definitely of secondary interest. However, the D-machine is sufficiently complex to provide a realistic picture of the subtleties and the details of microprogramming.

3.1.2 Vertical versus Horizontal Microprogramming

Two general approaches are used in the implementation of microprogramming concepts: vertical microprogramming and horizontal microprogramming. With *vertical microprogramming,* each M-instruction specifies a single discrete microoperation, and a microroutine exists as a relatively long sequence of M-instructions that are executed serially. With *horizontal microprogramming,* each M-instruction specifies several microoperations that are executed in parallel.

Advantages and disadvantages exist to each approach. For vertical microprogramming, the advantages and disadvantages are:

Advantages	Disadvantages
Easy to microprogram.	Execution of microroutines takes many machine cycles.
Instruction bits are fully utilized.	Doesn't take advantage of the inherent parallelism of hardware.

For horizontal microprogramming, the advantages and disadvantages are:

Advantages	Disadvantages
Execution of microroutine takes relatively few microinstructions.	Difficult to microprogram.
Takes advantage of hardware parallelism.	Instruction bits are not fully utilized unless algorithm is "tightly" programmed.

Both approaches possess desirable advantages, and one would naturally prefer those features of both sets. As described in the succeeding paragraphs, the D-machine employs vertical *and* horizontal attributes and therefore provides an ideal vehicle for the study of microprogramming.

3.2 SYSTEM STRUCTURE

The D-machine is introduced in several stages. This chapter covers the overall structure of the system, the functions performed by many of the D-machine components, and the manner in which the system operates. Subsequent chapters cover the use of the simulator, use of the translator, and microprogram operations.

3.2.1 Organization of the D-Machine

The organization of the D-machine is given in Figure 3.1. The system is composed of three major hardware subsystems and two control memories, listed as follows:

1. The logic unit
2. The control unit
3. The memory control unit
4. The microprogram memory
5. The nanoprogram memory

The logic, control, and memory control units are introduced here. Memory is covered in the next section.

The *logic unit* executes D-machine microinstructions, as directed by the control unit. Functions performed by the logic unit are arithmetic and logical operations, shifting operations, and data input and output operations to S-memory and peripheral devices. (The control memory of the D-machine is used *only* for microprograms and *not* for S-programs and data.) The *control unit* directs the operation of the logic unit by controlling the commands, shift

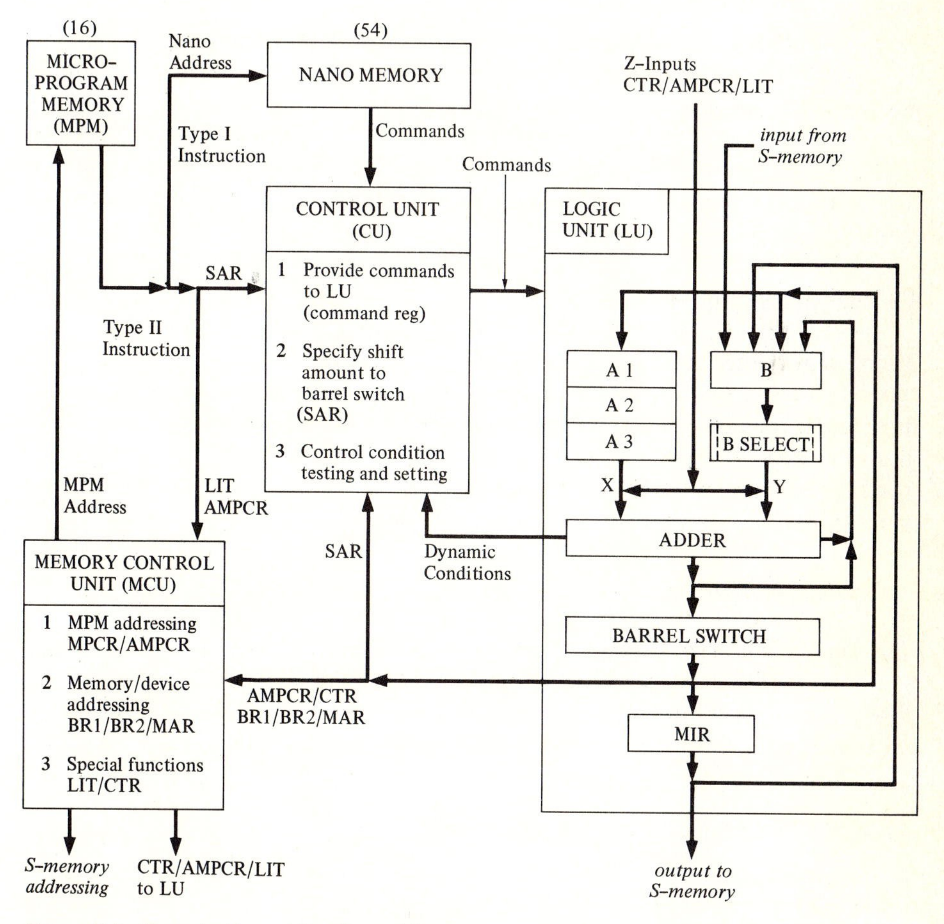

Figure 3.1 Organization of the D-machine.

amounts, and conditions that govern its operation. The *memory control unit* provides the means of addressing the microprogram memories, S-memory, and peripheral devices, maintains the current-address register, and supplies storage facilities for a literal value and a counter.

3.2.2 Control Storage

Control storage in the D-machine is split into the microprogram memory and the nanoprogram memory. The *microprogram memory* is narrow and contains an entry for each instruction in the microprogram. The use of microprogram memory is analogous to vertical microprogramming, since a relatively large number of ''small'' instructions are involved. Some M-instructions, held in microprogram memory, are self-contained and stand alone. Other M-instructions and in particular those that utilize the logic unit must be augmented by instruction bits that *effectively* control the logic unit. *Nanoprogram memory* is used to store the required instruction bits. Each microinstruction held in nanoprogram memory is wide and allows for parallel operations within the logic unit. Thus, the use of nanoprogram memory is analogous to horizontal microprogramming, as presented earlier. Only those M-instructions that require the use of nanoprogram memory point to it, so that control storage is not wasted. Moreover, if two M-instructions require identical nanoprogram instructions, called *N-instructions,* then each M-instruction can point to the same N-instruction.

Normally, microprogram memory is referred to as ''MPM''; nanoprogram memory is known as ''nano.''

3.3 MICROINSTRUCTIONS

Microinstructions in the D-machine are divided into two classes: type I and type II. Type I instructions utilize nanomemory, and type II instructions do not. Both types of instructions originate with an instruction held in microprogram memory.

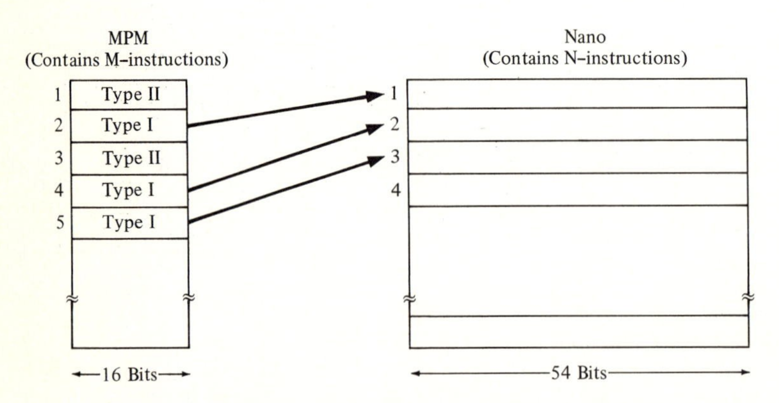

Figure 3.2 Overview diagram of the split instruction concept.

3.3.1 Split-Instruction Concept

Figure 3.2 gives an overview diagram of the split-instruction concept. Each set of operations executed by the D-machine originates with an M-instruction, where the "set" may include a single microoperation or a series of microoperations executed in parallel. *All operations that utilize the logic unit require an N-instruction held in nanoprogram memory.*

Each M-instruction is 16 bits wide, and five different instructions are defined. These instructions and their formats are shown in Figure 3.3. Four of the instructions are classed as type II; they are used to load D-machine registers. The fifth instruction is classed as type I; it gives the address in nanoprogram memory of a nanoinstruction.

3.3.2 Machine Cycle

The D-machine operates according to a fixed time interval, called a "clock." During each machine cycle, electricity generated by an electronic clock ripples through the system, causing information to be modified and selected as it passes through the various gates and switches.

During each clock (that is, each machine cycle), an M-instruction is read from the microprogram memory. As indicated above, the first few bits of the instruction specify its type. If it is a type II instruction, execution is completed during that clock, since all operands are contained in the M-instruction itself. If it is a type I instruction, then the nanomemory is accessed in the same cycle, but a second cycle is needed to execute the corresponding nanoinstruction. Thus, a type I microinstruction requires two clock intervals for execution; whereas a type II microinstruction requires one clock interval. The first clock

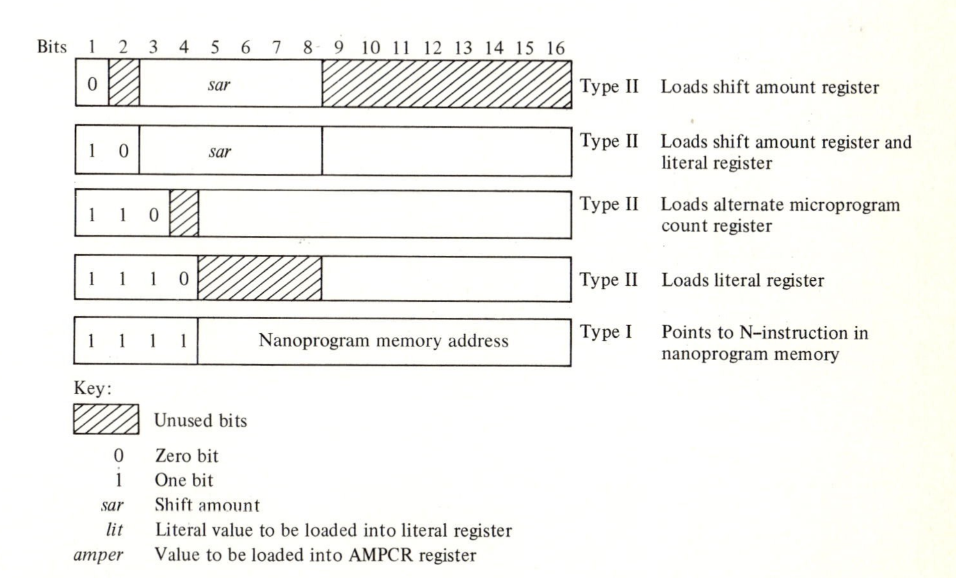

Figure 3.3 Form of M-instructions.

interval is referred to as *phase 1* of the execution of the microinstruction, and the second clock interval, if it exists, is referred to as *phase 3*.

Phase 3 of a type I microinstruction is overlapped with phase 1 of the next microinstruction, reducing the effective execution time so that it approaches one clock interval. The precise functions performed by the D-machine during phases 1 and 3 are covered in detail later, after additional introductory material is presented.

3.3.3 Instructions

During D-machine operation, type I and type II instructions are indicated by the setting of instruction bits in an M-instruction. These instructions are specified symbolically through the use of a microprogramming reference language. During actual microprogramming, a microprogram is initially written in a symbolic form known as TRANSLANG, to facilitate programming, and is then translated to binary machine-readable form by a conventional language processor program. For examples given in this text, the reference language is used. For examples run on the computer, TRANSLANG is used. Type II instructions are presented first because they are easier to describe and because they give insight into the nature of the reference language.

3.3.3.1 Type II A type II instruction loads any of three D-machine registers and can take any of the following four forms:

$$k \rightarrow \text{SAR}$$
$$k \rightarrow \text{LIT}$$
$$k \rightarrow \text{AMPCR}$$
$$k_1 \rightarrow \text{SAR}, k_2 \rightarrow \text{LIT}$$

where k is a decimal integer constant appropriate in magnitude to the register being loaded. For example, the statements

$$5 \rightarrow \text{LIT}$$
$$1 \rightarrow \text{SAR}$$
$$100 \rightarrow \text{AMPCR}$$

load the values 5, 1, and 100 into the literal register (LIT), the shift amount register (SAR), and the alternate microprogram count register (AMPCR), respectively. *In the statements, the key words* LIT, SAR, *and* AMPCR *are the names of D-machine registers and are not variables, as is the case with many programming languages.* The LIT register and SAR can both be loaded with a single type II statement, as follows:

$$\text{COMP } 0 \rightarrow \text{LIT}, 8 \rightarrow \text{SAR}$$

This statement loads the ones complement of 0, which is 255, into the LIT register and loads the value 8 into the SAR. The preceding statement and its interpretation imply that the width of the LIT register is 8 bits, which is a correct assumption. In general, the microprogrammer has to be aware of the width of each machine register in order to utilize the processing unit effectively.

3.3.3.2 Type I A type I instruction controls the operation of the logic, control, and memory control units of the D-machine, and always specifies (that is, points to) a 54-bit N-instruction in nanoprogram memory. Each N-instruction can indicate, *all at the same time,* the following types of operations:

Conditional test
Memory-device operation and condition adjust (conditionally or unconditionally)
Logic, control, or memory control unit operations (conditionally or unconditionally)

For example, the statement:

A1 + B L→A2

adds the contents of the A1- and B-registers, shifts the sum to the left, and places the result in register A2. The number of places to be shifted is governed by the contents of the SAR when the statement is executed. As another example,

MW2, IF MST THEN A3 + B + 1→A1 BEX, INC, SKIP ELSE JUMP

This statement specifies that the following operations are to be performed:

1 Unconditional S-memory write operation (MW2), that is, a write from the memory information register (MIR) in the D-machine to an S-memory location.

2 A conditional test (MST) of the most significant bit of the adder output of the preceding instruction. If that bit is set (that is, it is equal to 1), then the following operations are performed:

A3 + B + 1→A1	The contents of A3 plus the contents of B plus 1 replace the previous contents of A1.
BEX	A word is brought from the external data bus to the B-register.
INC	The value of the counter in the memory control unit is increased by 1.
SKIP	The successor instruction, (that is, the instruction to be executed next) is the current instruction plus 2. Thus, the next instruction is skipped.

If the MST bit is not set, then microprogram control is passed to the address specified in the AMPCR plus 1. This is specified with the key word JUMP.

Each facility of the D-machine is described in detail in subsequent sections. The preceding type II instructions are intended only to give a "flavor" for the kinds of operations that can be performed in the D-machine and do not demonstrate the parallelism available through the use of "horizontal" nanoinstructions. As used here, *parallelism* refers to the fact that basic machine functions can be executed simultaneously. Clearly, this feature makes microprogramming more difficult, but at the same time, it makes the computer more powerful. In general, the following specific operations can be performed in a single nanoinstruction:

1 Test a condition.
2 Set or reset a switch.
3 Initiate an external read/write operation.
4 Execute an operation in the adder component.
5 Shift the result of the adder operation.
6 Store the result of the adder and/or shift operation in one or more registers.
7 Increment the counter.
8 Transfer information among registers.
9 Complement the contents of the shift amount register.
10 Select the successor instruction to the current instruction.

The various classes of D-machine operations will become more meaningful after the components of the system are introduced.

3.3.4 A Note on Machine Specifications

The D-machine is not a hypothetical computer; it exists as a product of the Burroughs Corporation. Even though several variations of the basic machine exist, the D-machine simulator used in this book uses a particular version of the machine. For example, the width of the operational registers in the logic unit is 32 bits, and the shift address register (SAR) is 6 bits. Other registers have been assigned fixed sizes as well. As a marketable product, the D-machine can be constructed with logic-unit widths of 64, 56, 48, 40, 32, 24, 16, and 8 bits. Also several features of the actual D-machine are not described because they are outside the scope of a microprogramming primer. However, the major features of the D-machine that most directly relate to the microprogramming process are included in the simulator and in the translator. In fact, the simulator and translator contain options that are mentioned in this book but not introduced in a formal manner. D-machine features that are not covered are listed in a later chapter. Therefore, this book and the associated software should not be viewed as a definitive presentation of the total D-machine concept.

3.4 LOGIC UNIT

The major components of the logic unit are the adder, three A-registers, the B-register, the barrel switch, and the memory information register (MIR). The relationship of the components of the logic unit is depicted in Figure 3.1. The arrows in that diagram denote information flow, and an arrow between components indicates that a D-machine facility is available for causing information to take the indicated path. As mentioned previously, a few D-machine components are used before they are introduced, so that reference should be made to the diagram of the logic unit for clarification. However, *all* major functions and components of the D-machine are presented in this chapter.

3.4.1 Adder Component

The *adder* is 32 bits wide and permits two inputs: an X select and a Y select. The following operations can be performed on the X and Y inputs:

X
Y
X + Y
X + Y + 1
X − Y
X − Y − 1
NOT X
X⊕Y

where ⊕ denotes a logical operation, covered later, such as AND, OR, NAN(D), or NOR. The X and Y inputs are values, registers, or other constructs that serve as input specifications to the adder component.

3.4.1.1 X and Y Inputs Input values to the adder component are classed as follows:

A input: A1-, A2-, and A3-registers
B input: B-register with gating options (covered later)
Z input: AMPCR, CTR, and LIT registers

One aspect of microprogramming is to select the inputs that correspond to the X and Y operands.

The X select inputs can be the following:

0
A1-register
A2-register
A3-register
CTR register
LIT register

or, alternatively, the X select can be nonexistent. The Y select inputs can be the following:

0 value
1 value
B-register
CTR register
LIT register
AMPCR

and, alternatively, the Y select can be preceded by the prefix operator NOT that specifies that the ones complement of the Y select should be taken prior to the logic-unit operation. Some examples of adder operations are:

A2 + 1→
A1 AND LIT→
A3 − B − 1→
NOT CTR→
AMPCR→
A2 EQV B→
LIT + NOT CTR + 1→

It should be noted that these adder component examples are not necessarily complete since a destination for the adder output has not been specified.

3.4.1.2 Adder Input The A and B classes of input to the adder must be used as X select and Y select inputs, respectively. The width of each register is the same as the adder, and no special routing of register bits is involved. Outputs from the B-register can be gated, and this topic is covered in the description of the B-register.

The Z class of input to the adder is routed to specific bit positions in the adder as follows:

1 The output of the CTR register is routed to the most significant 8 bits of the adder; other bits are 0s.

2 The output of the LIT register is routed to the least significant 8 bits of the adder; other bits are 0s.

3 The output of the AMPCR is routed to the least significant 12 bits of the adder; other bits are 0s.

The set of Z inputs are the external inputs to the logic unit. External outputs of the logic unit include the Z-input registers as well as several other registers in the control and memory control units.

3.4.1.3 Adder Output Output of adder component can be routed to the barrel switch, which is used for shift operations, and to the B-register—by tapping the adder output before it reaches the barrel switch. Adder output to the B-register is described as B-register input.

3.4.1.4 Default Adder Operations An adder operation is performed during each clock interval. In the absence of a logic-unit operation, specified in a nanoinstruction, the adder performs the following operation:

$$0+0\rightarrow$$

This is an adder operation of 0 + 0 without a destination specification for the result. Thus, any subsequent operation that depends on a logic-unit operation for its completion can be executed successfully.

3.4.2 A-Registers

The D-machine includes three registers, known and referenced as A1, A2, and A3, that are used for temporary storage during microprogram execution and that serve as primary input to the adder. Any of the three registers can serve as the X input to the adder; however, only one of the A-registers can serve as input to a given logic-unit operation.

The only means of loading an A-register is as the output of the barrel switch, as in the following examples:

A3+1 L→A2
AMPCR→A1

In both examples, an A-register serves as a destination for the result of the logic-unit operation.

The latter example, that is, AMPCR→A1, illustrates an important point in microprogramming and how it differs from conventional computer programming. In conventional computer programming, it is sufficient to know that the contents of one register are placed in another register. In microprogramming, it is necessary for the microprogrammer to be aware of the flow of information through the various components of the processing unit. Knowledge of information flow is needed for determining the operations that can be performed, for microprogram optimization, for timing, and for the effective use of subsequent microinstructions.

3.4.3 B-Register

The B-register is the primary Y select input to the adder, and it serves as the external input interface. The B-register also may be loaded as the destination of a logic-unit operation. The width of the B-register is 32 bits, which is the same as the A-registers and the adder.

3.4.3.1 B-Register Output Output of the B-register serves as a Y select input to the adder. However, the B-register differs from the A-registers because it has true/false/complement selector gates. The selection gates control the most significant bit (that is, the leftmost bit), the least significant bit (that is, the rightmost bit), and the remaining central bits (that is, those that are between the most significant and least significant bits). When no gating is specified, the contents of the B-register are used in true form, as in the following example:

$$A1 + B \rightarrow AMPCR$$

Gating is specified through a subscript that is translated into bit settings in the corresponding nanoinstruction. Each of the three parts of the B-register is selected independently, and the register specification takes the form

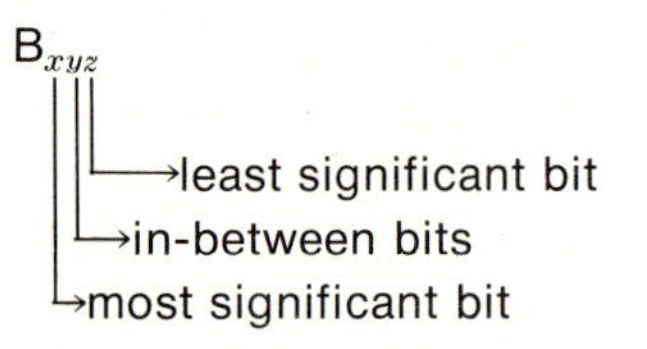

The options for B-register gating are

T true contents
F ones complement of the contents
0 zero output
1 one output

For example, the following list demonstrates some B select operations:

B-register specification	Meaning
B_{T00}	Most significant bit true; remaining bits 0.
B_{001}	Least significant bit 1; remaining bits 0.
B_{FTT}	Complement most significant bit; remaining bits true.
B_{000}	All bits 0.
B_{111}	All bits 1.
B_{FFF}	All bits complemented (ones complement)
B_{TTT}	All bits true; equivalent to B without a subscript.

The biggest use of B-register gating is to generate constants, mask values, and to select specific fields within the B-register.

3.4.3.2 B-Register Input B-register input can originate from the external switch interlock or from the logic unit. External input results from either an S-memory read or an input from a peripheral device. Peripheral devices are not used in this primer, and all external input is from S-memory.

3.4.3.2.1 External External input from S-memory is covered briefly here and in more detail in a later chapter. In order to do an S-memory read, the following steps must be performed:

1 Send the S-memory address to the memory control unit.
2 Initiate a read operation in the logic unit to fetch a word from S-memory.
3 When the read is complete, move the data from the switch interlock into the B-register.

As an example, suppose that register A1 contained the address of a word in S-memory. The following D-machine statements would read that word into the B-register:

```
A1→MAR1                          (1)
MR1                              (2)
IF RDC THEN BEX ELSE WAIT        (3)
```

Statement (1) transfers the S-memory address to a memory address register, statement (2) initiates the S-memory read operation, and statement (3) checks for read completion (that is, RDC). When the read is complete, that is, RDC is true, then the BEX operation moves the word from S-memory from the switch interlock to the B-register. The successor instruction to the true case is the next M-instruction. The successor instruction to the false case is a repetition of the IF statement. The latter process continues until the read *is* complete.

3.4.3.2.2 Input from the Logic Unit The B-register may be loaded from within the logic unit in one of the following ways:

1 As the output of the barrel switch, for example,

```
A1 AND LIT R→B
```

2 As the adder output tapped before it enters the barrel switch, for example,

```
A1 + LIT R→A2,BAD
```

3 From the memory information register (MIR) output, for example,

```
A1 + LIT R→A2,BMI
```

4 As the barrel switch output ORed (that is, logical or) with either the adder, switch interlock, or MIR output, for example,

```
A1+LIT R→A2,BBA    [BSW ∨ adder]
A1+LIT R→A2,BBE    [BSW ∨ external]
A1+LIT R→A2,BBI    [BSW ∨ MIR]
```

In all these cases, the B-register is a destination register in the sense that it is loaded as the result of the logic-unit clock cycle. As the output of the barrel switch, case 1, the B-register participates directly in the adder/barrel-switch (BSW) operation. In cases 2, 3, and 4, the B-register is loaded in a separate but possibly related operation that executes in parallel with the adder/BSW operation. The B-register may participate in the adder operation and may also be a destination register, as in the following example:

```
A1+B→A2,BMI
```

In this example, the previous contents of B are used in the adder operation; the previous contents of the MIR register replace the contents of the B-register when the execution of the above statement is complete.

3.4.4 Barrel Swtich

The *barrel switch* component provides the capability of shifting a word to the right or to the left by the amount specified in the shift amount register (SAR). Input is from the adder. Three options are available:

L end-off left shift
R end-off right shift
C circular right shift

Output of the barrel switch can go to any of the following registers: A1, A2, A3, B, MIR, BR1, BR2, MAR, CTR, SAR, and AMPCR. The A1-, A2-, A3-, B-, and MIR registers take the full barrel switch output. The BR1 and BR2 registers, not mentioned yet, take the second least significant byte from the barrel switch, while the MAR, CTR, and SAR take the least significant byte. The AMPCR takes the least significant 12 bits of the barrel switch output.

All adder output goes through the barrel switch to the specified destination register, regardless of whether a shift operation is specified. If no shift is specified in a statement, the translator inserts automatically a no-shift-type indicator in the nanoinstruction.

3.4.5 Memory Information Register

The *memory information register* (MIR) serves as a buffer for words written to S-memory or a peripheral device. The MIR serves the same function as the storage buffer register mentioned in Chapter 2.

The MIR is always loaded from the barrel switch as a destination register, as in the following example:

A1→MIR

The process of writing to S-memory involves four distinct steps:

1 Moving the data to be written to the MIR
2 Establishing the S-memory address in the memory control unit
3 Initiating the write operation
4 Checking that the switch interlock has accepted the information

Suppose that register A3 contains an S-memory address and that register A1 contains a word to be written to that address. The following statements would perform the specified write operation:

```
A3→MAR1                          (1)
A1→MIR                           (2)
MW2                              (3)
IF SAI THEN STEP ELSE WAIT       (4)
```

Statements (1) and (2) establish the S-memory address and place the word to be written in the MIR, respectively. Statement (3) initiates the write operation, and statement (4) causes the D-machine to wait until the "switch accepts information" (SAI) indicator is set. The contents of the MIR can also be placed in the B-register through the use of the BMI key word, as presented above.

3.4.6 Note on Logic-Unit Operations

The syntax and semantics of logic-unit operations are given in a later chapter. Before the details can be presented, however, it is necessary to introduce the other major units of the D-machine, to present the various fields of the nanoinstruction format, to give meaningful examples of microprogramming, and to tell how to use the translator and the simulator.

3.5 MEMORY CONTROL UNIT

The memory control unit provides microprogram addressing and S-memory and peripheral device addressing and supplies Z-class inputs to the adder of the logic unit. In the latter case, the Z-class inputs contain the CTR and LIT registers. A schematic of the memory control unit and the control unit is given in Figure 3.4

3.5.1 Microprogram Addressing

The memory control unit contains two registers for addressing the microprogram memory (MPM). (Clearly, the nanoprogram memory is referenced through type I instructions.) The microprogram count register (MPCR) serves as the current-address register. During the execution of an M-instruction, the

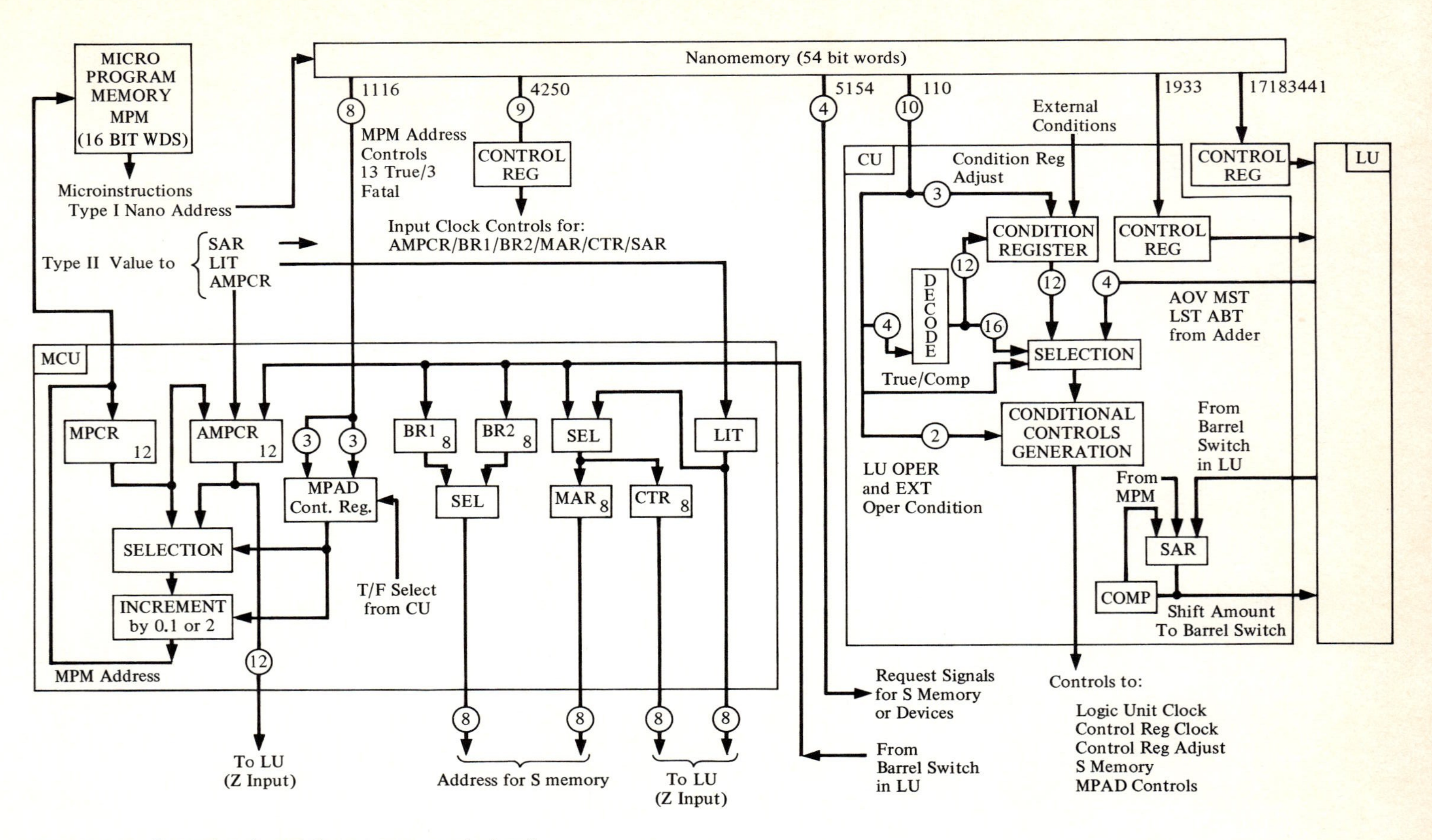

Figure 3.4 Control unit and the memory control unit.

MPCR is incremented by 0, 1, or 2 depending upon the successor to the current instruction.

The alternate microprogram count register (AMPCR) serves as an alternate to the MPCR and is used during program control operations. The AMPCR may be used as input to the adder and as an output destination register from the barrel switch.

The following successors to the current instruction are provided:

WAIT	Repeat the current instruction.
STEP	Step to the next sequential M-instruction and continue execution.
SKIP	Skip the next sequential M-instruction and continue execution.
SAVE	Save the current MPCR address in the AMPCR and step to the next sequential M-instruction.
CALL	Transfer microprogram control to the M-instruction in microprogram memory located at the address contained in the AMPCR *plus* 1, that is, (AMPCR) + 1. The current address (held in the MPCR) is saved in the AMPCR.
EXEC	Out-of-line execution of the instruction located in microprogram memory at the address contained in the AMPCR *plus* 1, that is, (AMPCR) + 1. Execution continues with the completion of the current instruction.
RETN	Transfer control to the instruction located in microprogram memory at the address contained in the AMPCR *plus* 2, that is, (AMPCR) + 2. Execution continues from that instruction.
JUMP	Transfer control to the instruction located in microprogram memory at the address contained in the AMPCR *plus* 1, that is, (AMPCR) + 1. Execution continues from that instruction.

In general, the default successor for both true and false conditions is the STEP command, and in all cases except EXEC, the new microprogram memory address is placed in the MPCR. Type II instructions do not affect instruction sequencing, and the implicit successor is STEP.

3.5.2 S-Memory Addressing

S-memory addressing is provided through three registers in the memory control unit: the BR1, BR2, and MAR. BR1 and BR2 serve as base registers and normally contain the second least significant byte of an S-memory address. The memory address register (MAR) serves as a deplacement from the address value in a base register and contains the least significant byte of an S-memory address. The BR1, BR2, and MAR can be loaded separately from the barrel switch or collectively through the MAR1 and MAR2 pseudoregisters, which are defined as follows:

BR1	MAR

MAR1 pseudoregister

BR2	MAR

MAR2 pseudoregister

When MAR1 and MAR2 are used as destination registers, the full 16-bit register (that is, BR1 or BR2 concatenated with MAR) is loaded from the barrel switch, and contains the least significant 16 bits of the barrel switch output. When BR1, BR2, and MAR are loaded separately from the barrel switch, BR1 and BR2 receive the second least significant byte of the barrel switch output and the MAR receives the least significant byte of the barrel switch output. The MAR1 and MAR2 pseudoregisters are used with S-memory read and write operations as follows:

Register	S-Memory read command	S-Memory write command
MAR1	MR1	MW1
MAR2	MR2	MW2

As an example of how the above concepts are used, consider the following problem:

> S-machine registers are stored in S-memory. BR1 points to the high-order byte of the 16-bit address of the registers. A1 contains the register number which can be 0, 1, 2, etc. The operation is to add the value contained in register A3 to the S-machine register, specified by A1, and store the result back in S-memory.

A short microprogram segment to perform the stated operation is given as follows:

```
A1→MAR
MR1
IF RDC THEN BEX ELSE WAIT
A3+B→MIR
MW1
IF SAI THEN STEP ELSE WAIT
```

In this example, BR1 would have been loaded previously, perhaps in an initialization routine, with the indicated base address. On the other hand, assume that register A2 contained an effective address and it were desired to add the contents of register A3 to the contents of that address location and place the sum back in the location. A short microprogram segment to perform the latter operation is given as follows:

```
A2→MAR1
MR1
IF RDC THEN BEX ELSE WAIT
A3+B→MIR
MW1
IF SAI THEN STEP ELSE WAIT
```

The microprogram segments are essentially the same except that MAR is loaded in the first case and MAR1 is loaded in the latter case.

The memory address register (MAR) can also be loaded directly from the LIT register without requiring an adder operation through the use of the LMAR command, as in the following microprogram segment:

```
A1+B→A3,LMAR
3→LIT
```

In this case, the value 3 is placed in the MAR. This is the first example of a case in which a register is loaded with a type II instruction after it is used in a type I instruction. Because of the timing characteristics of the D-machine and the phase 1 overlap, mentioned above, the value 3 is placed in the LIT register before the LMAR takes place. This is an example of good microprogramming practice. If the 3→LIT were placed before the LMAR, as follows,

```
3→LIT
A2+B→A3,LMAR
```

then three clock intervals would be necessary to complete the A2+B→A3 and LMAR commands. If the 3→LIT is placed after the LMAR,

```
A2+B→A3,LMAR
3→LIT
```

then only two clock intervals are required for the entire set of operations.

3.5.3 Counter Register

The *counter register* (CTR) is an 8-bit counter in the memory control unit. The CTR can be loaded in two ways: as the output of the barrel switch, such as

```
A3→CTR
```

or directly from the LIT register without requiring an adder operation through the use of the LCTR command, as in the following microprogram segment:

```
A1+B→A3,LCTR
3→LIT
```

In this case, the ones complement of the value 3 is placed in the CTR, which is the binary value 11111100. *In fact, the CTR is always loaded with the ones complement of the source field, regardless of the method of assignment.*

The CTR cannot be loaded directly with a type II instruction.

3.5.3.1 Increment The CTR can be used in an adder operation in the following manner:

```
A3 + NOT CTR→B
```

Whenever the true value of the CTR is needed, the NOT CTR must be used. The CTR may also be incremented without using the adder through the use of the INC command, as follows:

```
A1 + B→A3,INC
```

The INC command always adds a true 1 to the ones complement counter value. Thus, after the statements of the following program segment were executed:

```
A1 + B→A3,LCTR
3→LIT
INC
```

the CTR would contain the binary value 11111101.

3.5.3.2 Overflow The counter register (CTR) overflows from all 1s, that is, 255 (decimal), to all 0s and sets the counter overflow indicator, which can be tested with the counter overflow (COV) indicator as follows:

```
INC
 .
 .
 .
IF COV THEN...
```

As an example of how the CTR operates, consider the following example:

```
A1 + B→A3,LCTR
3→LIT
...
INC...
IF COV THEN...
```

A value of 3 complemented is originally placed in the CTR, and the contents of CTR exist as follows for the successive iterations:

	CTR value	
Initially:	11111100	
After first increment:	11111101	
After second increment:	11111110	
After third increment:	11111111	
After fourth increment:	00000000	"overflow"

The counter overflow (COV) condition can be tested following or concurrently with the increment counter (INC) command; it indicates that the counter has overflowed or is in the process of overflowing.

3.5.4 Literal Register

The *literal register* (LIT) is an 8-bit register in the memory control unit. The LIT register can be loaded with only a type II instruction and is one method of entering a constant value into a microprogram. Several examples follow:

```
9→LIT
COMP 0→LIT, 15→SAR
```

The LIT register can be used as either an input to the adder or a source register for the LCTR and LMAR commands.

3.6 CONTROL UNIT

The control unit contains four sections that collectively control the operation of the D-machine: the shift system, the condition system, the command system, and the timing system. The major components of the control unit are depicted in Figure 3.4. Timing has been introduced and briefly discussed. The timing system is covered in more detail in a later chapter.

3.6.1 Shift System

The *shift address register* (SAR) and the barrel switch operate together to provide an end-off or end-around shift capability. For right shift operations, the number of places to be shifted is placed in the SAR. For left shift operations, the twos complement of the number of places is placed in the SAR. For shift amounts that originate as type II instructions, the twos complement is provided by the translator as follows:

Type II instruction	Action performed
3→SAR	True value 3 for right and circular shift
COMP 5→SAR	Twos complement of 5 for left shift

The use of the SAR as a destination register, however, requires a more careful look at the contents of the SAR.

Table 3.1 Shift Amounts and Their Complements for a 32-Bit Machine
(X-Bit Is Ignored by the Hardware)

Shift amount	SAR contents: Right shift (true amount)	SAR contents: Left shift (complement)
0	000X00	000X00
1	01	111X11
2	10	10
3	↓ 11	01
4	001X00	↓ 00
5	01	110X11
6	10	10
7	↓ 11	01
8	010X00	↓ 00
9	01	101X11
10	10	10
11	↓ 11	01
12	011X00	↓ 00
13	01	100X11
14	10	10
15	↓ 11	01
16	100X00	↓ 00
17	01	011X11
18	10	10
19	↓ 11	01
20	101X00	↓ 00
21	01	010X11
22	10	10
23	↓ 11	01
24	110X00	↓ 00
25	01	001X11
26	10	10
27	↓ 11	01
28	111X00	↓ 00
29	01	000X11
30	10	10
31	↓ 11	↓ 01

3.6.1.1 Shift Amounts and Their Complements As mentioned earlier in this chapter, the D-machine is designed for different logic-unit widths, and this flexibility is reflected in the contents of the shift amount register (SAR). For a 32-bit machine, the shift amount and their complements are given in Table 3.1. For example, a right shift of 6 places requires that the following value be placed in the SAR:

001X10

where the X bit is ignored by the hardware. Similarly, a left shift of 3 places requires that the following value be placed in the SAR:

111X01

where again, the X bit is ignored by the hardware. In the former case, the microprogrammer writes 6→SAR, and the language processor generates the correct SAR value. In the latter case, the microprogrammer writes COMP 3→SAR, and the language processor computes the twos complement of 3 and determines the correct SAR value.

When the SAR is loaded from the barrel switch as a destination operator, the shift amount is not adjusted automatically. Therefore, incorrect results will be obtained unless the X bit (see Table 3.1) is inserted into the shift amount before it is sent to the SAR.

3.6.1.2 SLIT If it is expected that the contents of the LIT will be moved to the SAR, then it is possible to avoid the task of shifting the X bit into the shift amount by using the SLIT key word. For example, if a right shift of 5 places is required, then the following correct and incorrect program segments could be written:

Incorrect	**Correct**
5→LIT	5→SLIT
...	...
LIT→SAR	LIT→SAR

The key word SLIT indicates that a shift amount is to be inserted into the LIT register and that a correct shift value should be placed in the literal assignment instruction.

3.6.1.3 CSAR The CSAR command is a means of complementing the contents of the SAR without using the adder and the barrel switch. The CSAR serves as a destination register, as in the following example:

A1 + B→A2, CSAR

A note on complements is in order. Complement operators to the SAR and SLIT register, such as,

COMP 3→SAR
COMP 7→SLIT

always take the twos complement. Complement operators to the AMPCR and LIT register, such as,

COMP 20→AMPCR
COMP 0→LIT

always take the ones complement.

3.6.2 Condition System

The condition system is used to execute commands on a conditional basis. Both conditional and unconditional operations can be included in the same statement, and the conditional part of a statement can utilize either the IF or the WHEN option. Conditions are classed as static or dynamic.

3.6.2.1 Static Conditions Static conditions are set during the course of machine operation and are reset by testing. Static conditions include:

SAI — *Switch interlock accepts information* This condition is used with a write operation and indicates that the operation is logically complete.

RDC — *Read complete* This condition is used with a read operation and indicates that the data are available for entry to the B-register with the BEX command.

COV — *Counter overflow* This condition is set when the CTR overflows from all 1s to all 0s.

LC1 — *Local condition 1*
LC2 — *Local condition 2*
LC3 — *Local condition 3*
Local conditions 1 through 3 provide Boolean conditions that are set with the SET LC1, SET LC2, and SET LC3 commands, respectively.

The SAI, RDC, and COV conditions are set implicitly as a result of the execution of other commands. The LC1, LC2, and LC3 conditions are set explicitly with the SET command. Once a static condition is set, it continues to be set until it is tested, regardless of the intervening statements.

3.6.2.2 Dynamic Conditions Dynamic conditions are established dynamically from the adder output of phase 3 of the previous instruction using the logic unit. Dynamic conditions are maintained only until the next logic-unit operation, when they are changed dynamically. Dynamic conditions include:

AOV — *Adder overflow* The condition is set in an adder operation by a carry-out of the most significant bit.

LST — *Least significant* This condition is set when the least significant output bit of the adder is 1. If the bit is 0, the condition is not set.

MST — *Most significant* This condition is set when the most significant output bit of the adder is 1. If the bit is 0, the condition is not set.

ABT — *All bits true* This condition is set when all output bits of the adder are 1. If at least one output bit is 0, the condition is not set.

A dynamic condition established in one statement must be tested in the next type I statement that is executed.

All static and dynamic conditions may be prefixed with NOT, which indicates that the ones complement of the condition is taken before the conditional part of the statement is executed.

3.6.2.3 IF Statement The IF statement has the general format:

IF *condition* THEN *commands, true successor* ELSE *false successor*

where "condition" is one of the options mentioned previously. Some examples are:

```
IF COV THEN A1+B→A2, BEX, SET LC1, LCTR ELSE JUMP
IF NOT ABT THEN SKIP ELSE STEP
IF LC1 THEN A1→MIR, LMAR ELSE RETN
```

Another topic, which is covered in detail later, involves the physical placement of information in a destination register. In a type I statement such as

A2+1→A2

the result of the adder/BSW operation is not physically placed in register A2 until the next logic-unit operation is encountered in a type I statement. Consider the following microprogram segment in which the AOV condition tests false:

B_{000}→A2 (1)
A2+1→A2 (2)
IF AOV THEN A2→MIR, INC, STEP ELSE STEP (3)
A2+1→A3 (4)
STEP (5)

A 0 value is assigned to A2 in statement (1). In statement (2), 1 is added to the contents of A2, but the replacement is not made until the next logic-unit operation. Therefore, in statement (3), the contents of MIR are not replaced, and the CTR is not incremented. However, in statement (4), the destination operator of statement (2) is replaced because statement (4) implicitly specifies a true condition and causes a logic-unit operation to be executed. A 1 is added to the contents of A2 and the result is placed in A3. Statement (5) is a "no operation" statement that causes statement (4) to be completed.

Recall that a static condition is reset by testing. An IF clause without a THEN clause and an ELSE clause causes the condition to be reset but does not specify conditional operations. For example, in the statement

A1+B→A2, IF LC1

the adder/BSW operation A1 + B→A2 is performed unconditionally, LC1 is reset, and the implicit successor is STEP. This option provides a means of resetting a condition without using a separate statement to do it.

3.6.2.4 WHEN Statement The WHEN statement is a simplified form of the IF statement. Consider an IF statement of the form:

IF *condition* THEN *commands* STEP ELSE WAIT

This particular form of the statement is used frequently with memory read and write operations and can be replaced with a simplified statement of the form:

WHEN *condition* THEN *commands*

The statements are operationally equivalent. The true successor to the true condition is STEP; the false successor to the false condition is WAIT. The following statement demonstrates the use of the WHEN statement:

WHEN RDC THEN BEX, INC

In a statement, the key word WHEN can be optionally preceded by one or more commands that are executed unconditionally.

3.6.3 Command System

During the translation of a type I instruction to a 54-bit nanoinstruction, each command is represented by the setting of 1 or more bits in the nanoinstruction.

				Group A	
Nanoinstruction Bits		1–7		8–10	51–54
☐,	IF	*condition*	THEN	*condition-adjust*,	*external-op*,
		LC 1/2/3		SET LC 1/2/3	MR1/2
		SAI		*	MW1/2
		RDC			*
		ABT			
		AOV			
		COV			
		LST			
		MST			

☐ Group A or B operators may be executed unconditionally or conditionally. If they are placed before the conditional test, they are executed unconditionally.
* Other options exist in the D-machine. They are listed briefly at the end of the book.

Figure 3.5 General form of a type I instruction.

Specific bit settings are covered later, along with their respective meanings. Knowledge of the format of a nanoinstruction is not necessary to do microprogramming, but is needed for a complete understanding of the microprogramming process.

The general form of a type I instruction is given in Figure 3.5. The objective of the figure is to communicate the fact that commands in a type I instruction can be executed either unconditionally or conditionally. In Figure 3.5, commands that set conditions and perform external operations are referred to as group A, and logic-unit, memory control unit, and control-unit commands are referred to as group B. Because extra bit positions in a nanoinstruction are at a premium, the conditional/unconditional option applies collectively to group A and collectively to group B. Thus, for example, it is *not* possible to write

A1 + B→A2, IF ABT THEN INC

because A1 + B→A2 and INC are both group B commands. However, it *is* possible to write

A1 + B→A2, IF ABT THEN MR1 ELSE STEP

because A1 + B→A2 is a group B command and MR1 is an external operation.

The control signals from a nanoinstruction that represent commands to be performed are stored in a 36-bit control register in the control unit. Therefore, the control information is readily available when it is necessary to repeat an instruction because of timing.

Group B				
17–41	42–50	11–13		14–16
LU	*MCU/CU*	*true successor*	ELSE	*false successor*
A1/2 select	Controls for:	WAIT		WAIT
B1/2 select	AMPCR	STEP		STEP
Adder function	BR1/2	SAVE		SAVE
Shift selection	MAR	SKIP		SKIP
Destination(s)	CTR, INC	JUMP		JUMP
	SAR, CSAR	EXEC		EXEC
		CALL		CALL
		RETN		RETN

3.7 FINAL REMARK

This chapter obviously represents a heavy dose of technical information about microprogramming and the D-machine. Clearly, a set of pertinent examples is needed and should be expected. They do exist, but they have been placed in the next chapter. This organization of the subject matter allows the reader to use this chapter for reference and the next chapter for examples.

VOCABULARY

The reader should be familiar with the following terms and acronyms in the context in which they were used in the chapter:

Terms	Acronyms		
Vertical microprogramming	SAR	BBA	SKIP
Horizontal microprogramming	LIT	BBI	WAIT
D-machine	MPCR	BMI	STEP
Logic unit	AMPCR	SLIT	SAVE
Control unit	CTR	CSAR	CALL
Memory control unit	L		EXEC
Microprogram memory	R	IF	JUMP
Nanoprogram memory	C	THEN	RETN
S-memory	A1	ELSE	
Control storage	A2	WHEN	
M-instruction	A3		
N-instruction	B	NOT	
Clock	BR1	COMP	
Phase 1	BR2		
Phase 3	MAR		
Type I instruction	MIR		
Type II instruction	MR1		
Condition	MR2		
External operation	MAR1		
Adder	MAR2		
X select input	MW1		
Y select input	MW2		
A input	MST		
B input	LST		
Z input	AOV		
Barrel switch	ABT		
Prefix operator	COV		
Complement operator	SAI		
Ones complement	RDC		
Twos complement	LC1		
Successor	LC2		
Destination	LC3		
Condition-adjust operation	SET		
Gating	BEX		

Shift amount register
Counter register
Memory information register
Memory address register
Literal register
Counter overflow
Least significant bit
Most significant bit
Static condition
Dynamic condition
Command

INC
LCTR
LMAR
BAD
BBE

QUESTION SET

1. Using what you know about computers and simulation, compare the use of a simulator with the use of an actual microprogrammable computer. What advantages does the simulator have?
2. Is the hypothetical microprogrammable computer introduced in Chapter 1 a vertically or horizontally programmed machine?
3. Name the two control memories used in the D-machine.
4. Name the three major hardware subsystems of the D-machine. In general, what function does each subsystem perform?
5. What is the width in bits of an M-instruction? An N-instruction?
6. What is wrong with the following type II instruction? $5 \rightarrow$ CTR
7. In what way is the execution of microinstructions overlapped in the D-machine?
8. What would be an effective measure of nanoinstruction efficiency?
9. List the registers in the logic unit and the memory control unit.
10. What is wrong with the following adder statements?

$$\mathrm{B} + \mathrm{A1} \rightarrow \mathrm{MIR}$$
$$1 + \mathrm{B} \rightarrow \mathrm{A1}$$

11. Explain the result of the following instruction:

$$\mathrm{CTR} + 1 \rightarrow \mathrm{A1}$$

12. Give the numerical equivalent to the following register specifications:

$$\mathrm{B}_{000}$$
$$\mathrm{B}_{001}$$
$$\mathrm{B}_{111}$$
$$\mathrm{B}_{011}$$
$$\mathrm{B}_{100}$$

13. Explain the difference between the MPCR and the AMPCR.
14. What condition is used to check the MR1 operation? The MW1 operation?
15. What is the magnitude of the largest literal value that can be placed in the LIT register?
16. What method can be used to determine how large MPM can be on the D-machine? How large *can* it be?

17 The MAR2 register is the concatenation of what registers?
18 Distinguish between a destination and a successor.
19 List the steps required to write a word to S-memory.
20 What does the SAR contain after the following type II instruction is executed?

5→SAR

21 Distinguish between a static and a dynamic condition.
22 Give the equivalent IF statement to the following WHEN statement:

WHEN RDC THEN BEX

23 In what way are the SKIP and RETN successors similar?
24 What simple operation does the following statement perform?

A1 + NOT 0→A1

25 Name the conditions that relate to adder output.

EXERCISES

1. Write statements to perform the following:
   - **a** Move the value 5 to the LIT register, and 12 to the SAR register.
   - **b** Check the most significant bit of the adder output. If it is true, go to the next statement; otherwise, jump to the contents of AMPCR plus 1.
   - **c** Take the ones complement of the contents of register A1 and place the result in the B-register.
2. Write microprogram segments to perform the following:
   - **a** Exchange the values of the A1- and B-registers.
   - **b** Move the contents of location 123 in S-memory to location 321 in S-memory.
   - **c** Register BR1 points to 16 fixed-point registers in S-memory. Add the contents of register 3 to register 2 and place the result in register 2.
3. Register A3 contains an S-machine instruction with an operation code in the first 8 bits of the instruction. It is necessary to right-justify the operation code in register-B as follows:

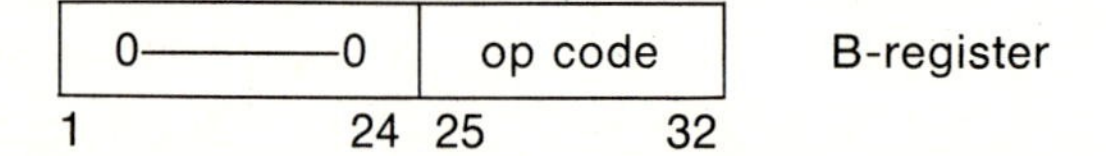

   Write a statement or a program segment to perform the data manipulation.
4. Write a statement or program segment to exchange the values in the B-register and the MIR.
5. Write a statement or program segment to add the contents of registers A1 and A2 and place the result in register A3.

Chapter 4

Microprogram Operations

4.1 OVERVIEW

The objective of Chapter 3 was to introduce the microprogrammed computer and to cover the structure of microinstructions. The objective of this chapter is to introduce the type of microprogram operations that are normally contained in microprograms, along with a presentation of nanoinstruction codes. The chapter also includes several examples of microprogramming methodology.

4.1.1 Program Structure

A microprogram is composed of a set of statements that specify the basic machine operations to be performed. The only required statement in a microprogram is the END statement, which is required by the translator to terminate processing. The translator generates an M-instruction of 4000 (in hexadecimal) for the END statement, which is recognized by the simulator as a "halt" command.

The following microprogram writes the value 1234 to location 1234 in S-memory:

```
AMPCR→MAR1, MIR
1234→AMPCR
MW1, IF SAI
WHEN SAI THEN STEP
END
```

a Translation

```
>>>>> TRANSLANG D MACHINE MICRØTRANSLATØR

ENTER FILENAME FØR HEX? F41HEX
SUPPRESS BIT PATTERNS?(1=SUPPRESS)? 1
SUPPRESS HEX LISTING?(1=SUPPRESS)? 1
IF INPUT IN FILE ENTER 1? 31
ENTER SØURCE FILENAME? FIG41

0000        AMPCR = MAR1, MIR $
0001        1234 = AMPCR $
0002        MW1, IF SAI $
0003        WHEN SAI THEN STEP $
0004        END $


THE TØTAL NUMBER ØF ERRØRS =      0

EXECUTE (Y/N)? N
```

b Execution

```
DMACH1     (CØMPILED)  05 JAN 76   16:29


ENTER SAME FILENAME FØR HEX? F41HEX
ØUTPUT REGISTERS AND S MEMØRY IN INTEGER(1) ØR ØCTAL(2)? 1
INPUT S MEMØRY IN INTEGER(1) ØR ØCTAL IN Ø11 FØRMAT(2)? 1
STARTING ADDRESS =? 0
MAXIMUM NUMBER ØF CLØCKS TØ SIMULATE=? 10
NUMBER ØF CLØCKS BETWEEN ØUTPUT PØINTS=? 1

ENTER ØUTPUT LINES DESIRED      1-ADDRESSES AND CLØCK
2- A1,A2,A3,B    3- MIR,SAR,LIT,CTR,AMPCR     4- BR1,BR2,MAR,BMAR,GC1,GC2
 5- CØNDITIØNS
ENTER NUMBER ØF ØUTPUT LINES DESIRED? 5

BEGIN ØUTPUT AT MPM ADDRESS=? 4
END ØUTPUT AT MPM ADDRESS=? 4
ENTER 1 FØR S MEMØRY DUMP WHEN PRØGRAM TERMINATES? 1

ENTER S MEMØRY VALUES IN CØNSECUTIVE BLØCKS
ENTER 9999 FØR STARTING ADDRESS WHEN FINISHED


STARTING S MEMØRY ADDRESS=? 1234
FINAL S MEMØRY ADDRESS FØR THIS BLØCK=? 1234
SMEM(1234)=? 0


STARTING S MEMØRY ADDRESS=? 9999



END ØF SIMULATIØN - REGISTERS CØNTAIN


P(1) ADDR. =    3      P(3) ADDR. =    3      CLØCK =     6
A1 =           0       A2 =           0       A3 =           0       B =          0
MIR =       1234       SAR = 0        LIT =   0       CTR =  0       AMPCR =1234
BR1 =   4        BR2 =   0        MAR =210        BMAR = 1234       GC1=0   GC2=0
LC1=0  LC2=0  MST=0  LST=0  ABT=0  AØV=0  CØV=0  SAI=1  RDC=0  INT=0
```

Figure 4.1 Example of a complete microprogram that was executed using the translator and simulator.

```
MEMØRY DUMP REQUESTED

ENTER VALUES AS DØNE IN MEMØRY INPUT (9999 FØR STARTING ADDRESS WHEN
FINISHED)

STARTING S MEMØRY ADDRESS=? 1234
FINAL S MEMØRY ADDRESS FØR THIS BLØCK=? 1234


S MEMØRY(1234) TØ S MEMØRY(1234) =


      1234
STARTING S MEMØRY ADDRESS=? 9999
```

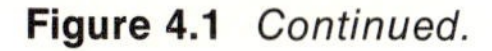

Figure 4.1 *Continued.*

This is a complete microprogram, even though it does not perform a particularly useful function. It was run on the translator/simulator, and the printout is given in Figure 4.1. Even though the translator and simulator have not been covered, an idea of the available facilities is fairly evident. [The biggest difference between the reference language and the machine-readable syntax is that an equals sign (=) is substituted for the replacement arrow (→) and that each statement must terminate with a dollar sign ($).]

4.1.2 Statement Labels

The use of a statement label permits the MPM address of an instruction to be referenced in a type II instruction. The statement label is used in the type II instruction to load the AMPCR for use in a subsequent type I instruction that uses the AMPCR as the source of the next MPM address. The AMPCR must be explicitly loaded before it is referenced, as follows:

$$\underline{\text{label}} - 1 \rightarrow \text{AMPCR}$$

.

.

.

______, JUMP

The JUMP command causes microprogram control to be transferred to the contents of the AMPCR *plus* 1, that is, in symbolic notation

$$(\text{AMPCR}) + 1$$

The following microprogram, for example, writes all 1s to the first 10 locations of S-memory:

0→A1, LCTR	(1)
9→LIT	(2)

a Translation

```
>>>>> TRANSLANG D MACHINE MICRØTRANSLATØR

ENTER FILENAME FØR HEX? F42HEX
SUPPRESS BIT PATTERNS?(1=SUPPRESS)? 1
SUPPRESS HEX LISTING?(1=SUPPRESS)? 1
IF INPUT IN FILE ENTER 1? 31
ENTER SØURCE FILENAME? FIG42

0000        0 = A1, LCTR $
0001        9 = LIT $
0002        RPT - 1 = AMPCR $
0003        NØT 0 = MIR, INC $
0004    RPT. A1 + 1 = A1, MAR1 $
0005        MW1, IF SAI $
0006        WHEN SAI THEN STEP $
0007        IF NØT CØV THEN INC, JUMP ELSE STEP $
0008        END $


THE TØTAL NUMBER ØF ERRØRS =     0

EXECUTE (Y/N)? N
```

b Execution

```
2) DMACH1    (CØMPILED)  05 JAN 76  17:10


ENTER SAME FILENAME FØR HEX? F42HEX
ØUTPUT REGISTERS AND S MEMØRY IN INTEGER(1) ØR ØCTAL(2)? 2
INPUT S MEMØRY IN INTEGER(1) ØR ØCTAL IN Ø11 FØRMAT(2)? 2
STARTING ADDRESS =? 0
MAXIMUM NUMBER ØF CLØCKS TØ SIMULATE=? 75
NUMBER ØF CLØCKS BETWEEN ØUTPUT PØINTS=? 1

ENTER ØUTPUT LINES DESIRED     1-ADDRESSES AND CLØCK
2- A1,A2,A3,B    3- MIR,SAR,LIT,CTR,AMPCR    4- BR1,BR2,MAR,BMAR,GC1,GC2
 5- CØNDITIØNS
ENTER NUMBER ØF ØUTPUT LINES DESIRED? 5

BEGIN ØUTPUT AT MPM ADDRESS=? 8
END ØUTPUT AT MPM ADDRESS=? 8
ENTER 1 FØR S MEMØRY DUMP WHEN PRØGRAM TERMINATES? 1

ENTER S MEMØRY VALUES IN CØNSECUTIVE BLØCKS
ENTER 9999 FØR STARTING ADDRESS WHEN FINISHED


STARTING S MEMØRY ADDRESS=? 9999



END ØF SIMULATIØN - REGISTERS CØNTAIN


P(1) ADDR. =    7     P(2) ADDR. =    6      CLØCK =    55
A1=00000000012     A2=00000000000     A3=00000000000      B =00000000000
MIR =37777777777     SAR = 0        LIT =   9       CTR =   0       AMPCR =    3
BR1 =   0      BR2 =   0       MAR = 10       BMAR =    10       GC1=0   GC2=0
LC1=0   LC2=0   MST=0   LST=0   ABT=0   AØV=0   CØV=0   SAI=1   RDC=0   INT=0
```

Figure 4.2 Microprogram depicting a loop and the use of a statement label.

```
MEMØRY DUMP REQUESTED

ENTER VALUES AS DØNE IN MEMØRY INPUT (9999 FØR STARTING ADDRESS WHEN
FINISHED)

STARTING S MEMØRY ADDRESS=? 1
FINAL S MEMØRY ADDRESS FØR THIS BLØCK=? 15


S MEMØRY(    1) TØ S MEMØRY(   15) =


37777777777  37777777777  37777777777  37777777777  37777777777

37777777777  37777777777  37777777777  37777777777  37777777777

00000000000  00000000000  00000000000  00000000000  00000000000

STARTING S MEMØRY ADDRESS=? 9999
```

Figure 4.2 *Continued.*

```
       RPT-1→AMPCR                              (3)
       NOT 0→MIR, INC                           (4)
RPT:   A1+1→A1, MAR1                            (5)
       MW1, IF SAI                              (6)
       WHEN SAI THEN STEP                       (7)
       IF NOT COV THEN INC, JUMP ELSE STEP      (8)
       END                                      (9)
```

Register A1 is used to keep a running count of the S-memory address, and the counter register (CTR) is used to keep track of the number of iterations through the loop. Statement (1) performs initialization by placing a 0 value in A1 and the contents of the LIT register, which is loaded in statement (2), into the CTR. Recall here that the ones complement of the LIT goes to the CTR. Statement (3) places the address value of label RPT *minus* 1 into the AMPCR. The branch address will then be to RPT. Statement (4) moves all 1s to the MIR and increases the value of CTR by 1. Statement (5) increases A1 by 1 and moves that value to the MAR1 register, which is used as an S-memory address. Recall here that MAR1 is the concatenation of register BR1 and MAR. Statement (6) initiates a memory write operation with the MW1 command and resets SAI by testing. Statement (7) waits until the memory write is accepted by the switch interlock and then steps to the next instruction. It should be noted that the use of the MW1 command specifies that MAR1 will be used as an S-memory address. If the MW2 command were used, then MAR2, the concatenation of BR2 and MAR, would be implicitly specified as the S-memory address. Statement (8) checks for CTR overflow. If the CTR has not overflowed, then the value of CTR is incremented by 1 and branches to RPT. If the CTR has overflowed, control passes to statement (9), which ends the microprogram.

The statement label is a series of letters and digits, the first of which must be alphabetic. The statement label is separated from the body of the statement by a colon (:).

The above microprogram was run on the translator/simulator, and the printout is given in Fig. 4.2. In the computer version, the colon used to separate a statement label from the body of the statement is replaced by a period.

4.1.3 Efficiency

In microprogramming, efficiency, measured in the number of clocks necessary to execute a microprogram, is of prime importance. Initially, it is difficult to write an efficient microprogram because experience is generally lacking. However, even professional microprogrammers do not simply "dash off" an efficient microprogram. Usually, a microprogram goes through a process of successive refinement over an extended period of time until the required number of clocks is minimized. Initially, it is important to include the needed function in a microprogram. After the function is there, then efficiency can be improved.

As an example, recall the preceding microprogram used as an example of looping and the use of statement labels. The microprogram initially may have been written as the initial version given in Figure 4.3. After successive refinement, the microprogram may take the form of the other versions given in the same figure.

4.1.4 Complements and Logical Negation

Complements are used in type II instructions, and logical negation is used in type I statements. In type II instructions, the form of complement is dependent upon the target register. For the LIT and the AMPCR registers, that is,

```
COMP n→LIT
COMP n→AMPCR
```

where n is a nonnegative integer, the ones complement of n is taken and then the required number of bits (8 for the LIT and 12 for the AMPCR) is placed in the register. For the SAR and SLIT registers, that is,

```
COMP n→SAR
COMP n→SLIT
```

the twos complement of n is placed in the SAR and LIT register, respectively. (Recall here that the use of SLIT means that the LIT register is loaded but that the extra bit, mentioned in Chapter 3, is inserted, so that a subsequent operation of the form LIT→SAR will be meaningful.)

Logical negation (that is, NOT) is an operator used in type I logical expressions, and it denotes the bit-by-bit complement, performed by converting all 1 bits to 0 bits and all 0 bits to 1 bits. In the preceding example, the type I statement

```
NOT 0→MIR
```

	Initial microprogram		After some improvement		Final version
	0→ A1		0→ A1		0→A1, LCTR
	LIT→ CTR		LIT→ CTR		9→LIT
	9→LIT		9→LIT		RPT−1→AMPCR
RPT:	A1+1→A1		RPT−1→AMPCR		NOT 0→MIR, INC
	INC		NOT 0→MIR	RPT:	A1+1→A1, MAR1
	FIN−1→AMPCR		INC		MW1, IF SAI
	IF COV THEN JUMP ELSE STEP	RPT:	A1+1→A1, MAR1		WHEN SAI THEN STEP
	A1→MAR1		MW1, IF SAI		IF NOT COV THEN INC, JUMP ELSE STEP
	MW1, IF SAI		WHEN SAI THEN STEP		END
	RPT−1→AMPCR		IF COV THEN SKIP ELSE STEP		
	WHEN SAI THEN JUMP		INC, JUMP		
FIN:	STEP		END		
	END				

Figure 4.3 The process of successive refinement to improve the efficiency of a microprogram.

specifies the ones complement of 0, which is a word of all 1s. Clearly, $B_{111} \rightarrow$ MIR is equivalent to the above statement.

Two destination registers in type I statements involve complements. LCTR specifies that the ones complement of the contents of the LIT is placed in the counter, whereas CSAR specifies that the twos complement of the prior contents of the SAR are placed in the SAR.

4.2 LOGIC-UNIT OPERATIONS

Logic-unit operations are grouped into six classes: logic operations, arithmetic operations, conditions, shift operations, destination specifications, and successor control.

4.2.1 Logical Operations

Logical operations in the D-machine are summarized in Table 4.1 and are specified in nanoinstructions through the appropriate bit settings given in Figure 4.4. For example, the logical expression

A1 AND LIT→A3

is denoted in a nanoinstruction by the following bits (see Figure 4.4):

A1:

17	18	19
1	0	1

Adder X input

LIT:

20	21	22	23	24	25	26
0	0	0	0	1	0	1

Adder Y input

AND:

28	29	30	31
1	0	1	1

Adder operation

A3:

34	35	36
0	0	1

A register input from BSW (barrel switch)

If the instruction had been written as

A1 AND LIT→A3, CTR

then the following bits would have been set as well:

CTR:

46	47	48
1	0	1

The translator takes care of providing the appropriate bit settings in a nanoinstruction. In fact, the bits cannot be set manually. The only means that the mi-

MICRO CONTROLS

<table>
<tr><td>1</td><td>2</td><td>3</td><td>4</td><td>5</td><td>6</td><td>7</td><td>8</td><td>9</td><td>10</td><td>11</td><td>12</td><td>13</td><td>14</td><td>15</td><td>16</td></tr>
<tr><td>ø</td><td>ø</td><td colspan="6">* SAR</td><td>ø</td><td>ø</td><td>ø</td><td>ø</td><td>ø</td><td>ø</td><td>ø</td><td>ø</td></tr>
<tr><td>1</td><td>0</td><td colspan="6">SAR</td><td colspan="8">LIT</td></tr>
<tr><td>1</td><td>1</td><td>0</td><td>ø</td><td colspan="12">* AMPCR</td></tr>
<tr><td>1</td><td>1</td><td>1</td><td>0</td><td>ø</td><td>ø</td><td>ø</td><td>ø</td><td colspan="8">LIT</td></tr>
<tr><td>1</td><td>1</td><td>1</td><td>1</td><td colspan="12">* NANO ADDRESS</td></tr>
</table>

ø Unused
* Shorter fields are right justified

NANO CONTROLS

Parentheses surround optional lexic units, provided by default.

1 2 3 4	Condition Tested Result is Boolean end
0 0 0 0	GC1
0 0 0 1	GC2
0 0 1 0	LC1
0 0 1 1	LC2
0 1 0 0	MST
0 1 0 1	LST
0 1 1 0	ABT
0 1 1 1	AOV
1 0 0 0	COV
1 0 0 1	SAI
1 0 1 0	RDC
1 0 1 1	LC3
1 1 0 0	EX1
1 1 0 1	INT
1 1 1 0	EX2
1 1 1 1	EX3

5	FT Condition Value
0	NOT $\overline{\text{end}}$=:SC
1	– end=:SC

6	Logic Unit Conditional
0	Do Unconditionally
1	Do Conditionally if SC

7	Ext Op (MDOP/CAJ) Conditional
0	Do Unconditionally
1	Do Conditionally if SC

8 9 10	Condition adjust -- CAJ
0 0 0	--
0 0 1	SET LC2
0 1 0	SET GC2
0 1 1	RESET GC
1 0 0	SET INT
1 0 1	SET LC3
1 1 0	SET GC1
1 1 1	SET LC1

11 12 13 Then Part Used if SC=1	Successor to MPAD Ctls	14 15 16 Else Part Used if SC=0
0 0 0	WAIT	0 0 0
0 0 1	(STEP)	0 0 1
0 1 0	SAVE	0 1 0
0 1 1	SKIP	0 1 1
1 0 0	JUMP	1 0 0
1 0 1	EXEC	1 0 1
1 1 0	CALL	1 1 0
1 1 1	RETN	1 1 1

17 18 19	Adder X Input
0 0 0	(0)
0 0 1	LIT
0 1 0	ZEXT
0 1 1	CTR
1 0 0	Z
1 0 1	A1
1 1 0	A2
1 1 1	A3

20	21	22	23	24	25	26	Adder Y Input
0	0	-	-	-	-	-	B0--
0	1	-	-	-	-	-	BT--
1	0	-	-	-	-	-	BF--
1	1	-	-	-	-	-	B1--
-	-	0	0	0	-	-	B-0-
-	-	1	0	0	-	-	B-T-
-	-	-	-	-	0	0	B--0
-	-	-	-	-	0	1	B--T
-	-	-	-	-	1	0	B--F
-	-	-	-	-	1	1	B--1
Comp	1	0	0	Comp			B-F-*
Comp	0	0	0	Comp			B-1-*
0	0	0	0	1	0	1	LIT
0	0	0	1	0	0	0	ZEXT
0	1	0	1	1	0	0	CTR
0	1	1	0	1	0	1	Z
0	0	1	1	0	0	1	AMPCR

*Use Adder Operation with Complement Y

27		Inhibit Carries into Bytes
0	--	Allow
1	IC	Inhibit

28 29 30 31	Adder Operation				Logic
0 0 0 0	X	+	Y		
0 0 0 1	X	NOR	Y		$\bar{X}\,\bar{Y}$
0 0 1 0	X	NRI	Y		$\bar{X}$ Y
0 0 1 1	X +	Y +	1		
0 1 0 0	X	NAN	Y		$\bar{X} \vee \bar{Y}$
0 1 0 1	X	OAD	Y		X + (X v Y)
0 1 1 0	X	XOR	Y		$X\,\bar{Y} \vee \bar{X}\,Y$
0 1 1 1	X	NIM	Y		$X\,\bar{Y}$
1 0 0 0	X	IMP	Y		$\bar{X} \vee Y$
1 0 0 1	X	EQV	Y		$X\,Y \vee \bar{X}\,\bar{Y}$
1 0 1 0	X	AAD	Y		X + (XY)
1 0 1 1	X	AND	Y		X Y
1 1 0 0	X -	Y -	1		$X + \bar{Y}$
1 1 0 1	X	RIM	Y		$X \vee \bar{Y}$
1 1 1 0	X	OR	Y		X v Y
1 1 1 1	X	-	Y		$X + \bar{Y} + 1$

32 33		Shift Type Selection for BSW
0 0	--	No Shift
0 1	R	Right End Off
1 0	L	Left End Off
1 1	C	Right Circular

34 35 36		A Register Input from BSW
0 0 0	--	No Change
1 - -	A1	
- 1 -	A2	
- - 1	A3	

37 38 39 40		B Register Input Select
0 0 0 0	--	No Change
0 0 0 1	BC4	Comp 4 Bit Carries
1 0 0 0	BAD	Adder
1 0 0 1	BC8	Comp 8 Bit Carries
1 0 1 0	BBA	BSW v Adder
1 0 1 1	B	BSW
1 1 0 0	BEX	External
1 1 0 1	BMI	MIR
1 1 1 0	BBE	BSW v External
1 1 1 1	BBI	BSW v MIR

41		MIR Input from BSW
0	--	No Change
1	MIR	

42		AMPCR Input from BSW
0	--	No Change
1	AMPCR	

43 44 45 46		Mem Dev Address Input
0 0 0 -	--	No Change
- - 1 0	LMAR	From LIT
- - 1 1	MAR	From BSW
- 1 0 -	BR2	From BSW
- 1 1 1	MAR2	From BSW
1 - 0 -	BR1	From BSW
1 - 1 1	MAR1	From BSW

46 47 48		Counter Input
- 0 0	--	No Change
0 0 1	LCTR	From LIT*
1 0 1	CTR	From BSW*
- 1 0	INC	+1

*Ones Complement

49 50		SAR Input
0 0	--	No Change
0 1	CSAR	Complement
1 0	SAR	From BSW

51 52 53 54		Mem Dev Op--MDOP
0 0 0 0	--	No Change
0 0 1 0	MR1	
0 0 1 1	MR2	
0 1 1 0	MW1	
0 1 1 1	MW2	
1 0 0 0	DL1	
1 0 0 1	DL2	
1 0 1 1	DR1	
1 0 1 1	DR2	
1 1 0 0	DU1	
1 1 0 1	DU2	
1 1 1 0	DW1	
1 1 1 1	DW2	

Figure 4.4 Nanoinstructions—bit setting.

Table 4.1 Logical Operations
(Bitwise Operations Are Computed as Follows: $R_i \leftarrow X_i \oplus Y_i$, where R_i Is the Result Bit and $\oplus$ Is the Logical Operation Involved)

Logical operation	Symbolic operations	Logical definition	Bitwise equivalent
Nor (not or)	X NOR Y	$\overline{X} \wedge \overline{Y}$	$X \not\vee Y$
Not reverse imply	X NRI Y	$\overline{X} \wedge Y$	$X < Y$
And	X AND Y	$X \wedge Y$	$X \wedge Y$
Not imply	X NIM Y	$X \wedge \overline{Y}$	$X > Y$
Exclusive or	X XOR Y	$(X \wedge \overline{Y}) \vee (\overline{X} \wedge Y)$	$X \neq Y$
Equivalence	X EQV Y	$(X \wedge Y) \vee (\overline{X} \wedge \overline{Y})$	$X = Y$
Imply	X IMP Y	$\overline{X} \vee Y$	$X \leqslant Y$
Nand (not and)	X NAN Y	$\overline{X} \vee \overline{Y}$	$X \not\wedge Y$
Reverse imply	X RIM Y	$X \vee \overline{Y}$	$X \geqslant Y$
Inclusive or	X OR Y	$X \vee Y$	$X \vee Y$
Negation	NOT X	$\overline{X}$	
Negation	NOT Y	$\overline{Y}$	

croprogrammer has for writing microprograms is to use the TRANSLANG microprogramming language.

4.2.2 Arithmetic Operations

Arithmetic operations in the D-machine are summarized in Table 4.2 and are specified in nanoinstructions through appropriate bit settings. Again, the nanoinstruction summary, given in Figure 4.4, is used.

For example, the arithmetic expression

$$A2 + AMPCR \rightarrow B$$

is denoted in a nanoinstruction by the following bits (see Figure 4.4):

A2: Adder X input

17	18	19
1	1	0

AMPCR: Adder Y input

20	21	22	23	24	25	26
0	0	1	1	0	0	1

+: Adder operation

28	29	30	31
0	0	0	0

B: B-register input select

37	38	39	40
1	0	1	1

Similarly, the expression

$$LIT - B \rightarrow AMPCR$$

Table 4.2 Arithmetic Operations

Addition operation	Symbolic operation	Logical equivalent
Addition	X+Y	
Subtraction	X−Y	$X+\overline{Y}+1$
Or add	X OAD Y	$X+(X \vee Y)$
And add	X AAD Y	$X+(X \wedge Y)$
	X+Y+1	
	X−Y−1	$X+\overline{Y}$

is specified in a nanoinstruction as

	Bits	Values	
LIT:	17 18 19	0 0 1	Adder X input
B:	20 21 22 23 24 25 26	0 1 1 0 0 0 1	Adder Y input
−:	28 29 30 31	1 1 1 1	Adder operation
AMPCR:	42	1	AMPCR input from BSW

Some instructions require a substitution by the translator. The expression $A1+1 \rightarrow MIR$, for example, is equivalent to $A1+B_{001} \rightarrow MIR$, and corresponds to the following nanoinstruction bit settings:

	Bits	Values	
A1:	17 18 19	1 0 1	Adder X input
B_{001}:	20 21 22 23 24 25 26	0 0 0 0 0 1 1	Adder Y input
+:	28 29 30 31	0 0 0 0	Adder operation
MIR:	41	1	MIR input from BSW

In the absence of an adder operation, the translator generates the default operation $0+0 \rightarrow$. During each clock interval, as implied previously, the machine cycles through an adder operation, places the adder or barrel switch output in the specified destination (if any), and chooses a successor instruction. The task of the microprogrammer is to set appropriate bits in the nanoinstructions so that the machine performs the required sequence of operations.

4.2.3 Conditions

A condition may be effective on a conditional or an unconditional basis—depending upon nanoinstruction bit settings. Three D-machine functions can be performed conditionally or unconditionally: the logic-unit operation, the external operation, and the selection of the successor instruction.

In the execution of a nanoinstruction, the *condition* is tested first. Depending upon its truth value, subsequent D-machine functions are performed. For example, in the statement

IF COV THEN A1→MIR STEP ELSE SKIP

the following nanoinstruction bits are set (using Figure 4.4):

IF COV:

1	2	3	4
1	0	0	0

Condition test; result is Boolean *cnd*

5
1

Condition value (true condition)

6
1

Logic unit conditional (do conditionally)

STEP ELSE SKIP:

True

11	12	13
0	0	1

<u>Successor</u>

14	15	16
0	1	1

False

A1:

17	18	19
1	0	1

Adder X input

20	21	22	23	24	25	26
0	0	0	0	0	0	0

Adder Y input

28	29	30	31
0	0	0	0

Adder operation

MIR:

41
1

MIR input from BSW

As another example, consider the statement

LIT+AMPCR→AMPCR IF ABT THEN MW1 STEP ELSE RETN

In this case, the adder/BSW operation is done unconditionally, but the external operation (MW1) is done conditionally, as reflected in the following nanoinstruction bit settings:

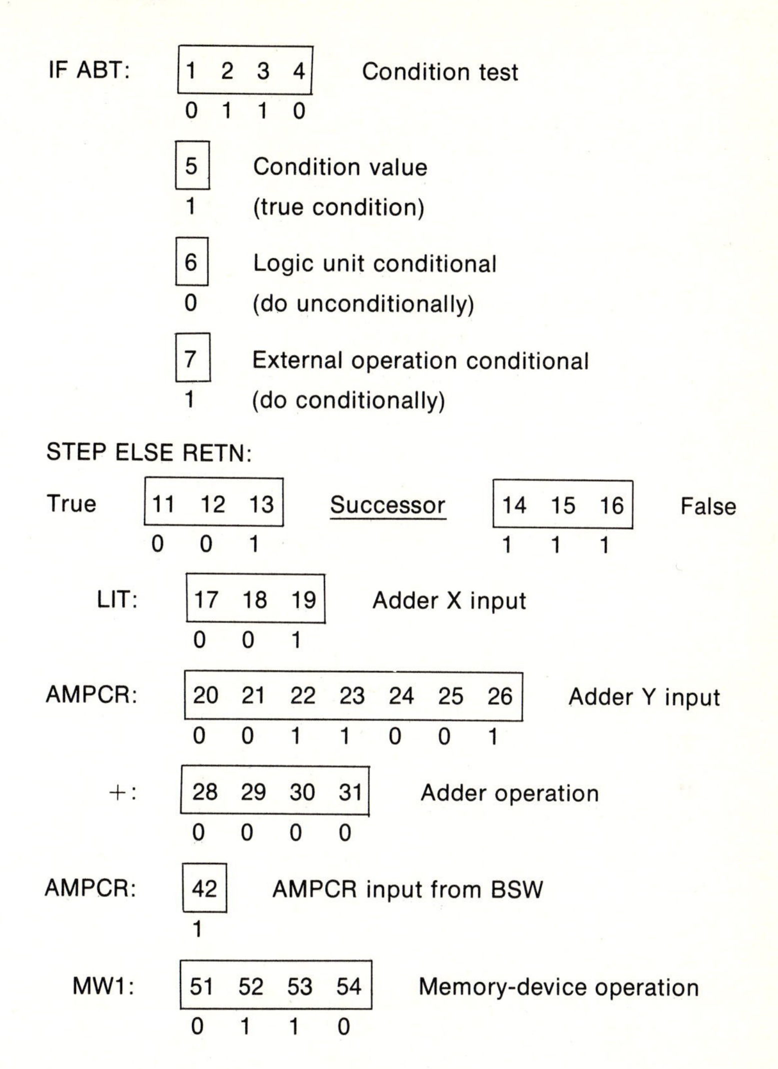

In the absence of a condition test, a default option of NOT MST is generated by the translator, and bits are set to perform logic-unit and external operations on an unconditional basis.

The *condition-adjust* specification is used to set an indicator, as in the following statement:

SET LC3

The nanoinstruction bit settings for this statement are

SET LC3:

8	9	10
1	0	1

The condition-adjust operation is governed by the external operation condition.

4.2.4 Shift Operations

Shift operations are performed in the barrel switch and apply to the output of the adder. The shift amount is always the value in the shift amount register (SAR) when the shift operation is executed. When a right shift is desired, a true value is placed in the SAR, as follows:

A1 R→B
3→SAR

When a left shift is desired, a complemented value is placed in the SAR, as follows:

A1 L→B
COMP 3→SAR

Circular shifts are always performed to the right, and a true value is placed in the SAR.

A shift operation is specified by an appropriate bit setting in a nanoinstruction. For example, in the statement

A1 R→B

the nanoinstruction bit settings are as follows (see Figure 4.4):

A1: Adder X input

17	18	19
1	0	1

Adder Y input

20	21	22	23	24	25	26
0	0	0	0	0	0	0

Adder operation

28	29	30	31
0	0	0	0

R: Shift-type selection

32	33
0	1

B:

37	38	39	40
1	0	1	1

The shift is considered to be a logic-unit operation. When no shift is specified in a statement, the "no shift" option is selected by the translator, and bits 32 and 33 of the nanoinstruction are set to 0.

4.2.5 Destination Specifications

Destination specifications may denote input to the following groups: A-register, B-register, MIR, AMPCR, memory-device address, CTR, and the SAR. Each of the above groups may be specified in a single instruction, but entries within a group, except for A input, are mutually exclusive. For example, a single instruction, such as the following

A2 + LIT→A1, A3, BEX, MIR, AMPCR, MAR1, INC, CSAR

can specify several destination specifications. In fact, the nanoinstruction bit settings for this instruction are:

Adder Operations

A2: Adder X input

17	18	19
1	1	0

LIT: Adder Y input

20	21	22	23	24	25	26
0	0	0	0	1	0	1

+: Adder operation

28	29	30	31
0	0	0	0

Destination Specifications

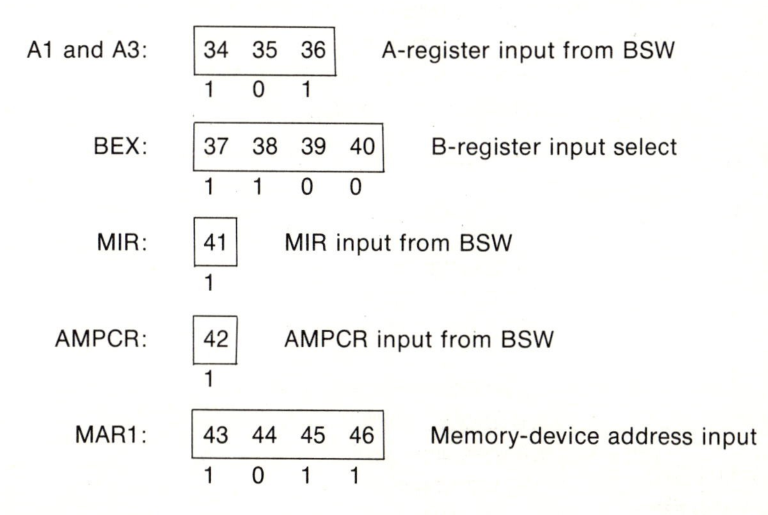

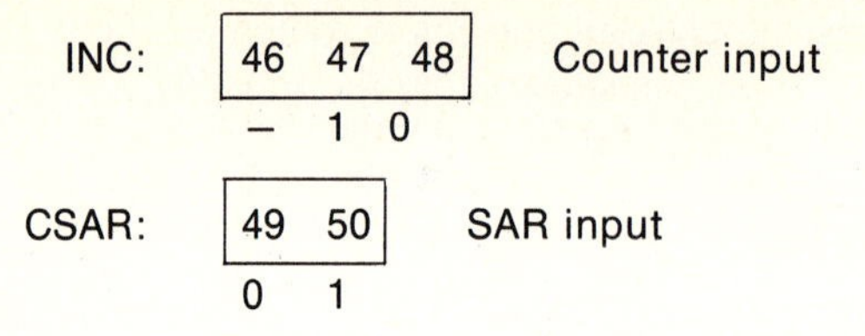

As indicated, bit 46 of a nanoinstruction is shared between the memory-device address input and the counter input. Therefore, the following restrictions are necessary:

1 If counter input is CTR, then memory-device address input may not be MAR, MAR1, or MAR2.

2 If memory-device address input is LMAR, then counter input may not be CTR.

The default option for a destination specification is a 0 placed in the appropriate bit position, which indicates a "no change" operation.

4.2.6 Successor Control

The successor to a statement is controlled by the condition test, which allows a true and a false successor. The only exception is the SAVE command, which implicitly specifies a STEP successor. Successor control options are summarized in Table 4.3.

4.3 MICROPROGRAMMING METHODS

This section contains a potpourri of microprogramming methods intended to give some indication of how the D-machine can be used to the fullest advantage. By working through the methods, the reader should gain insight into the process of microprogramming.

Table 4.3 Summary of Successor Control Options

Successor	Next MPM address	Next content of MPCR	Next content of AMPCR
WAIT	(MPCR)	(MPCR)	–
STEP	(MPCR)+1	(MPCR)+1	–
SKIP	(MPCR)+2	(MPCR)+2	–
SAVE	(MPCR)+1	(MPCR)+1	(MPCR)
CALL	(AMPCR)+1	(AMPCR)+1	(MPCR)
EXEC	(AMPCR)+1	(MPCR)	–
JUMP	(AMPCR)+1	(AMPCR)+1	–
RETN	(AMPCR)+2	(AMPCR)+2	–

Key: – unchanged
(x) denotes contents of x

4.3.1 Generation of Constant Values

In a microprogram, a constant value can originate in one of three ways:

1. From S-memory
2. Through literal assignment
3. As the result of an adder operation

When the value originates from S-memory, it is obtained with a memory read command, covered later.

4.3.1.1 Literal Assignment Constants generated through literal assignment originate in MPM memory and are assigned with the following type II instructions:

$$n \rightarrow \text{LIT}$$
$$m \rightarrow \text{AMPCR}$$

Constants generated through literal assignment are right-justified in their respective registers with zero fill on the left.

4.3.1.2 Signed-Magnitude versus Twos Complement Representation In the definition of an S-machine, the computer architect may select signed-magnitude representation or twos complement representation for fixed-point values. Either option may be selected through microprogrammed implementation.

With *signed-magnitude representation,* a numeric value is expressed in true form, prefixed by a sign digit, as follows:

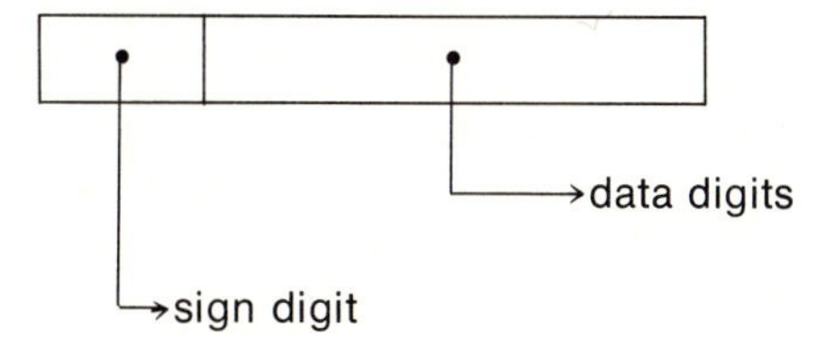

In binary, the sign digit is usually 0 for a positive value and 1 for a negative value. Using 8-bit words, for example, the signed-magnitude representation of the values +6 and −6 is given as follows:

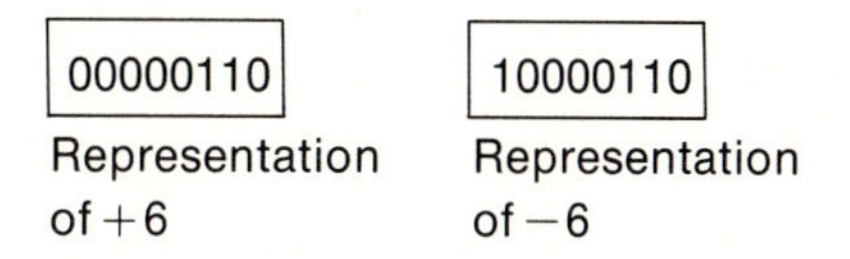

It follows that microprograms that operate on values, such as these, must incorporate the signs and method of representation. Algorithms for addition and subtraction of values represented in signed-magnitude form are given as follows:

Addition	Subtraction
1 If the values to be added have like signs, add the magnitudes of the values and give the sum the common sign.	**1** Change the sign of the subtrahend.
2 If the values to be added have unlike signs, compute the difference of the magnitudes of the values and give the result the sign of the value with the largest magnitude.	**2** Add the minuend and the modified subtrahend.

In general, signed-magnitude representation requires a more complicated set of microroutines than twos complement representation. However, the fact that values are stored in true form facilitates input and output conversion, resulting in slightly less complicated S-programs. Signed-magnitude representation is most commonly used when the accumulator registers are not used for indexing and addressing.

With *twos complement representation,* positive values are stored in true form and negative values are stored in twos complement form, as in the following binary 8-bit representation of the values +6 and −6.

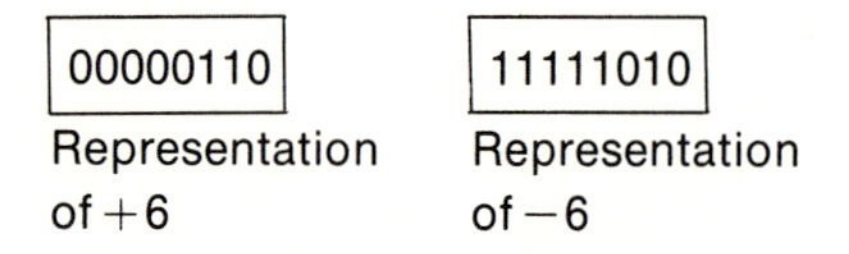

Because it is relatively easy to develop the twos complement of a binary value[1] since arithmetic operations on values stored in twos complement form can be executed without regard to sign, addition and subtraction operations are straightforward. Addition is a simple binary and operation, as demonstrated in the following examples:

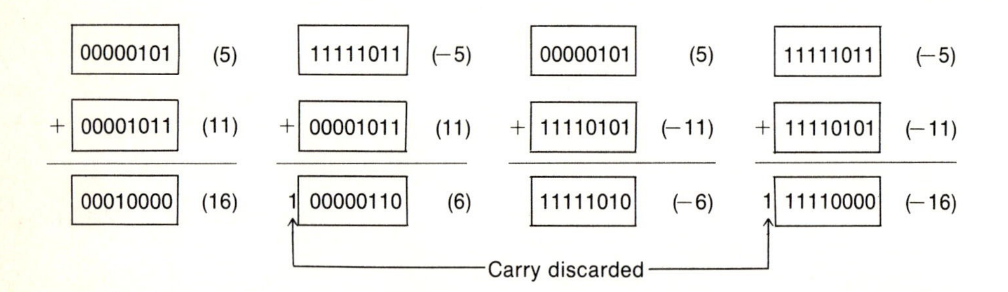

Subtraction is performed by taking the twos complement of the subtrahend and adding it to the minuend, as demonstrated in the following examples:

[1] The twos complement is formed by changing each 1 bit to a 0 bit, and each 0 bit to a 1 bit, and by adding 1 to the result.

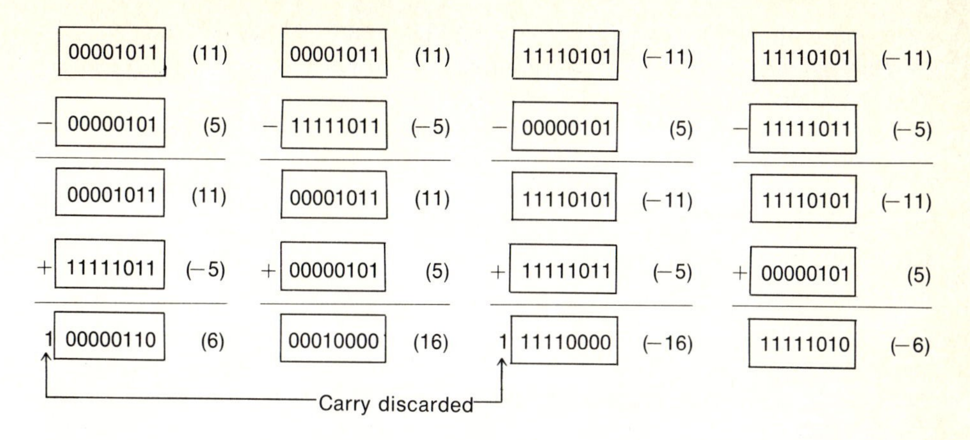

In general, twos complement representation requires a simpler set of microroutines than needed with signed-magnitude representation, but the fact that negative values are stored in twos complement form complicates input and output conversion. Twos complement representation is used when general-purpose registers are used for indexing, addressing, and fixed-point arithmetic.

4.3.1.3 Adder-generated Constants Several constants and functions on an operand can be generated by using the B-register as the Y select input to the adder. The following is a useful set of these constants and functions:

Constant or function	Y select for twos complement representation	Y select for signed-magnitude representation	Example
−2	−1−1	$+B_{101}+1$	A1−1−1→ or $A1+B_{101}+1\rightarrow$
−1	−1	B_{101}	A1−1→ or $A1-B_{101}\rightarrow$
0	0	0	0→
1	1	1	1→
2	+1+1	+1+1	A1+1+1→
−B	−B	B_{FTT}	−B→ or $B_{FTT}\rightarrow$
not B	NOT B		NOT B→
sign B		B_{T00}	$A1 \vee B_{T00}\rightarrow$
abs B		B_{0TT}	$A1+B_{0TT}\rightarrow$
neg B		B_{1TT}	$A1+B_{1TT}\rightarrow$

It is generally faster to use adder-generated constants than to use literal assignment or to read them from S-memory.

4.3.1.4 Constants Generated through the Barrel Switch Constants can also be generated by a combination of literal assignment and the use of shift operations. This method has the following format:

LIT C→A1
n→SAR,v→LIT

where n is the number of places to be shifted and v is a literal value. For example, the value 237 can be placed in the high-order byte of register A1 by the following statements:

```
LIT C→A1
8→SAR,237→LIT
```

The operation is then completed during the next logic-unit operation.

Special constants of the form 2^n can be generated through the use of the following format:

```
1 C→destination
COMP n→SAR
```

For example, the value $2^4 = 16$ is generated in the B-register as follows:

```
1 C→B
COMP 4→SAR
```

Alternatively, a bit can be set in the nth position from the leftmost position with the following format:

```
1 C→destination
n→SAR
```

For example, the statements

```
1 C→MIR
15→SAR
```

place a 1 bit in the fifteenth position from the left in the MIR.

4.3.2 Exchanging the Values in Registers

In a microprogrammable processing unit, the number of machine registers that can be used in logic-unit operations is usually limited. This fact, coupled with restrictions on adder input, makes it frequently necessary to exchange the values in registers. In general, the operation is relatively straightforward, except that an extra register for the exchange operation is usually not available.

4.3.2.1 Exchange without a Temporary Register Use of the XOR logic operation in the following manner allows the values of two registers to be interchanged:

```
reg#1 XOR reg#2→reg#1
reg#1 XOR reg#2→reg#2
reg#1 XOR reg#2→reg#1
```

For example, the statements

A1 XOR B→A1
A1 XOR B→B
A1 XOR B→A1

exchange the values in A1 and B.

4.3.2.2 Exchange B-Register and MIR The values in the B-register and the MIR can be exchanged, as follows:

B→MIR, BMI

The BMI command is particularly useful in D-machine microprogramming since it is the only method of moving a word from the MIR to other logic-unit registers.

4.3.2.3 Exchange A- and B-Registers Using the MIR Since the MIR does not participate as an adder input to logic-unit operation, it can be used as a temporary register in an A- and B-register exchange operation. The following statements exchange the values of the A1- and B-registers:

A1→MIR
B→A1, BMI

Use of the MIR register is preferred over the use of the XOR operation, given earlier, since two instead of three instructions are required.

4.3.3 Comparison Operations

Conventional operations can be microprogrammed using the following relations, with registers A1 and B as models:

Comparison	Adder operation	True condition
$A1<B$	$A1-B$	NOT AOV
$A1\leq B$	$A1-B-1$	NOT AOV
$A1\neq B$	A1 EQV B	NOT ABT
$A1=B$	A1 EQV B	ABT
$A1\geq B$	$A1-B$	AOV
$A1>B$	$A1-B-1$	AOV

The conventions assume that values are stored using twos complement representation.

It should be noted that the true conditions may appear to be incorrect unless the manner in which the D-machine performs arithmetic is taken into consideration. The true conditions *are correct,* and the D-machine uses complement arithmetic. Also, the following relations exist:

$$-B \equiv +B_{FFF} + 1$$
$$-B - 1 \equiv +B_{FFF}$$

As an example, assume 8-bit registers, the following values,

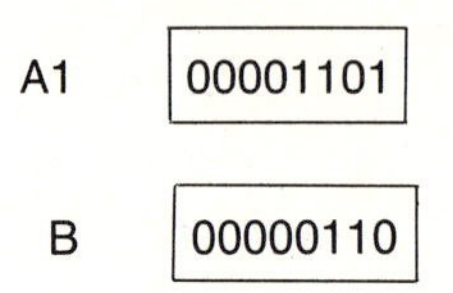

and a test for the condition: A1 ≥ B. The comparison is calculated as follows:

$$A1 - B \equiv A1 + B_{FFF} + 1$$

It is executed as

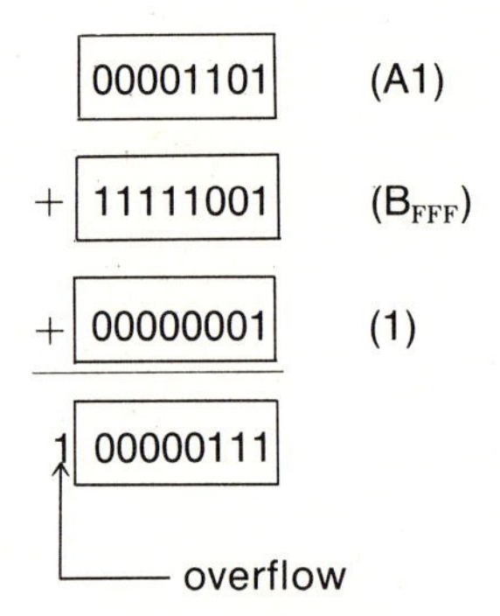

Therefore, the test for adder overflow (AOV) is appropriate. If the contents of A1 had been less than the contents of B, then no adder overflow would have occurred.

4.3.4 Looping

Looping is an important aspect of microprogramming because many S-machine operations are performed on a bit-by-bit basis. Several techniques for controlling the execution of a loop are presented.

4.3.4.1 Method of Leading Decisions The method of leading decisions tests the control parameters before a loop is executed and uses the following skeleton:

```
       TEST − 1→AMPCR
       ..., CALL
LOOP:  ...
TEST:  IF condition THEN ..., JUMP
```

where the ellipses (. . .) denote one or more type I instructions. The CALL command branches to the conditional statement and establishes the loop address for subsequent iterations. The following microprogram segment multiplies two positive integers by repeated addition and uses the method of leading decisions, which is desirable in the event that the multiplier is 0.

```
    INIT: LIT R→A1,BAD        % LOAD 10 TO B AND
       10→LIT, 1→SAR          % 5 TO A1
COMMENT LOOP STARTS HERE
       TEST−1→AMPCR
       0→A2, CALL        % BRANCH TO TEST
 LOOP: A2+B→A2           % PRODUCT IN A2
 TEST: A1−1→A1
       IF AOV THEN JUMP       % BACK TO LOOP
```

In the microprogram segment, A1 contains the multiplicand, B contains the multiplier, and A2 contains the product. The microprogram segment has been run on the translator/simulator, and the printout is given in Figure 4.5. The above microprogram in the reference language and the same program in TRANSLANG demonstrate the use of the comment, contained on the same line or as a separate statement. Also, when the ELSE option is omitted in an IF statement, an ELSE STEP successor is assumed by default.

4.3.4.2 Fixed Iterations The following skeleton permits a loop to be executed exactly n times:[1]

```
        n→CTR
        TEST−1→AMPCR
        ..., INC, CALL
LOOP:   ...
        ...
TEST:   IF NOT COV THEN ..., INC, JUMP
```

where the same conventions regarding the ellipses and CALL statement exist as in the previous skeleton. The following microprogram segment adds the five values in S-memory locations 65 through 69 and places the sum in S-memory location 70:

```
B001 L→A2, LCTR
5→LIT, COMP 6→SAR
TEST−1→AMPCR
0→A1, INC, CALL
```

[1] It is recognized that the statement n→CTR is not a valid statement except for special values of n. It is used to denote that the CTR is loaded with a value. The next example gives a valid case.

a Translation

```
>>>>> TRANSLANG D MACHINE MICRØTRANSLATØR

ENTER FILENAME FØR HEX? F45HEX
SUPPRESS BIT PATTERNS?(1=SUPPRESS)? 1
SUPPRESS HEX LISTING?(1=SUPPRESS)? 1
IF INPUT IN FILE ENTER 1? 31
ENTER SØURCE FILENAME? FIG45

0000    INIT. LIT R = A1, BAD $ LØAD 10 TØ B AND
0001        10 = LIT, 1 = SAR   $ 5 TØ A1
0002        CØMMNT LØØP STARTS HERE $
0002        TEST - 1 = AMPCR $
0003        0 = A2, CALL $ BRANCH TØ TEST
0004    LØØP. A2 + B = A2 $ PRØDUCT IN A2
0005    TEST. A1 - 1 = A1 $
0006        IF AØV THEN JUMP $ BACK TØ LØØP
0007        END $

THE TØTAL NUMBER ØF ERRØRS =     0

EXECUTE (Y/N)? N
```

b Execution

```
2) DMACH1     (CØMPILED)   07 JAN 76   17:40


ENTER SAME FILENAME FØR HEX? F45HEX
ØUTPUT REGISTERS AND S MEMØRY IN INTEGER(1) ØR ØCTAL(2)? 1
INPUT S MEMØRY IN INTEGER(1) ØR ØCTAL IN Ø11 FØRMAT(2)? 1
STARTING ADDRESS =? 0
MAXIMUM NUMBER ØF CLØCKS TØ SIMULATE=? 30
NUMBER ØF CLØCKS BETWEEN ØUTPUT PØINTS=? 1

ENTER ØUTPUT LINES DESIRED      1-ADDRESSES AND CLØCK
2- A1,A2,A3,B    3- MIR,SAR,LIT,CTR,AMPCR     4- BR1,BR2,MAR,BMAR,GC1,GC2
 5- CØNDITIØNS
ENTER NUMBER ØF ØUTPUT LINES DESIRED? 5

BEGIN ØUTPUT AT MPM ADDRESS=? 7
END ØUTPUT AT MPM ADDRESS=? 7
ENTER 1 FØR S MEMØRY DUMP WHEN PRØGRAM TERMINATES?



ENTER S MEMØRY VALUES IN CØNSECUTIVE BLØCKS
ENTER 9999 FØR STARTING ADDRESS WHEN FINISHED


STARTING S MEMØRY ADDRESS=? 9999



END ØF SIMULATIØN - REGISTERS CØNTAIN


P(1) ADDR. =     6       P(3) ADDR. =     6       CLØCK =     22
A1 =4294967295        A2 =          50        A3 =          0        B =          10
MIR =           0        SAR = 1        LIT = 10        CTR =  0        AMPCR =    3
BR1 =  0      BR2 =  0        MAR =  0        BMAR =     0        GC1=0   GC2=0
LC1=0   LC2=0   MST=1   LST=1   ABT=1   AØV=0   CØV=0   SAI=0   RDC=0   INT=0
```

Figure 4.5 Microprogram to perform integer multiplication by repeated addition. A1 contains the multiplicand (initially), B contains the multiplier, and A2 contains the product (after execution is complete).

```
LOOP:   MR2
        WHEN RDC THEN BEX
        A1+B→A1, MIR
TEST:   IF NOT COV THEN A2+1→A2, MAR2, INC, JUMP
WRITE:  A2+1→MAR2
        MW2, IF SAI
        WHEN SAI THEN STEP
```

In the microprogram segment, A2 contains the running count of the S-memory location, and A1 contains the sum. The microprogram segment has been run on the translator/simulator, and the printout is given in Figure 4.6.

4.3.5 Shifting

In an emulator, shifting operations are particularly useful for executing double-register fixed-point operations and for field isolation during instruction decoding. Because these functions are performed frequently, an efficient method of doing them is a major contributor to overall system efficiency.

4.3.5.1 Double-length Shift Assume that the A1- and B-registers are *logically* one double-width register, as follows:

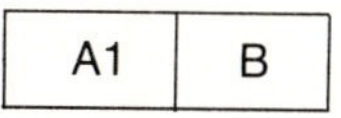

A double-length shift to the right operates as follows:

1 The rightmost bits of A1 are shifted into B.
2 A1 is filled on the left with 0s.
3 The rightmost bits of B are shifted off.

Assuming 6-bit registers, for simplicity, a 2-bit shift to the right would execute as follows:

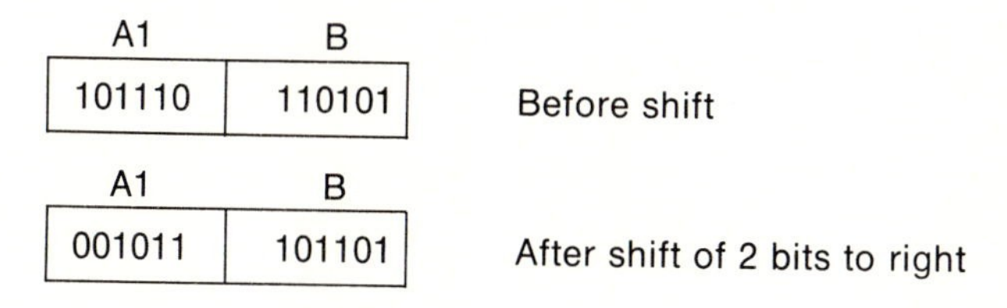

A microprogram skeleton to shift the registers to the right by the amount given in the SAR is given as follows:

```
B R→MIR
A1 L→, BBI
A1 R→A1
```

a Translation

```
>>>>> TRANSLANG D MACHINE MICRØTRANSLATØR

ENTER FILENAME FØR HEX? F46HEX
SUPPRESS BIT PATTERNS?(1=SUPPRESS)? 1
SUPPRESS HEX LISTING?(1=SUPPRESS)? 1
IF INPUT IN FILE ENTER 1? 31
ENTER SØURCE FILENAME? FIG46

0000        B001 L = A2, LCTR $ FØRM 64 IN A2
0001        5 = LIT, CØMP 6 = SAR $
0002        TEST - 1 = AMPCR $
0003        0 = A1, INC, CALL $
0004     LØØP. MR2 $
0005        WHEN RDC THEN BEX $
0006        A1 + B = A1, MIR $
0007     TEST. IF NØT CØV THEN A2 + 1 = A2, MAR2, INC, JUMP $
0008     WRITE. A2 + 1 = MAR2 $
0009        MW2, IF SAI $
0010        WHEN SAI THEN STEP $
0011        END $

THE TØTAL NUMBER ØF ERRØRS =     0

EXECUTE (Y/N)? N
```

b Execution

```
2) DMACH1     (CØMPILED)  07 JAN 76   17:52


ENTER SAME FILENAME FØR HEX? F46HEX
ØUTPUT REGISTERS AND S MEMØRY IN INTEGER(1) ØR ØCTAL(2)? 1
INPUT S MEMØRY IN INTEGER(1) ØR ØCTAL IN Ø11 FØRMAT(2)? 1
STARTING ADDRESS =? 0
MAXIMUM NUMBER ØF CLØCKS TØ SIMULATE=? 50
NUMBER ØF CLØCKS BETWEEN ØUTPUT PØINTS=? 1

ENTER ØUTPUT LINES DESIRED      1-ADDRESSES AND CLØCK
2- A1,A2,A3,B    3- MIR,SAR,LIT,CTR,AMPCR    4- BR1,BR2,MAR,BMAR,GC1,GC2
 5- CØNDITIØNS
ENTER NUMBER ØF ØUTPUT LINES DESIRED? 5

BEGIN ØUTPUT AT MPM ADDRESS=? 11
END ØUTPUT AT MPM ADDRESS=? 11
ENTER 1 FØR S MEMØRY DUMP WHEN PRØGRAM TERMINATES? 1

ENTER S MEMØRY VALUES IN CØNSECUTIVE BLØCKS
ENTER 9999 FØR STARTING ADDRESS WHEN FINISHED


STARTING S MEMØRY ADDRESS=? 65
FINAL S MEMØRY ADDRESS FØR THIS BLØCK=? 70
SMEM(   65)=? 4
SMEM(   66)=? 2
SMEM(   67)=? 6
SMEM(   68)=? 5
SMEM(   69)=? 9
SMEM(   70)=? 0


STARTING S MEMØRY ADDRESS=? 9999
```

Figure 4.6 Microprogram to sum the five values in S-memory locations 65 through 69 and place the sum in S-memory location 70. A1 contains the running count of the S-memory locations, and A2 contains the sum.

```
END ØF SIMULATIØN - REGISTERS CØNTAIN

P(1) ADDR. =  10       P(3) ADDR. =  10       CLØCK =    31
A1 =          26     A2 =            69     A3 =          0      B =          9
MIR =          26      SAR =26         LIT =  5      CTR =  0      AMPCR =    3
BR1 =  0       BR2 =  0      MAR = 70       BMAR =    70       GC1=0   GC2=0
LC1=0  LC2=0  MST=0  LST=0  ABT=0  AØV=0  CØV=0  SAI=1  RDC=1  INT=0

MEMØRY DUMP REQUESTED

ENTER VALUES AS DØNE IN MEMØRY INPUT (9999 FØR STARTING ADDRESS WHEN
FINISHED)

STARTING S MEMØRY ADDRESS=? 65
FINAL S MEMØRY ADDRESS FØR THIS BLØCK=? 70

S MEMØRY(  65) TØ S MEMØRY(  70) =

        4           2           6           5           9

       26
STARTING S MEMØRY ADDRESS=? 9999
```

Figure 4.6 *Continued.*

The destination command, BBI, or's the output of the barrel switch with the MIR and places the result in the B-register. Using a SAR value of 2, the reader should verify the microprogram skeleton with the above contents of A1 and B.

For a double-length left shift, assume the registers are concatenated *logically,* as follows:

B	A1

A double-length shift to the left operates as follows:

1 The leftmost bits of A1 are shifted into B.
2 A1 is filled on the right with zeros.
3 The leftmost bits of B are shifted off.

Again, assuming 6-bit registers for simplicity, a 2-bit shift to the left would execute as follows:

B	A1	
101110	110101	Before shift

B	A1	
111011	010100	After shift of 2 bits to the left

A microprogram skeleton to shift the registers to the left by the word length (twos) complement of the contents of the SAR is given as follows:

```
B L→MIR
A1 R→, BBI
A1 L→A1
```

Thus, to shift two places to the left, a shift value of

```
COMP 2→SAR
```

is needed. The reader should again verify the microprogram skeleton with the above contents of B and A1.

4.3.5.2 Field Isolation Isolation of bits within a field of a word is normally accomplished by shifting and masking. Given the following general problem:

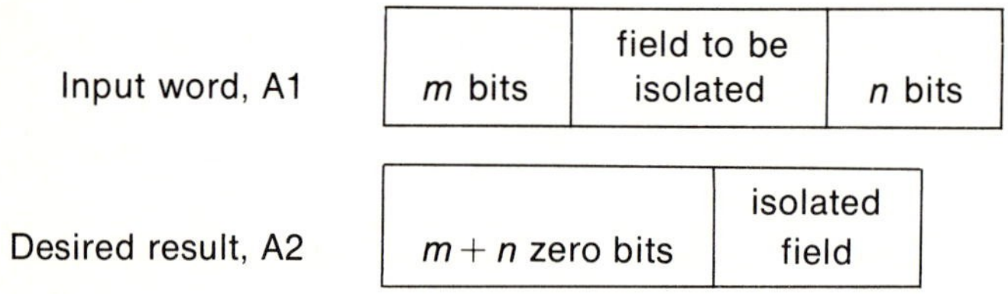

Input word, A1	m bits	field to be isolated	n bits

Desired result, A2	$m + n$ zero bits	isolated field

The simplest method is to shift to the left, end off m places, followed by a right end-off shift of $m + n$ places, as follows:

```
A1 L→A2
COMP m→SAR
A2 R→A2
m+n→SAR
```

A potentially more efficient method is to use a mask combined with shifting, as follows:

```
NOT 0 R→B
m→SAR
A1 AND B R→A2
n→SAR
```

The potential efficiency of this technique exists in the fact that the first two instructions serve only to construct a mask, which could be developed using several methods including literal assignment. A circular shift followed by a mask operation could also be used as follows:

A1 C→A2
n→SAR, k→LIT
A2 AND LIT→A2

where $k = 2^w - 1$ and w is the width of the field to be isolated. If k exceeds 8 bits, then the AMPCR can be used instead of the LIT.

4.3.6 Miscellaneous Techniques

Effective use of the logical operations can help in the development of an efficient microprogram. For example, a frequently used method of doubling the value of an A-register is as follows:

A1→B
A1+B→A1

A more efficient technique is available with the *or add* (OAD) instruction as follows:

A1 OAD 0→A1

Using the same logical operation, the next-to-most-significant bit of a register can be tested as follows:

A1 OAD 0→
IF MST THEN ...

A variety of additional techniques are introduced throughout the remainder of this book as microprogramming topics are introduced.

VOCABULARY

The reader should be familiar with the following terms in the context in which they were used in the chapter:

Statement label
Microprogram efficiency
Complement
Logical negation
Logical operation
Arithmetic operation
Condition
Condition-adjust specification
Shift operation
Destination specification
Successor
Constant
Signed-magnitude representation
Twos complement representation
Exchange
Loop
Method of leading decisions
Double-length shift
Field isolation

QUESTION SET

The following questions test your comprehension of the subject matter. All questions can be answered from the text directly or possibly through a logical extension of the subjects presented. Some questions would be suitable for discussion sessions.

1. Give two methods of keeping count of the number of iterations in a microprogram loop.
2. When does $COMP_n$ mean twos complement, and when does it mean ones complement?
3. Does the logical operator NOT take the one or twos complement?
4. What is the "first," or prime, ingredient of an effective microprogram?
5. What are the three basic microprogram functions that can be performed conditionally or unconditionally?
6. In a nanoinstruction, what do bits 28 to 31 specify?
7. For a right-shift operation, is the shift amount placed in the SAR in true form or complement form?
8. What bit is shared in a nanoinstruction, and what functions share it?
9. What successor command is not conditional?
10. What are three methods of generating a constant?
11. Assume that a value in signed-magnitude representation is contained in the B-register. What mathematical function does the specification B_{0TT} perform?
12. How can information be moved from the MIR to other machine registers?
13. What is the primary advantage of the method of leading decisions?

EXERCISES

1. Write a microprogram to sum the first *n* locations of S-memory, where *n* can be any value from 0 to 255.
2. Give a bit-by-bit example, using hypothetical 8-bit registers, for each of the following operations:

    X NRI Y
    X NIM Y
    X EQU Y
    X IMP Y
    X RIM Y

3. Show *what* nanoinstruction bits are set for the following statements:

    A1 + 1→MIR, BEX
    IF ABT THEN INC, JUMP ELSE SKIP
    MR1, IF COV THEN B→MIR, RETN ELSE JUMP
    A1 AND B→A2, AMPCR, MAR, B, MIR
    LCTR, INC

4. S-memory locations 100 and 101 contain the values H and I, respectively. Write a microprogram segment to compute

$$H+2*I$$

and store the result in S-memory location 102.

5 Write a microprogram segment to isolate the field occupying bits 20 to 27 of register A1 and place the result right-justified in register A2.

6 Registers A1 and B contain integer values in signed-magnitude representation. Write a microprogram segment to compare the contents of A1 and B and branch to symbolic location REPEAT if $A1 \geq B$.

Chapter 5

Introduction to Emulation

5.1 OBJECTIVES

The objective of this chapter is to demonstrate the characteristics of a simple emulator. In a practical sense, the chapter ties together many of the concepts presented earlier and serves as a point of reference in the presentation of microprogramming.

Emulation is the primary application of microprogramming, even though substantial use of the methodology is used in the development of device/controllers and modern laboratory equipment. Special microprogramming techniques are required to support emulation, and a presentation of those techniques is a secondary objective of this chapter.

5.2 MICROPROGRAMMING TECHNIQUES RELEVANT TO EMULATION

Emulation normally involves the use of base registers for MPM and S-memory addressing, tables of literal assignments that serve as "jump tables," the effective use of S-memory operations, and methods of performing related operations in an efficient manner. In general, the concepts and methods exist independently of a particular microprogrammed computer.

5.2.1 Base Registers

Recall that the concatenation of the BR*i* registers and the MAR form a 16-bit address, with either BR1 or BR2 pointing to a 256-word block of S-memory. Thus, BR1 or BR2 can be used as a *base register* for S-memory addressing, as in base/index/displacement addressing, or as a base register that points to accumulator registers held in S-memory.

5.2.1.1 S-Memory Access Typically, therefore, S-memory is addressed for two reasons:

1 To access S-machine registers, that is, general-purpose registers, floating-point registers, etc.
2 To access S-memory for data words (that is, operands) and for instruction words (that is, S-machine instructions)

It is necessary to establish an arbitrary but useful convention for assigning the BR1 and BR2 registers to a particular type of access. The following arbitrary convention is offered:

BR1 points to S-machine registers in S-memory.
BR2 points to instructions and data in S-memory.

Therefore, BR1 is always loaded explicitly, as in the following statement:

```
A1→BR1
```

and, accordingly, the MAR is also assigned a value explicitly. On the other hand, BR2 is always loaded implicitly—as the high-order part of an S-memory address—as in the following statement:

```
A2 + 1→MAR2
```

in which the BR2 and MAR registers are both loaded.

5.2.1.2 Loading the Memory Address Register Two methods are generally available for loading the MAR for use in S-machine register operations. When the S-machine register is known independently of the S-program, then the following skeleton may be used:

```
LMAR, ...
S-machine-register – #→LIT
```

as in the following example,

```
A1 + 1→A2,LMAR
4→LIT
```

When the S-machine register is not known independently of the S-program, it may be field-isolated in a D-machine register and assigned to the MAR through a type I instruction using the following skeleton:

S-machine-register→MAR

as in the statement

B→MAR

The LMAR command moves the contents of the LIT to the MAR without going through the adder or the barrel switch.

Collectively, the concatenation of either BR1 or BR2 with the MAR is referred to as *BMAR*.

5.2.2 S-Memory Read and Write Operations

The procedures for S-memory read and write operations given in earlier chapters were *precisely* correct but simplified. There is more to it.

5.2.2.1 General Specifications The first major consideration is that two kinds of information are involved in S-memory operations: addresses and data. Consider the following skeleton, which will always work and was used previously:

```
S-memory address→MAR2
MR2, ...
...
WHEN RDC THEN BEX, ...
```

(Clearly, several instructions may be placed between the MR2 and the WHEN statement, and in a real-time operating environment this facility provides overlap.) In reality, however, two steps are involved with a read operation:

1 The memory address is accepted from the BMAR by the switch interlock.

2 The data word is placed on the external input bus[1] so that it can be read into the B-register with the BEX command.

With a write operation, a single step is involved, which is the acceptance of the BMAR and the data word in the MIR by the switch interlock.

5.2.2.2 Amplification of the Read Operation During a read operation, it is possible to use the BMAR address prior to read completion by using the following skeleton:

[1] This is called the *external data interface*, or XDI.

Skeleton	Comment
S-memory-address→MAR2	
MR2, ..., IF SAI	Resets SAI
...	At least one intervening instruction
WHEN SAI THEN ...	Address can now be changed
...	
WHEN RDC THEN BEX, ...	Data available

However, overlapped operations are designed for multiple-processor systems and are rarely used (or needed) with the D-machine simulator.

5.2.2.3 Amplification of the Write Operation The correct skeleton for the S-memory write operation is as follows:

Skeleton	Comment
S-memory-address→MAR2	
data→MIR	
MW2, ..., IF SAI	Initiate write and reset SAI
...	At least one intervening instruction
WHEN SAI THEN ...	MIR and MAR may be changed

It takes one intervening instruction to set SAI after a read or write operation. Otherwise, a WHEN SAI statement that immediately follows the read or write instruction will be delayed. (Incidentally, this is the case in Figure 4.1 in which the WHEN SAI immediately follows the MW1 command.)

It is possible to load the MIR and the MAR with one type I instruction, as demonstrated in the following skeleton:

```
logic-operation→MIR,LMAR
S-machine-register – #→LIT
MW1, ..., IF SAI
```

It is not possible to move the contents of the BR1, BR2, and MAR back to the logic unit, but it is possible to move the contents of the MIR to the B-register with the BMI and BBI commands.

5.2.2.4 Timing Since there is no device contention with S-memory operations, the following skeleton may be used:

```
MR1, ..., BEX
WHEN RDC THEN ...
```

so that when a "true" condition is encountered by the D-machine, the BEX command is completed.

In general, when a destination register is specified in a type I instruction, that destination register is replaced when the next true condition is received. However, logic-unit and memory-device operations are executed during the normal phase 3 cycle. In the preceding example, therefore, the MR1 is executed immediately, and the BEX is executed when the RDC condition is true.

5.2.2.5 Multiple Reads of the Same Data After an S-memory read operation, repeated BEX commands without an intervening read provide repeated access to the same data word from the external device interface (XDI). In the following skeleton, for example,

```
S-memory-address→MAR2
MR2
...
BEX
...
BEX
```

each BEX moves a replica of the same data to the B-register, whereas in

```
S-memory-address – 1→MAR2
MR2
...
BEX
....
S-memory-address –2→MAR2
MR2
...
BEX
```

a different data word is accessed with each BEX command.

5.2.3 Literal Tables

Since constant values, such as table entries, cannot be stored in a microprogram, each occurrence of the use of a constant value, regardless of whether it represents a data item or an address, must be moved to a register with a type I or a type II instruction. Therefore, a table in the S-program sense is normally implemented as a list of literal assignment statements in microprogramming. In S-machine programming, a table entry is referenced with a load instruction. In microprogramming, a table entry is placed in a machine register with the EXEC instruction. Table references in S-machine programming and in microprogramming are depicted in Figure 5.1.

5.2.3.1 Jump Table A *jump table* takes the form:

```
labelA – 1→AMPCR
labelB – 1→AMPCR
      .
      .
      .
labelK – 1→AMPCR
```

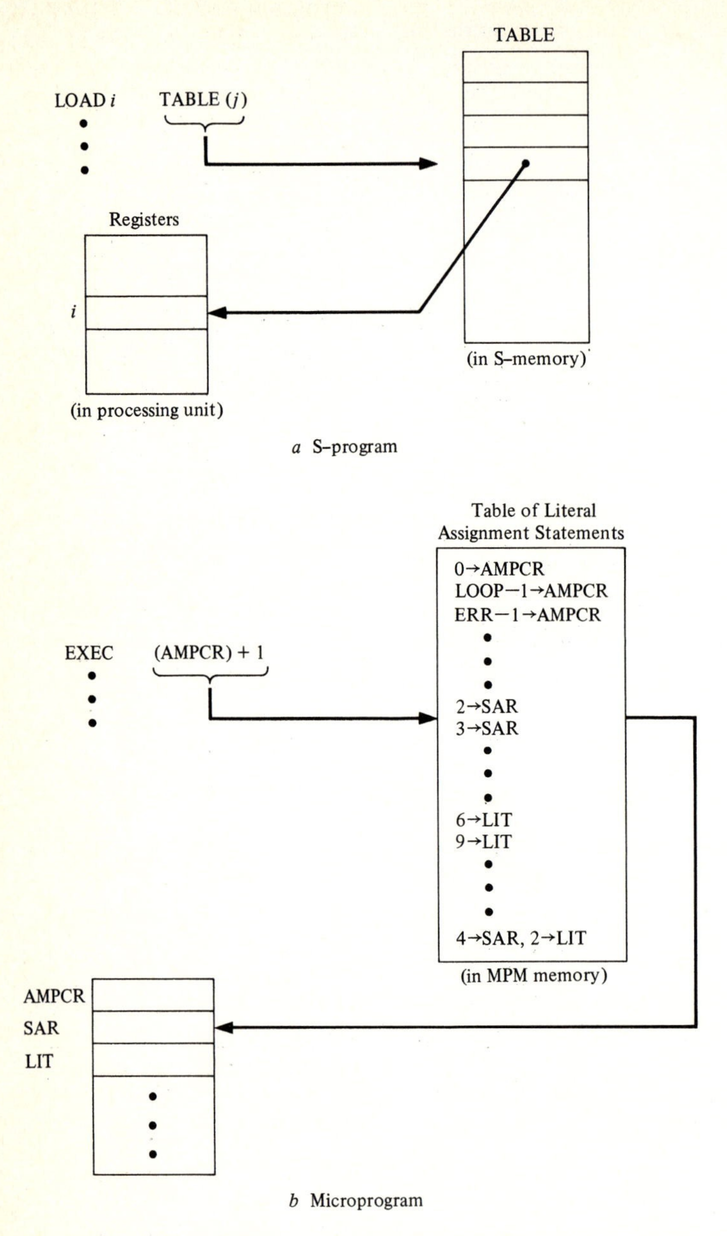

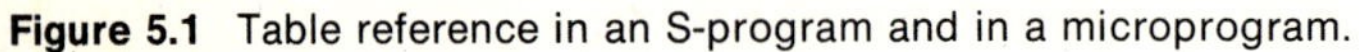

Figure 5.1 Table reference in an S-program and in a microprogram.

where the labels are statement labels in a microprogram and the -1 (that is, *label* -1) compensates for the fact that D-machine branch addresses are always to the contents of the AMPCR + 1 [that is, (AMPCR) + 1]. To reference the table, we use a sequence of statements such as

```
A1 + AMPCR→AMPCR
base − 1→AMPCR
EXEC
JUMP
```

where A1 contains the table offset. The statement *base* $-$ 1→AMPCR places the base address of the table in the AMPCR, and the statement A1 + AMPCR→ AMPCR puts the address of the desired literal assignment instruction in the AMPCR. Next, the EXEC instruction executes the instruction in the jump table at (AMPCR) + 1, that is, the desired MPM location to which program control will be passed, in an out-of-line mode. Execution continues with the instruction following EXEC. Lastly, the JUMP command passes program control to the statement label specified in the jump table at the offset contained in A1. If a return is expected from the branch command, then CALL should be used instead of JUMP. An example of the use of a jump table is given in Figure 5.2.

	Microprogram	Comments
TBL:	ABLE−1→AMPCR	
	BAKER−1→AMPCR	Jump table
	CHARLY−1→AMPCR	
	. . .	
	1→A2	Offset of 1 to A2
	A2+AMPCR→AMPCR	Compute literal location
	TBL−1→AMPCR	
	EXEC	Place jump address in AMPCR
	JUMP	Pass control to (AMPCR)+1
ABLE:	———	
	———	
	———	
	———	
BAKER:	———	Control passes to here
	———	
	———	
	———	
CHARLY:	———	
	———	
	———	
	———	

Figure 5.2 Example of the use of a jump table.

5.2.3.2 EXEC Command In the summary of successor control options, given in Table 4.3, the "next content of the MPCR" for the EXEC command is (MPCR), as with the WAIT command, whereas the STEP command has an entry of (MPCR) + 1. This is a specification of the fact that the EXEC command is performed first, followed by the remainder of the statement. This design allows mask, shift, and operand values to be selected from a literal table in the instruction in which they are used. For example, consider the following microprogram segment:

```
1 SAR, 3→LIT                    (1)
2 SAR, 7→LIT                    (2)
3 SAR, 15→LIT                   (3)
...
table index→AMPCR               (4)
...
A3 AND LIT R→..., EXEC          (5)
```

Statements (1), (2), and (3) represent a literal table. Statement (4) places the MPM address of a table entry in the AMPCR. Statement (5) executes the literal assignment statement out of line, placing mask and shift values in the LIT and SAR, respectively, and then performs the AND operation with the newly determined operands. Using the LIT register as a mask value governs only the rightmost 8 bits of an adder operation; the leftmost 24 bits are 0s. If a larger mask is required along with the flexibility of using the EXEC command, the AMPCR can be used in a literal assignment statement and in the logical operation. It provides a means of using a 12-bit mask.

5.3 DESIGN OF A SIMPLE EMULATOR

This section presents a simple emulator and a corresponding set of microroutines.[1] A complete analysis of the microroutines is given in the next section. Although the microprogram given is correct, it assumes a D-machine with a logic unit of 16 bits, for simplicity, and will not run on our translator/simulator, which is programmed as a 32-bit machine. An expanded 32-bit version of the same emulator with multiple registers is given in Chapter 9.

5.3.1 Characteristics of the S-Machine

The S-machine is a one-address computer with a single accumulator. Each instruction word is 16 bits wide, as is the accumulator. The instruction format is:

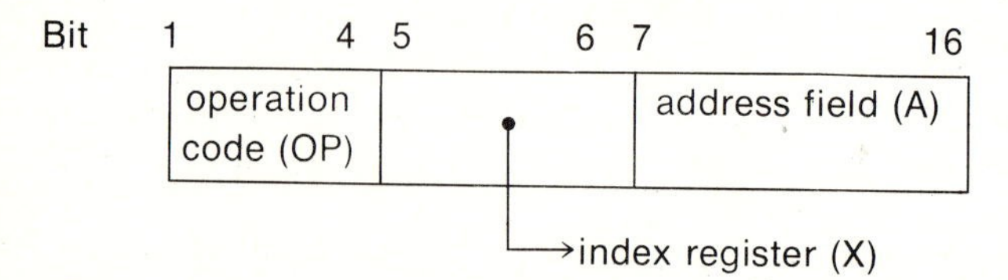

[1] The emulator was designed and microprogrammed by Dr. Earl Reigel of the Burroughs Corporation.

Table 5.1 Machine Operations for the Emulator for a One-Address Computer

Name	Operation code	Mnemonic	Description	Symbolic notation
Load	0001	LD	Load the contents of S-memory address A+(X) into the accumulator (ACCUM).	(A+(X))→(ACCUM)
Store	0010	ST	Store the contents of the accumulator in S-memory address A+(X).	(ACCUM)→(A+(X))
Branch	0011	BR	Branch to the instruction at S-memory address A+(X).	→A+(X)
Test zero	0100	TZ	If the contents of the accumulator are all 0s, branch to S-memory address A+(X).	→A+(X) if ACCUM=0
Test least bit	0101	TL	If the lower order (that is, least bit or rightmost bit) of the accumulator is 1, branch to S-memory address A+(X).	→A+(X) if $\text{ACCUM}_{\text{bit }16}$=1
Decrement	0110	DEC	Decrement the contents of S-memory address A+(X) by 1.	(A+(X))−1→(A+(X))
Increment	0111	INC	Increment the contents of S-memory address A+(X) by 1.	(A+(X))+1→(A+(X))
Shift	1000	SHF	Circular shift the contents of the accumulator 1 bit to the right.	

Thus, the operation-code field is 4 bits, the index register is 2 bits, and the address field is 10 bits. Eight different machine operations are defined in Table 5.1.

5.3.2 S-Machine Mapping

When an S-machine is mapped onto a microprogrammed computer, certain conventions must be established for representing the S-machine registers. Clearly, the level of efficiency of the emulator is dependent upon the degree to which the microprogrammed processor matches the S-machine.

The following assignments are used in the emulator:

1 A1 in the D-machine is used as a current-address register.

2 A2 in the D-machine is used as the instruction register and for temporary storage during instruction processing.

```
DRTRY:  ERR-1→AMPCR                                  (1)
        ERR-1→AMPCR                                  (2)
        LD-1→AMPCR                                   (3)
        ST-1→AMPCR                                   (4)
        BR-1→AMPCR                                   (5)
        TZ-1→AMPCR                                   (6)
        TL-1→AMPCR                                   (7)
        DEC-1→AMPCR                                  (8)
        INC-1→AMPCR                                  (9)
        SHF-1→AMPCR                                  (10)
IFETCH: A1→MAR2                                      (11)
        MR2, A1+1→A1, BEX                            (12)
        WHEN RDC THEN B C→A2                         (13)
        10→SAR, 3→LIT                                (14)
        A2 AND LIT→MAR                               (15)
        MR1, B R→AMPCR                               (16)
        12→SAR                                       (17)
        A2 R→A2                                      (18)
        6→SAR                                        (19)
        BEX, EXEC                                    (20)
        WHEN RDC THEN A2+B→A2, MAR2, JUMP            (21)
    LD: MR2, BEX                                     (22)
        IFETCH-1→AMPCR                               (23)
        WHEN RDC THEN B→A3, JUMP                     (24)
    ST: A3→MIR                                       (25)
        MW2, IF SAI                                  (26)
        IFETCH-1→AMPCR                               (27)
        WHEN SAI THEN JUMP                           (28)
    BR: IFETCH-1→AMPCR                               (29)
        A2→A1, RETN                                  (30)
    TZ: NOT A3→                                      (31)
        IFETCH-1→AMPCR                               (32)
        IF ABT THEN A2→A1 RETN ELSE JUMP             (33)
    TL: A3→                                          (34)
        IFETCH-1→AMPCR                               (35)
        IF LST THEN A2→A1 RETN ELSE JUMP             (36)
   DEC: MR2, B111→A2, BEX                            (37)
        IFETCH-1→AMPCR                               (38)
        WHEN RDC THEN A2+B→MIR                       (39)
        MW2, IF SAI                                  (40)
        WHEN SAI THEN JUMP                           (41)
   INC: MR2, BEX                                     (42)
        IFETCH-1→AMPCR                               (43)
        WHEN RDC THEN 0+B+1→MIR                      (44)
        MW2, IF SAI                                  (45)
        WHEN SAI THEN JUMP                           (46)
   SHF: IFETCH-1→AMPCR                               (47)
        1→SAR                                        (48)
        A3 C→A3, JUMP                                (49)
```

Figure 5.3 Emulator microprogram for the S-machine described in this chapter.

3 A3 in the D-machine is used as the accumulator of the S-machine.
4 BR1 points to the index registers in S-memory.

In this example, the word sizes of both machines are assumed to be the same. All other considerations are subordinated to a clear and straightforward presentation of the example.

5.3.3 Emulator Microprogram

The emulator microprogram is given in Figure 5.3. An S-program is assumed to have been placed in S-memory, and the contents of register A1 initially point to the first instruction to be executed. Similarly, BR1 is set by an initialization microroutine to point to the set of four index registers numbered 00, 01, 10, and 11. It is further assumed, for simplicity, that register 00 actually exists and can be used for indexing.

Lastly, the directory (that is, the jump table) of literal assignments refers to an error microroutine at symbolic address ERR. It is not present in the microprogram.

The microprogram is analyzed in the next section.

5.4 ANALYSIS OF THE EMULATOR MICROPROGRAM

From an overall viewpoint, the emulator microprogram (Figure 5.3) is structured very similarly to a conventional S-program in symbolic machine language. The emulator is composed of a directory, a fetch routine, and an execution cycle routine for each type of instruction. Control of the S-machine always originates with and returns to the fetch routine.

5.4.1 Directory

The directory, listed as follows,

```
DRTRY:  ERR - 1→AMPCR     (1)
        ERR - 1→AMPCR     (2)
        LD - 1→AMPCR      (3)
        ST - 1→AMPCR      (4)
        BR - 1→AMPCR      (5)
        TZ - 1→AMPCR      (6)
        TL - 1→AMPCR      (7)
        DEC - 1→AMPCR     (8)
        INC - 1→AMPCR     (9)
        SHF - 1→AMPCR     (10)
```

exists as a list of literal assignment statements and serves as a jump table to the execution cycle microroutines in the emulator. Each literal assignment statement involves address arithmetic at the time of translation to hexadecimal D-machine instructions. Thus, the expression LD − 1, for example, gives the MPM address of LD *minus* 1. If LD were assigned an MPM address of 21, then execution of the statement

LD − 1→AMPCR

would place the value 20 in the AMPCR.

It should be emphasized that the literal assignment statements must be explicitly executed by the D-machine, in order that they can place a value in the AMPCR.

Recall that each type I or type II instruction is represented by an M-instruction in microprogram memory (MPM). Type II instructions are contained entirely in microprogram memory, and type I instructions require a corresponding nanoinstruction. Therefore, each statement in the emulator corresponds to an M-instruction. MPM addresses start with 0 and run upward. There are 49 statements in the emulator, so that the corresponding M-instructions are placed in MPM addresses 0 through 48.

The directory is placed at the beginning of microprogram memory for a particular reason. Look at statements (16) and (20) of the emulator. The numerical operation code is used as the index into the jump table. Statement (16) isolates the operation-code field, and because the directory is located at the beginning of microprogram memory, it is not necessary to add a base address to it which would take another instruction. When statement (20) is executed, the EXEC command executes the statement, out of line, at the MPM address of the operation code, plus 1. In the case of the load instruction with an operation code of 1, the EXEC statement executes the literal assignment statement at location 2 of microprogram memory, which is the LD − 1→AMPCR statement.

5.4.2 Fetch Routine

The fetch routine, listed as follows,

```
IFETCH:  A1→MAR2                                   (11)
         MR2, A1+1→A1, BEX                         (12)
         WHEN RDC THEN B C→A2                      (13)
         10→SAR, 3→LIT                             (14)
         A2 AND LIT→MAR                            (15)
         MR1, B R→AMPCR                            (16)
         12→SAR                                    (17)
         A2 R→A2                                   (18)
         6→SAR                                     (19)
         BEX, EXEC                                 (20)
         WHEN RDC THEN A2+B→A2, MAR2, JUMP         (21)
```

is designed to read the next instruction, update the current-address register, decode the instruction and isolate the various fields, compute the effective address, and branch to the necessary execution cycle routines.

Statement (11) prepares to fetch the next instruction by placing its address (from the current-address register) to the MAR2 register for an S-memory read. Statement (12) initiates the read and updates the current-address register. When the read is complete, statement (13), the instruction in B, is circularly shifted to the right to isolate the index register field, and the B- and A2-registers are as follows:

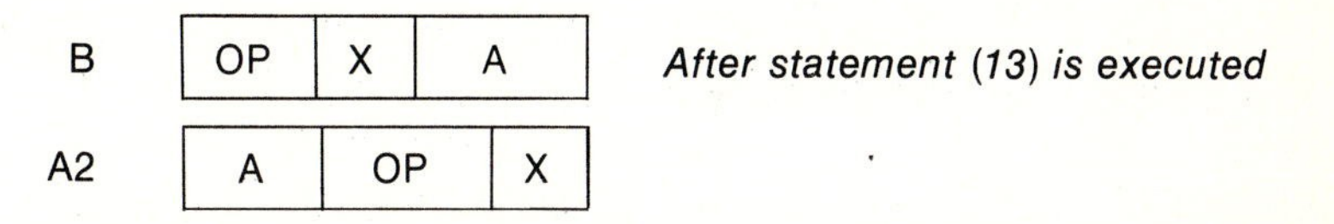

Statement (15) masks off the address(A) and operation-code (OP) fields and moves the index register number to the MAR. Thus, the contents of the MAR are X, or symbolically, (MAR) = X. Statement (16) initiates a read of the S-memory address in ⟨BR1,MAR⟩ to obtain the contents of the index register and also isolates the operation-code field in the AMPCR, as follows:

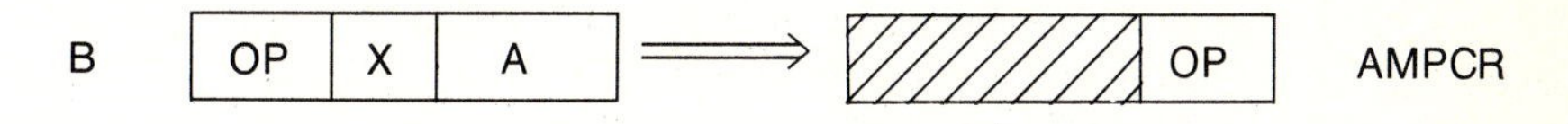

Statement (18) isolates the address field in A2, as follows:

A2 before | A | OP | X | ⟹ | A | A2 after

In statement (20), the contents of the index register are moved from the external device interface (XDI) to the B-register, and the EXEC command is used to place the (address − 1) of the appropriate microroutine for the current instruction in the AMPCR. Because of D-machine timing, the BEX of statement (20) is not completed until the RDC condition of statement (21) is true. When that occurs, the B-register contains the contents of the index register, or symbolically, (B) = (X). Recall that register A2 contains the address field of the instruction. Statement (2) adds the contents of A2 and B to form the effective address and places it in A2 for temporary storage and in MAR2 for subsequent fetch and write operations. Lastly, statement (21) branches to the execution cycle microroutine.

5.4.3 Load Routine

The load routine, listed as follows,

```
LD:  MR2, BEX                           (22)
     IFETCH − 1→AMPCR                   (23)
     WHEN RDC THEN B→A3, JUMP           (24)
```

fetches the operand, places it in the accumulator, and branches to the fetch routine. Symbolically, the operation is (A + (X))→(ACCUM). Statement (22) performs the S-memory read of the effective address placed in the MAR2 by the fetch routine. Statement (24) places the operand in the accumulator (that is, register A3) and passes control to the fetch routine to fetch the next instruction and continue.

5.4.4 Store Routine

The store routine, listed as follows,

```
ST:  A3→MIR                                (25)
     MW2, IF SAI                           (26)
     IFETCH − 1→AMPCR                      (27)
     WHEN SAI THEN JUMP                    (28)
```

places the contents of the accumulator in the effective address, that is, (ACCUM)→(A + (X)), and branches to the fetch routine. Statement (25) moves the contents of the accumulator to the MIR in preparation for an S-memory write operation. Statement (26) resets the SAI condition and initiates the write operation. When the write operation is complete in statement (28), control is passed to the fetch routine.

5.4.5 Branch Routine

The branch routine, listed as follows,

```
BR:  IFETCH − 1→AMPCR                      (29)
     A2→A1, RETN                           (30)
```

moves the effective address to the current-address register and returns to the fetch routine. In statement (30), the effective address in register A2 is moved to the current-address register in A1. The return to the fetch routine is made with the RETN command in order to skip the first statement in it. This technique saves the execution of one instruction because the effective address, which is now the new current address, has already been placed in the MAR2 by the last statement in the fetch routine.

5.4.6 Test Zero Routine

The test zero routine, listed as follows,

```
TZ:  NOT A3→                                       (31)
     IFETCH − 1→AMPCR                              (32)
     IF ABT THEN A2→A1 RETN ELSE JUMP              (33)
```

branches to the effective address if the bits in the accumulator (that is, D-machine register A3) are all 0s. Statement (31) moves the contents of the accumulator to the adder and takes the ones complement of it. This is performed with the unary operator NOT. If the bits of the adder are all true, this means the bits of the accumulator were all 0s. In statement (33), the all-bits-true (ABT) condition is tested, and if true, then execution proceeds as in the execution of the branch instruction. Otherwise, control is passed back to the fetch routine with the JUMP command, and execution of the S-program continues with the next sequential S-machine instruction after the TZ instruction.

5.4.7 Test Least-Bit Routine

The test least-bit routine, listed as follows,

```
TL:  A3→                                          (34)
     IFETCH−1→AMPCR                               (35)
     IF LST THEN A2→A1 RETN ELSE JUMP             (36)
```

branches to the effective address if the rightmost bit of the accumulator is 1. Statement (34) moves the contents of the accumulator, that is, D-machine register A3, to the adder. The least bit is tested in statement (36) with the LST condition, and if it is true, the branch is processed as in the execution of the branch instruction. Otherwise, control is passed back to the fetch routine with the JUMP command, and execution of the S-program continues with the next sequential S-machine instruction after the TL instruction.

5.4.8 Decrement and Increment Routines

The decrement routine, listed as follows,

DEC: MR2, B_{111}→A2,BEX (37)
IFETCH−1→AMPCR (38)
WHEN RDC THEN A2+B→MIR (39)
MW2, IF SAI (40)
WHEN SAI THEN JUMP (41)

fetches the contents of the effective address, decrements that value by 1, and returns it to the same address in S-memory. Statement (37) initiates the fetch operation and moves a word consisting of all 1s to A2. When the read is complete in statement (39), the contents of B are decremented by 1, using the following identity:

$$B - 1 \equiv B + (2^{16} - 1)$$

If register B contained 5, for example, then these calculations are used:

```
    1 1 1 1 1 1 1 1 1 1 1 1 1 1 1 1    A2
  + 0 0 0 0 0 0 0 0 0 0 0 0 0 1 0 1    B
  ---------------------------------
  1 0 0 0 0 0 0 0 0 0 0 0 0 0 1 0 0
  ↑
  └─Carry ignored
```

The result of the adder operation is placed in the MIR for the S-memory write operation that is initiated in statement (40). The MW2 command in statement (40) is performed unconditionally, and the IF SAI clause resets the SAI condition that may have been left in an on condition by a previous S-memory read or write operation. When the write operation, statement (41), is complete, control is returned to the fetch routine.

The increment routine, listed as follows,

```
INC:  MR2, BEX                              (42)
      IFETCH - 1→AMPCR                      (43)
      WHEN RDC THEN 0 + B + 1→MIR           (44)
      MW2, IF SAI                           (45)
      WHEN SAI THEN JUMP                    (46)
```

is similar to the decrement routine except that the contents of the B-register in statement (44) are incremented instead of decremented. The unusual expression $0 + B + 1$ is used in statement (44) because an X select operand is needed.

5.4.9 Shift Routine

The shift routine, listed as follows,

```
SHF:  IFETCH - 1→AMPCR                      (47)
      1→SAR                                 (48)
      A3 C→A3, JUMP                         (49)
```

shifts circularly the contents of the S-machine accumulator, that is, D-machine register A3, one position to the right. The shift operation is performed in statement (49), and microprogram control is then passed back to the fetch routine. The SAR is loaded in statement (48) prior to the shift operation, and so the shift microroutine is self-contained. The situation brings up an important point. If the contents of the SAR were changed before the execution of the circular shift were completed in statement (49), the result might be altered. *A good rule of thumb is to avoid loading the SAR and LIT in the first lines of a microroutine. Always put a type I instruction first.*

VOCABULARY

The reader should be familiar with the following terms in the context in which they were used in the chapter:

Base register
Effective address
Multiple read

Literal table
Jump table
Literal assignment
Accumulator
Current-address register
Instruction register
Directory

QUESTION SET

The following questions test your comprehension of the subject matter. All questions can be answered from the text directly or possibly through a logical extension of the subjects presented. Some questions would be suitable for discussion sessions.

1 Give two reasons why S-memory is accessed.
2 Give two areas that can be used for temporary storage, besides the A1-, A2-, A3-, and B-registers.
3 Why must an entry in a jump table be executed?
4 Would it be possible to write an emulator if there were only one BR*i* register?
5 In an input operation, precisely what functions do the MR*i* and BEX commands perform?
6 What does the EXEC command execute?
7 What is meant by the assertion that "the word size of both machines is the same"?
8 Why is it a good idea to put a type I instruction as the first instruction in a microroutine?

EXERCISES

1 Add a variable-length right-shift operation to the emulator, in which the effective address is the shift amount.
2 Add an ADD instruction to the emulator, which operates symbolically as follows:

$$(\text{ACCUM}) + (\text{A} + (\text{X})) \rightarrow (\text{ACCUM})$$

3 Modify the emulator so that the directory is at the end of the microprogram.
4 Assume an S-machine with the following instruction format for the MOVE instruction:

Bit	1 — 4	6 — 10	11 — 16
	OP code	address 1 (A_1)	address 2 (A_2)

The operation code for MOVE is 0110, and the instruction is described symbolically as follows: $(A_1) \rightarrow (A_2)$. Write a miniemulator to execute this instruction.

Chapter 6

The Translator

6.1 OVERVIEW

This is a short chapter that describes how to use the TRANSLANG translator, and it also includes supporting information on the syntax of the reference and the symbolic hardware languages and a description of hexadecimal microcode.

An overview of the translation process is depicted in Figure 6.1. Two modes of operation are available:

1 The symbolic microprogram is entered along with control information from the terminal or the card reader.

2 The symbolic microprogram is prestored, and only control information is entered from the terminal or the card reader.

The translator can be used in either the batch-processing or the time-sharing modes of operation. However, all examples have been run in the time-sharing mode of operation to demonstrate the manner in which the user interacts with the translator.

Short microprograms are entered from the terminal; long microprograms are prestored in the time-sharing system. The TRANSLANG system supports both methods of entering microprograms.

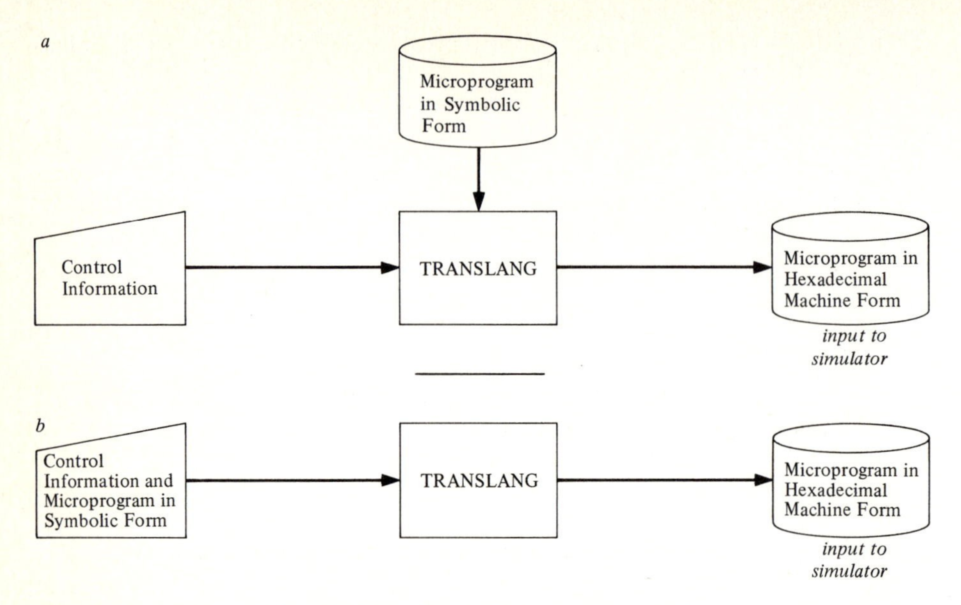

Figure 6.1 Overview of the TRANSLANG translation process. (*a*) Prestored microprogram is in symbolic form. (*b*) Symbolic microprogram is not prestored.

6.2 MICROPROGRAMMING LANGUAGES

The microprogramming reference language has been described informally in preceding chapters. It is described here in Backus-Naur form. The TRANSLANG language was presented only briefly; it is presented in more detail here so that the user can enter microprograms with a minimum of lexical errors.

6.2.1 Backus-Naur Form

When dealing with computer languages, it is frequently desirable to distinguish between a syntactically valid statement and a syntactically invalid statement. A language used to describe another language is known as a *metalanguage*. In the computer field, a metalanguage is used by programmers when constructing programs and by systems programmers when developing processors for programs written in a computer language.

The first well-known metalanguage was *Backus-Naur form* (BNF), developed to describe ALGOL 60; it is widely used today. BNF incorporates three metasymbols from which language definitions are constructed:

Symbol	Meaning
::=	"Is defined to be"
|	Read as "or"
⟨ ⟩	Angular brackets that specify the name of something. All other symbols serve as literals and stand for themselves.

Through the use of these metasymbols and a few operating conventions, a language can be described.

As an example, consider the definition of a number in ordinary computer usage. Typical occurrences of a computer number are 45, 621.4, −57, 1.23E−4, −.0003, and .96E+17. The definition of a number in BNF starts with a description of the basic constituents upon which a structure of definitions is developed. The following statements are used in BNF to describe a number:

```
⟨digit⟩ ::= 0|1|2|3|4|5|6|7|8|9
⟨unsigned integer⟩ ::= ⟨digit⟩|⟨unsigned integer⟩⟨digit⟩
⟨integer⟩ ::= ⟨unsigned integer⟩|+⟨unsigned integer⟩|−⟨unsigned integer⟩
⟨decimal fraction⟩ ::= .⟨unsigned integer⟩
⟨exponent part⟩ ::= E⟨integer⟩
⟨decimal number⟩ ::= ⟨unsigned integer⟩|⟨decimal fraction⟩|
                     ⟨unsigned integer⟩⟨decimal fraction⟩
⟨unsigned number⟩ ::= ⟨decimal number⟩|⟨decimal number⟩⟨exponent part⟩
⟨number⟩ ::= ⟨unsigned number⟩|+⟨unsigned number⟩|−⟨unsigned number⟩
```

The methodology employs left recursion, as demonstrated in the definition of an unsigned integer, which is repeated as follows:

```
⟨unsigned integer⟩ ::= ⟨digit⟩|⟨unsigned integer⟩⟨digit⟩
```

which means that an unsigned integer is a digit or a series of digits. Two constructs placed in succession are considered to be juxtaposed.

6.2.2 Reference Language

The description of the microprogramming reference language is divided into three types of productions: higher-level productions, operational productions, and lower-level productions. The mode of definition is top to bottom, which means that a definition is presented before the definitions of the constructions of which it is composed.

Definitional statements are numbered sequentially for reference.

6.2.2.1 Higher-Level Productions A microprogram consists of a series of type I or type II instructions, followed by an END statement.

```
⟨program⟩ ::= ⟨program body⟩⟨end line⟩                                  (1)
⟨program body⟩ ::= ⟨program line⟩|⟨program body⟩⟨program line⟩          (2)
⟨program line⟩ ::= ⟨comment line⟩|⟨instruction⟩                         (3)
⟨comment line⟩ ::= COMMENT ⟨comment string⟩                             (4)
⟨instruction⟩ ::= ⟨label part⟩⟨literal assignment⟩|⟨label part⟩          (5)
                  ⟨nanoinstruction⟩
⟨label part⟩ ::= ⟨statement label⟩:|⟨empty string⟩                      (6)
⟨end line⟩ ::= END                                                      (7)
```

6.2.2.2 Operational Productions Operational productions consist of literal assignment and nanoinstructions, along with a definition of the constructs from which they are formed.

6.2.2.2.1 Literal Assignment Statements A literal assignment statement, classed as type II, executes in one clock interval and specifies the loading of selected D-machine registers.

```
⟨literal assignment⟩ ::= ⟨literal construct⟩|⟨literal construct⟩%           (8)
                         ⟨comment string⟩
⟨literal construct⟩ ::= ⟨literal⟩→AMPCR|⟨literal⟩→SAR|⟨literal⟩→             (9)
                        ⟨lit⟩|⟨literal⟩→SAR, ⟨literal⟩→⟨lit⟩|
                        ⟨literal⟩→⟨lit⟩,⟨literal⟩→SAR
⟨literal⟩ ::= ⟨integer⟩|COMP ⟨integer⟩|⟨statement label⟩|                     (10)
              ⟨statement label⟩−1
⟨lit⟩ ::= LIT|SLIT                                                            (11)
```

6.2.2.2.2 Nanoinstruction Statements Nanoinstructions that execute in two or more clock intervals are classed as type I and are used to specify D-machine operational functions.

```
⟨nanoinstruction⟩ ::= ⟨unconditional part⟩⟨conditional part⟩|                (12)
                      ⟨unconditional part⟩⟨conditional part⟩%
                      ⟨comment string⟩
⟨unconditional part⟩ ::= ⟨component list⟩                                    (13)
⟨component list⟩ ::= ⟨component⟩|⟨component list⟩,⟨component⟩|⟨empty⟩       (14)
⟨component⟩ ::= ⟨external op⟩|⟨logic op⟩|⟨successor⟩                         (15)
⟨external op⟩ ::= ⟨memory device op⟩|⟨set op⟩|⟨memory device op⟩,            (16)
                  ⟨set op⟩|⟨set op⟩,⟨memory device op⟩|⟨empty⟩
⟨memory device op⟩ ::= MR1|MR2|MW1|MW2                                        (17)
⟨set op⟩ ::= SET ⟨condition-adjust bit⟩                                       (18)
⟨condition-adjust bit⟩ ::= LC1|LC2|LC3                                        (19)
⟨logic op⟩ ::= ⟨adder op⟩⟨shift op⟩⟨destination list⟩                        (20)
⟨adder op⟩ ::= 0|1|⟨unary op⟩|⟨binary op⟩|⟨empty⟩                             (21)
⟨unary op⟩ ::= ⟨not⟩⟨X select⟩|⟨not Y select⟩                                 (22)
⟨not⟩ ::= NOT|⟨empty⟩                                                         (23)
⟨X select⟩ ::= 0|A1|A2|A3|CTR|LIT|⟨empty⟩                                     (24)
⟨not Y select⟩ ::= ⟨not⟩⟨Y select⟩                                            (25)
⟨Y select⟩ ::= 0|1|B|B⟨m⟩⟨c⟩⟨l⟩|CTR|LIT|AMPCR                                 (26)
⟨m⟩ ::= 0|1|T|F                                                               (27)
⟨c⟩ ::= 0|1|T|F                                                               (28)
⟨l⟩ ::= 0|1|T|F                                                               (29)
⟨binary op⟩ ::= ⟨X select⟩⟨operator⟩⟨not Y select⟩|⟨X select⟩+               (30)
                ⟨not Y select⟩+1|⟨X select⟩−⟨not Y select⟩−1
⟨operator⟩ ::= AND|OR|NAN|NOT|IMP|NIM|RIM|NRI|XOR|EQV|                        (31)
               +|−|OAD|AAD
```

⟨shift op⟩ ::= R|L|C|⟨empty⟩ (32)

⟨destination list⟩ ::= →|→⟨destination⟩|⟨destination⟩|
⟨destination list⟩,⟨destination⟩ (33)

⟨destination⟩ ::= A1|A2|A3|MIR|BR1|BR2|AMPCR|⟨input B⟩|
⟨input CTR⟩|⟨input MAR⟩|⟨input SAR⟩ (34)

⟨input B⟩ ::= B|BEX|BAD|BMI|BBE|BBA|BBI (35)

⟨input CTR⟩ ::= CTR|LCTR|INC (36)

⟨input MAR⟩ ::= MAR|MAR1|MAR2|LMAR (37)

⟨input SAR⟩ ::= SAR|CSAR (38)

⟨successor⟩ ::= WAIT|STEP|SKIP|SAVE|CALL|EXEC|JUMP|RETN (39)

⟨conditional part⟩ ::= ⟨IF clause⟩⟨THEN clause⟩⟨ELSE clause⟩|
⟨IF clause⟩|⟨WHEN clause⟩⟨THEN clause⟩|
⟨empty⟩ (40)

⟨IF clause⟩ ::= IF ⟨condition⟩ (41)

⟨condition⟩ ::= ⟨not⟩⟨basic condition⟩ (42)

⟨basic condition⟩ ::= LST|MST|AOV|ABT|COV|SAI|RDC|
⟨condition-adjust bit⟩ (43)

⟨THEN clause⟩ ::= THEN ⟨component list⟩ (44)

⟨ELSE clause⟩ ::= ELSE ⟨successor⟩|⟨empty⟩ (45)

⟨WHEN clause⟩ ::= WHEN ⟨condition⟩ (46)

6.2.2.3 Lower-Level Productions Lower-level productions consist of the miscellaneous constructs from which microprograms are composed, such as labels, constants, and comments.

⟨comment string⟩ ::= ⟨comment character⟩|⟨comment string⟩
⟨comment character⟩ (47)

⟨statement label⟩ ::= ⟨letter⟩|⟨statement label⟩⟨letter⟩|
⟨statement label⟩⟨digit⟩ (48)

⟨integer⟩ ::= ⟨digit⟩|⟨integer⟩⟨digit⟩ (49)

⟨letter⟩ ::= A|B|C|D|E|F|G|H|I|J|K|L|M|N|O|P|Q|R|S|T|U|V|W|X|Y|Z (50)

⟨digit⟩ ::= 0|1|2|3|4|5|6|7|8|9 (51)

⟨comment character⟩ ::= any character in the computer alphabet (52)

⟨empty⟩ ::= the null string of characters (53)

The only construct not introduced in previous chapters is the comment that can be included as a separate input line with the key word COMMENT or can be included on the same line as a type I or II statement by separating the instruction and comment parts with a percent symbol (%).

6.2.3 TRANSLANG

TRANSLANG is the machine-readable and processable version of the microprogramming reference language defined and used in earlier sections of the book. The objective of this text is to teach you to do microprogramming, and TRANSLANG is a means of actually running a microprogram on a computer.

```
REFERENCE LANGUAGE

LST: A-1→AMPCR
   BLOCK1-1→AMPCR
   FOX→AMPCR
INIT: AMPCR→BR1
   3000→AMPCR, 10→LIT
   0→A1, LMAR, SAVE
LOOP: A1+1→A1  % BODY OF MPPOG STARTS HERE
   MR1, INC, BEX
   WHEN RDC THEN B R→A3, MIR
   16→SAR
   MW1, IF SAI
   A3 AND B C→A3
   6→SAR  20→LIT
   COMMENT CHECK FOR WRITE COMPLETION, CLEANUP, AND RETURN
   WHEN SAI THEN LCTR, BMI
   A2 EQV B→CSAR
   SET LC2, IF ABT THEN NOT A3→A2, JUMP ELSE RETN
   END
```

```
TRANSLANG

LST. A - 1 = AMPCR $
    BLØCK1 - 1 = AMPCR $
    FØX = AMPCR $
INIT. AMPCR = BR1 $
    3000 = AMPCR, 10 = LIT $
    0 = A1, LMAR, SAVE $
LØØP. A1 + 1 = A1 $ BØDY ØF MPRØG STARTS HERE
    MR1, INC, BEX $
    WHEN RDC THEN B R = A3, MIR $
    16 = SAR $
    MW1, IF SAI $
    A3 AND B C = A3 $
    6 = SAR, 20 = LIT $
    CØMMNT CHECK FØR WRITE CØMPLETIØN, CLEANUP, AND RETURN $
    WHEN SAI THEN LCTR, BMI $
    A2 EQV B =, CSAR $
    SET LC1, IF ABT THEN NØT A3 = A2, JUMP ELSE RETN $
    END $
READY
```

Figure 6.2 A comparison of the lexical conventions used with the microprogramming reference language and TRANSLANG.

6.2.3.1 Character Set A minimal character set is needed to run TRANSLANG programs. In addition to the 26 letters and 10 digits, the following special characters are required: + − = . , $.

6.2.3.2 Lexical Conventions A TRANSLANG lexical convention exists for each construct in the reference language. Figure 6.2 lists a sample microprogram in reference language form and in TRANSLANG form. Although the example is meaningless from a programming point of view, it demonstrates most, if not all, cases that occur in microprogramming. The typographic differences between the two languages are summarized in Table 6.1. Lexical conventions for TRANSLANG are summarized as follows:

1 Input to the TRANSLANG processor is free form except that no spaces may be embedded in key words or statement labels. Spacing is significant, as outlined below.

2 The statement label, if present, is separated from the body of the statement with a period followed by at least one space.

3 The equals sign (=) is used for replacement, instead of the →; it must *always* be preceded and followed by at least one space.

4 All operator symbols, key words, or other language tokens must be preceded by at least one space and followed by at least one space or by a comma and at least one space. Thus, a comma followed by a space is equivalent to a space.

5 All statements must terminate with a currency symbol ($) preceded by at least one space.

6 A comment string may follow the currency symbol in a statement line.

7 The key word COMMNT must be used with a comment line.

If the microprogrammer inadvertently violates one of these conventions, the TRANSLANG processor produces an appropriate diagnostic message.

6.2.3.3 Description in BNF As with the reference language, the description of TRANSLANG is divided into three types of productions: higher-level productions, operational productions, and lower-level productions. Differences between the reference language and TRANSLANG are lexical in nature.

6.2.3.3.1 Higher-Level Productions A microprogram written in TRANSLANG consists of a series of type I or type II instructions, followed by an END statement. Each statement must terminate with a currency symbol ($) preceded by a space.

⟨program⟩ ::= ⟨program body⟩⟨end line⟩ (1)
⟨program body⟩ ::= ⟨program line⟩|⟨program body⟩⟨program line⟩ (2)
⟨program line⟩ ::= ⟨comment line⟩|⟨instruction⟩ (3)
⟨comment line⟩ ::= COMMNT ⟨comment string⟩ (4)
⟨instruction⟩ ::= ⟨label part⟩⟨literal assignment⟩|⟨label part⟩
⟨nanoinstruction⟩ (5)

Table 6.1 Typographic Differences between the Reference Language and TRANSLANG

Reference language	TRANSLANG	Function of character
:	.	Separates statement label and body of statement
→	=	Specifies assignment
%	$	Separates comment field from body of statement
COMMENT	COMMNT	Key word for comment line
B_{mcl}	BMCL	B-register gating (for example, B_{001} B001)

Note: All statements must terminate with a $ preceded by a blank character in TRANSLANG.

⟨label part⟩ ::= ⟨statement label⟩.|⟨empty string⟩ (6)
⟨end line⟩ ::= END $ (7)

6.2.3.3.2 Operational Productions Operational productions consist of literal assignment instructions and nanoinstructions. The use of space characters has not been represented, because the specification of each place that a space is needed would unnecessarily complicate the syntactical description. For the use of spaces, the reader should consult the lexical conventions given in the previous section.

Literal assignment statements

⟨literal assignment⟩ ::= ⟨literal construct⟩ $|⟨literal construct⟩ (8)
  $ ⟨comment string⟩
⟨literal construct⟩ ::= ⟨literal⟩=AMPCR | (9)
  ⟨literal⟩=SAR |
  ⟨literal⟩=⟨lit⟩|
  ⟨literal⟩=SAR, ⟨literal⟩=⟨lit⟩|
  ⟨literal⟩=⟨lit⟩, ⟨literal⟩=SAR
⟨literal⟩ ::= ⟨integer⟩| COMP ⟨integer⟩| (10)
  ⟨statement label⟩|
  ⟨statement label⟩−1
⟨lit⟩ ::= LIT|SLIT (11)

Nanoinstruction statements

⟨nanoinstruction⟩ ::= ⟨unconditional part⟩⟨conditional part⟩ $| (12)
  ⟨unconditional part⟩⟨conditional part⟩
  $ ⟨comment string⟩
⟨unconditional part⟩ ::= ⟨component list⟩ (13)
⟨component list⟩ ::= ⟨component⟩|⟨component list⟩,⟨component⟩| (14)
  ⟨empty⟩
⟨component⟩ ::= ⟨external op⟩|⟨logic op⟩|⟨successor⟩ (15)
⟨external op⟩ ::= ⟨memory device op⟩|⟨set op⟩|⟨memory device op⟩, (16)
  ⟨set op⟩|⟨set op⟩,⟨memory device op⟩|⟨empty⟩
⟨memory device op⟩ ::= MR1|MR2|MW1|MW2 (17)
⟨set op⟩ ::= SET ⟨condition-adjust bit⟩ (18)
⟨conditional adjust bit⟩ ::= LC1|LC2|LC3 (19)
⟨logic op⟩ ::= ⟨adder op⟩⟨shift op⟩⟨destination list⟩ (20)
⟨adder op⟩ ::= 0|1|⟨unary op⟩|⟨binary op⟩|⟨empty⟩ (21)
⟨unary op⟩ ::= ⟨not⟩⟨X select⟩|⟨not Y select⟩ (22)
⟨not⟩ ::= NOT|⟨empty⟩ (23)
⟨X select⟩ ::= 0|A1|A2|A3|CTR|LIT|⟨empty⟩ (24)
⟨not Y select⟩ ::= ⟨not⟩⟨Y select⟩ (25)
⟨Y select⟩ ::= 0|1|B|B⟨m⟩⟨c⟩⟨l⟩|CTR|LIT|AMPCR (26)
⟨m⟩ ::= 0|1|T|F (27)

⟨c⟩ ::= 0|1|T|F (28)

⟨l⟩ ::= 0|1|T|F (29)

⟨binary op⟩ ::= ⟨X select⟩⟨operator⟩⟨not Y select⟩|
⟨X select⟩+⟨not Y select⟩+1|
⟨X select⟩−⟨not Y select⟩−1 (30)

⟨operator⟩ ::= AND|OR|NAN|NOT|IMP|NIM|RIM|NRI|XOR EQV|
+|−|OAD|AAD (31)

⟨shift op⟩ ::= R|L|C|⟨empty⟩ (32)

⟨destination list⟩ ::= =|=⟨destination⟩|⟨destination⟩|
⟨destination list⟩,⟨destination⟩ (33)

⟨destination⟩ ::= A1|A2|A3|MIR|BR1|BR2|AMPCR|
⟨input B⟩|⟨input CTR⟩|⟨input MAR⟩|⟨input SAR⟩ (34)

⟨input B⟩ ::= B|BEX|BAD|BMI|BBE|BBA|BBI (35)

⟨input CTR⟩ ::= CTR|LCTR|INC (36)

⟨input MAR⟩ ::= MAR|MAR1|MAR2|LMAR (37)

⟨input SAR⟩ ::= SAR|CSAR (38)

⟨successor⟩ ::= WAIT|STEP|SKIP|SAVE|CALL|EXEC|JUMP|RETN (39)

⟨conditional part⟩ ::= ⟨IF clause⟩⟨THEN clause⟩⟨ELSE clause⟩
⟨IF clause⟩|⟨WHEN clause⟩⟨THEN clause⟩|
⟨empty⟩ (40)

⟨IF clause⟩ ::= IF ⟨condition⟩ (41)

⟨condition⟩ ::= ⟨not⟩⟨basic condition⟩ (42)

⟨basic condition⟩ ::= LST|MST|AOV|ABT|COV|SAI|RDC|
⟨condition-adjust bit⟩ (43)

⟨THEN clause⟩ ::= THEN ⟨component list⟩ (44)

⟨ELSE clause⟩ ::= ELSE ⟨successor⟩|⟨empty⟩ (45)

⟨WHEN clause⟩ ::= WHEN ⟨condition⟩ (46)

6.2.3.3.3 Lower-Level Productions Lower-level productions describe the basic constructs from which statements are formed.

⟨comment string⟩ ::= ⟨comment character⟩|
⟨comment string⟩⟨comment character⟩ (47)

⟨statement label⟩ ::= ⟨letter⟩|⟨statement label⟩⟨letter⟩|
⟨statement label⟩⟨digit⟩ (48)

⟨integer⟩ ::= ⟨digit⟩|⟨integer⟩⟨digit⟩ (49)

⟨letter⟩ ::= A|B|C|D|E|F|G|H I|J|K|L M|N|O|P|Q|R|S|T|U|V|W X|Y|Z (50)

⟨digit⟩ ::= 0|1|2|3|4|5|6|7|8|9 (51)

⟨comment character⟩ ::= any character in the computer alphabet
excluding $ (52)

⟨empty⟩ ::= the null string of characters (53)

In TRANSLANG, the maximum size of a statement label is set at 6 characters.

6.3 RUNNING THE TRANSLATOR

The process of running the translator to produce hexadecimal microcode that can be executed with the simulator involves two major steps:

1 Preparation and processing of the microprogram in symbolic form
2 Specifying the processing options desired

The entering of the symbolic microprogram is demonstrated through sample runs and involves the following microprogram, expressed in reference language:

```
       0→A1, SAVE
LOOP:  A1 and B R→A2
       2→SAR
       IF LST THEN MR1, BEX ELSE JUMP
       WHEN RDC THEN JUMP
       END
```

Again, the microprogram serves only to demonstrate a variety of useful statement types.

6.3.1 Processing Specifications

Four processing specifications are available with the TRANSLANG processor:

1 The name of the file to which the hexadecimal microcode should be written for subsequent loading into the D-machine simulator
2 Whether or not the bit patterns for each statement should be generated following that statement in the source listing
3 Whether or not a hexadecimal listing of the microcode should be generated when the processing of the symbolic microprogram is complete
4 If the input is to be read from a prestored source file

Item 1, the name of the hexadecimal file, is dependent upon the computer and operating system used, and it could range from an unlabeled tape to a named file on direct-access storage. The sample runs were made on the Dartmouth Timesharing System that uses named disk files. Item 2, the bit pattern for each statement, is of academic value in that it shows the result of the translation process. Except in special cases, it serves little practical purpose. Similarly, item 3, the hexadecimal listing of microcode, is primarily of academic interest, since it is cumbersome to read. However, it should be emphasized that each source statement, other than a comment line, is represented in the hexadecimal code. The final specification, item 4, concerns the origin of the symbolic microprogram. If the input is from cards, then the source program can reside in the input job stream. If terminal input is used, however, long microprograms should be prestored because of the difficulty in accurately entering a lengthy program.

```
>>>>> TRANSLANG D MACHINE MICRØTRANSLATØR

ENTER FILENAME FØR HEX? F63HEX
SUPPRESS BIT PATTERNS?(1=SUPPRESS)? 1
SUPPRESS HEX LISTING?(1=SUPPRESS)?
IF INPUT IN FILE ENTER 1?

0000    ?     0 = A1, SAVE $
0001    ? LØØP. A1 AND B R = A2 $
0002    ?     2 = SAR $
0003    ?     IF LST THEN MR1, BEX ELSE JUMP $
0004    ?     WHEN RDC THEN JUMP $
0005    ?     END $


THE TØTAL NUMBER ØF ERRØRS =      0


HEX TRANSLATIØN
ØUTPUT READY FØR SIMULATØR INPUT

ADDR    MPM         NANØ
  0     F000 0012 0000 4000 0000
  1     F001 0009 AC56 A000 0000
  2     0200
  3     F002 5E0C 0000 0C00 0800
  4     F003 A820 0000 0000 0000
  5     4000

EXECUTE (Y/N)? N
```

Figure 6.3 Sample run of the TRANSLANG processor. Options specified: (1) no bit patterns; (2) hexadecimal listing; and (3) source program not prestored.

6.3.2 Sample Runs

Figures 6.3 through 6.6 supply sample runs of the translator using the TRANSLANG processor running on the Dartmouth Time-sharing System (DTSS).[1] Information on DTSS is presented only to facilitate understanding the examples. The following DTSS commands are used:

Command	Explanation
OLD *name*	Brings an old program or data file into the user's workspace
RUN	Executes a program
NEW *name*	Used to create a new program or data file
SAVE	Saves the file name (data file or program) in the DTSS catalog
UNSAVE	Deletes a saved file
?	Used to prompt a user for input
BUILD	Used to build a file without sequence numbers
LIST	List a file on the terminal

In Figure 6.3, the sample program is entered from the terminal; no bit patterns are requested, but a hexadecimal listing is desired. The reader should

[1] It should be emphasized that the translator and simulator are standard FORTRAN IV programs and can be run on any computer that has a FORTRAN IV compiler.

```
>>>>> TRANSLANG D MACHINE MICRØTRANSLATØR

ENTER FILENAME FØR HEX? F64HEX
SUPPRESS BIT PATTERNS?(1=SUPPRESS)?
SUPPRESS HEX LISTING?(1=SUPPRESS)? 1
IF INPUT IN FILE ENTER 1?

0000    ?     0 = A1, SAVE $
N=0000 000 000 010 010 000 00000000 0000 00 100 0000 00 0000 0000 0000
MPM=1111000000000000

0001    ? LØØP. A1 AND B R = A2 $
N=0000 000 000 001 001 101 01100010 1011 01 010 0000 00 0000 0000 0000
MPM=1111000000000001

0002    ?     2 = SAR $
MPM=0000011000000000

0003    ?     IF LST THEN MR1, BEX ELSE JUMP $
N=0101 111 000 001 100 000 00000000 0000 00 000 1100 00 0000 0000 0010
MPM=1111000000000010

0004    ?     WHEN RDC THEN JUMP $
N=1010 100 000 100 000 000 00000000 0000 00 000 0000 00 0000 0000 0000
MPM=1111000000000011

0005    ?     END $

THE TØTAL NUMBER ØF ERRØRS =     0

EXECUTE (Y/N)? N
```

Figure 6.4 Sample run of the TRANSLANG processor. Options specified: (1) bit patterns requested; (2) no hexadecimal listing; and (3) source program not prestored.

```
NEW FIG65
READY

BUILD
SPEAK!

    0 = A1, SAVE $
LØØP. A1 AND B R = A2 $
    2 = SAR $
    IF LST THEN MR1, BEX ELSE JUMP $
    WHEN RDC THEN JUMP $
    END $
READY

SAVE
READY
```

Figure 6.5 Building of a symbolic microprogram file (that is, a source file) with the BUID command. LIST gives a listing of the file, and SAVE places the file name in the system catalog.

```
>>>>> TRANSLANG D MACHINE MICRØTRANSLATØR

ENTER FILENAME FØR HEX? F66HEX
SUPPRESS BIT PATTERNS?(1=SUPPRESS)? 1
SUPPRESS HEX LISTING?(1=SUPPRESS)?
IF INPUT IN FILE ENTER 1? 31
ENTER SØURCE FILENAME? FIG65

0000         0 = A1, SAVE $
0001    LØØP. A1 AND B R = A2 $
0002         2 = SAR $
0003         IF LST THEN MR1, BEX ELSE JUMP $
0004         WHEN RDC THEN JUMP $
0005         END $

THE TØTAL NUMBER ØF ERRØRS =     0

HEX TRANSLATIØN
ØUTPUT READY FØR SIMULATØR INPUT

ADDR   MPM         NANØ
  0    F000 0012 0000 4000 0000
  1    F001 0009 AC56 A000 0000
  2    0200
  3    F002 5E0C 0000 0C00 0800
  4    F003 A820 0000 0000 0000
  5    4000

EXECUTE (Y/N)? N
```

Figure 6.6 Sample run of the TRANSLANG processor. Options specified: (1) no bit patterns; (2) hexadecimal listing; and (3) source program prestored.

note that each TRANSLANG statement is preceded by a question mark (?), which is the prompting to enter the statement.

In Figure 6.4, the same program is entered. In this case, however, bit patterns are printed, and the hexadecimal listing is suppressed.

In Figure 6.5, a source program file is built with the BUILD command and is listed and saved with the LIST and SAVE commands, respectively. This will be the microprogram source file for the next figure.

In Figure 6.6, the TRANSLANG processor is run with a prestored symbolic microprogram. When a prestored source file is specified as an option, then the TRANSLANG processor prompts the user for the name of the source file, as shown in the figure.

6.4 HEXADECIMAL MICROCODE

At first glance, hexadecimal microcode appears to be an ominous thing to read. The objective of this section is to simplify the concept by describing and delineating several literal assignment and nanoinstructions.

6.4.1 Delineation of Literal Assignment Statements

Consider the following literal assignment statement:

2→SAR

The type II instruction for this statement is:

Bit	1	2	3	4	5	6	7	8	9	10	11	12	13	14	15	16
	0	(unused)	shift amount						(unused)							

The bit pattern for the statement is

MPM = 0000001000000000

which corresponds to the following hexadecimal representation:

0200

In a similar fashion, the literal assignment statement

COMP 3→SAR, 5→LIT

with an instruction format of

Bit	1	2	3	4	5	6	7	8	9	10	11	12	13	14	15	16
	1	0	shift amount						literal value							

has the following bit pattern:

MPM = 1011110100000101

which corresponds to the following hexadecimal representation:

BD05

When a literal assignment statement of the form

⟨statement label⟩ − 1→AMPCR

is used, however, the processing is slightly more involved. Consider the statement

LRK − 1→AMPCR

in the following microprogram:

MPM address	Statement
0	LKR − 1→AMPCR
1	MR1, BEX
2	LKR: A1 + 1→A1
3	WHEN RDC JUMP
...	...

The format for the literal assignment statement is

Bit	1	2	3	4	5	6	7	8	9	10	11	12	13	14	15	16
	1	1	0	(unused)	AMPCR value											

It would be expected that the statement LKR − 1→AMPCR would result in the value 1 being placed in the address field of the instruction. However, the bit pattern for the instruction is

MPM = 1100000000000000

which is the correct format without the correct address field. The situation results from the fact that the bit patterns are generated during the first pass over the program. After the first pass has been completed, the address-dependent fields are loaded so that the hexadecimal microcode reflects complete instructions. Thus, the hexadecimal microcode for the LRK − 1→AMPCR statement is

C001

In TRANSLANG, the only programmer-defined constructs are the statement labels; all other options can be resolved in a single pass over the program.

6.4.2 Delineation of Nanoinstruction Statements

Each type I instruction causes a microprogram instruction word and a nanoinstruction word to be generated by the TRANSLANG processor. The following microprogram—not necessarily an efficient one—writes the values 1 through 5 to S-memory locations 1000 through 1004, respectively:

```
INIT: AMPCR→A1, MAR2          %  A1 CONTAINS S-MEMORY ADDRESS
  1000→AMPCR
  1→A2, MIR, LCTR        %  A2 CONTAINS VALUE
  4→LIT
  SAVE
LOOP: MW2, IF SAI
  A1 + 1→A1, MAR2, INC
  WHEN SAI THEN STEP
  A2 + 1→A2, MIR, IF NOT COV THEN JUMP ELSE STEP
  END
```

```
>>>>> TRANSLANG D MACHINE MICRØTRANSLATØR

ENTER FILENAME FØR HEX? F67HEX
SUPPRESS BIT PATTERNS?(1=SUPPRESS)?
SUPPRESS HEX LISTING?(1=SUPPRESS)?
IF INPUT IN FILE ENTER 1? 31
ENTER SØURCE FILENAME? FIG67

0000    INIT. AMPCR = A1, MAR2 $ A1 CØNTAINS S MEMØRY ADDRESS
N=0000 000 000 001 001 000 00110010 0000 00 100 0000 00 0111 0000 0000
MPM=1111000000000000

0001         1000 = AMPCR $
MPM=1100001111101000

0002         1 = A2, MIR, LCTR $ A2 CØNTAINS VALUE
N=0000 000 000 001 001 000 00000110 0000 00 010 0000 10 0000 0100 0000
MPM=1111000000000001

0003         4 = LIT $
MPM=1110000000000100

0004         SAVE $
N=0000 000 000 010 010 000 00000000 0000 00 000 0000 00 0000 0000 0000
MPM=1111000000000010

0005    LØØP. MW2, IF SAI $
N=1001 100 000 001 001 000 00000000 0000 00 000 0000 00 0000 0000 0111
MPM=1111000000000011

0006         A1 + 1 = A1, MAR2, INC $
N=0000 000 000 001 001 101 00000110 0000 00 100 0000 00 0111 1000 0000
MPM=1111000000000100

0007         WHEN SAI THEN STEP $
N=1001 100 000 001 000 000 00000000 0000 00 000 0000 00 0000 0000 0000
MPM=1111000000000101

0008         A2 + 1 = A2, MIR, IF NØT CØV THEN JUMP ELSE STEP $
N=1000 000 000 100 001 110 00000110 0000 00 010 0000 10 0000 0000 0000
MPM=1111000000000110

0009         END $


THE TØTAL NUMBER ØF ERRØRS =      0


HEX TRANSLATIØN
ØUTPUT READY FØR SIMULATØR INPUT

ADDR    MPM       NANØ
  0     F000 0009 0640 401C 0000
  1     C3E8
  2     F001 0009 00C0 2081 0000
  3     E004
  4     F002 0012 0000 0000 0000
  5     F003 9809 0000 0000 1C00
  6     F004 0009 A0C0 401E 0000
  7     F005 9808 0000 0000 0000
  8     F006 8021 C0C0 2080 0000
  9     4000

EXECUTE (Y/N)? N
```

Figure 6.7 Translation of microprogram to demonstrate bit patterns and hexadecimal microcode for nanoinstructions.

and is used to demonstrate hexadecimal microcode for nanoinstructions. A printout of the translation of the program is given in Figure 6.7. Consider the first statement in the microprogram:

AMPCR→A1, MAR2

for which the following bit patterns are generated:

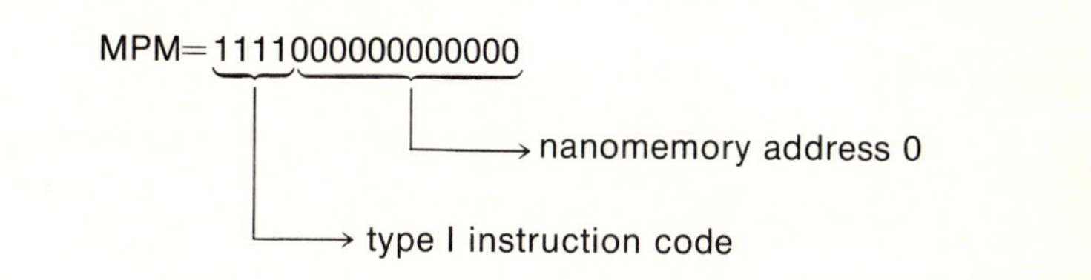

N=0000 000 000 001 001 000 00110010 0000 00 100 0000 00 0111 0000 0000

The corresponding hexadecimal microcode is determined as follows:

MPM=1111000000000000

F000

N=0000 000 000 001 001 000 00110010 0000 00 100 0000 00 0111 0000 0000

0009 0640 401C 0000 (hexadecimal)

As another example, consider the statement

1→A2, MIR, LCTR

for which the following bit patterns are generated:

MPM=1111000000000001

nanomemory address 1

type I instruction code

N=0000 000 000 001 001 000 00000110 0000 00 010 0000 10 0000 0100 0000

The corresponding hexadecimal microcode is determined as follows:

MPM=1111000000000001

F001

```
N=0000 000 000 001 001 000 00000110 0000 00 010 0000 10 0000 0100 0000
                        0009 00C0 2081 0000        (hexadecimal)
```

As a third example, consider the following conditional statement:

WHEN SAI THEN STEP

which is equivalent to

IF SAI THEN STEP ELSE WAIT

After translation, the following bit patterns are generated for the statement:

```
MPM=1111000000000101
     |      └──────→nanomemory address 3
     └──────→type I instruction code
```

```
N=1001 100 000 001 000 000 00000000 0000 00 000 0000 00 0000 0000 0000
```

which corresponds to hexadecimal microcode in the following manner:

```
MPM=1111000000000101
          F005
```

```
N=1001 100 000 001 000 000 00000000 0000 00 000 0000 00 0000 0000 0000
                        9808 0000 0000 0000        (hexadecimal)
```

As a final example, consider the statement:

A2 + 1→A2, MIR, IF NOT COV THEN JUMP ELSE STEP

which demonstrates unconditional and conditional components. The MPM instruction is straightforward and exists as follows:

MPM = 1111000000000110

The nanoinstruction requires a bit setting for the following options:

1. NOT condition
2. Unconditional logic-unit operation
3. True and false successors
4. Logic-unit operations

These options are demonstrated in the following nanoinstruction:

N = 1000 000 000 100 001 110 00000110 0000 00 010 0000 10 0000 0000 0000

which is equivalent to the following hexadecimal microcode:

MPM=1111000000000110

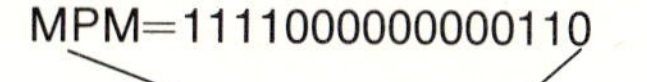

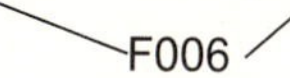

F006

N=1000 000 000 100 001 110 00000110 0000 00 010 0000 10 0000 0000 0000

8021 C0C0 2080 000 (hexadecimal)

The nature of microprogramming can now be stated more specifically. Each bit setting in an MPM or nanoinstruction causes the processing unit to react in a particular manner. The objective of microprogramming is to place the instructions in a meaningful sequence, and a microprogramming language simply facilitates the process.

VOCABULARY

The reader should be familiar with the following terms in the context in which they were used in the chapter.

Symbolic microprogram
Hexadecimal microcode
Backus-Naur form
Metalanguage
Reference language
Character set
TRANSLANG
Bit patterns
Hexadecimal listing
Prestored microprogram

QUESTION SET

1 What purpose does a syntactical description of a computer language serve?
2 What are the differences between the microprogramming reference language and TRANSLANG? List them and be specific.
3 In what way can bit patterns and hexadecimal microcode be used to improve the efficiency of a microprogram?
4 In the statement LOOP – 1→AMPCR, why is the bit pattern incorrect?
5 Consider a nanoinstruction and the fact that the number 54 is not a multiple of 4. How is hexadecimal microcode formed from a nanoinstruction bit pattern?

EXERCISES

1 Give six valid occurrences of a ⟨component list⟩.
2 Give three valid occurrences of a ⟨literal construct⟩.
3 Describe and delineate the bit patterns and hexadecimal microcode for the following statements given in Figure 6.7:

```
SAVE
MW2, IF SAI
A1+1→A1, MAR2, INC
```

4 Generate bit patterns for the following statements:

```
9→SAR
113→LIT, COMP 14→SAR
21→SLIT
```

5 Generate, describe, and delineate bit patterns and hexadecimal microcode for the following statements:

```
WHEN RDC THEN A2+B→A2, MAR2, JUMP
MR2, A1+1→A1, BEX
MR1, B R→AMPCR
IF ABT THEN A2→A1 RETN ELSE JUMP
```

Chapter 7

The Simulator

7.1 OVERVIEW

This chapter describes how to use the D-machine, how to load S-memory for execution, and how to understand the results of a simulator run. An overview of the process of executing a microprogram using the D-machine simulator is given in Figure 7.1. Because the D-machine simulator *is* a simulator, the printed output of a computer run is of prime importance. Because a microprogram contains no variables or storage access—just instructions—the printed output centers around two items:

1 The contents of machine registers during the execution of the microprogram

2 The content of S-memory before and after execution

Most processing options are concerned with the two types of printed results. Another reason for printed output is that microprograms, because of their innate complexity, frequently require debugging, and detailed information on microprogram execution is needed for this purpose.

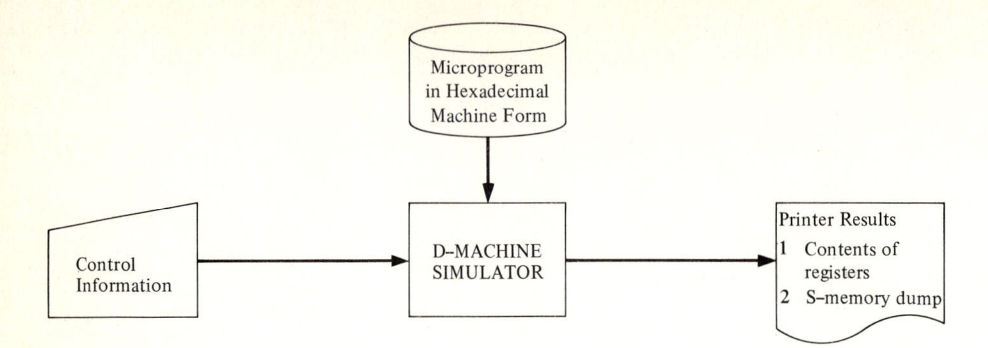

Figure 7.1 Overview of the process of executing a microprogram using the D-machine simulator.

7.2 RUNNING THE SIMULATOR

Input to the D-machine simulator, see Figure 7.1, is a file containing hexadecimal microcode along with control information that is entered from the terminal or the card reader. The required information is entered in response to the following requests for information:

(1) ENTER SAME FILENAME FOR HEX? ...
(2) OUTPUT REGISTERS AND S MEMORY IN INTEGER(1) OR OCTAL(2)? ...
(3) INPUT S MEMORY IN INTEGER(1) OR OCTAL IN O11 FORMAT(2)? ...
(4) STARTING ADDRESS = ? ...
(5) MAXIMUM NUMBER OF CLOCKS TO SIMULATE = ? ...
(6) NUMBER OF CLOCKS BETWEEN OUTPUT POINTS = ? ...
(7) ENTER OUTPUT LINES DESIRED 1-ADDRESSES AND CLOCK
2- A1, A2, A3, B 3- MIR, SAR, LIT, CTR, AMPCR
4- BR1, BR2, MAR, BMAR, GC1, GC2
5- CONDITIONS
ENTER NUMBER OF OUTPUT LINES DESIRED = ? ...
(8) BEGIN OUTPUT AT MPM ADDRESS = ? ...
END OUTPUT AT MPM ADDRESS = ?
ENTER 1 FOR S MEMORY DUMP WHEN PROGRAM TERMINATES? ...
(9) ENTER S MEMORY VALUES IN CONSECUTIVE BLOCKS
ENTER 9999 FOR STARTING ADDRESS WHEN FINISHED
STARTING S MEMORY ADDRESS = ? ...
FINAL S MEMORY ADDRESS FOR THIS BLOCK = ? ...
SMEM (...) = ? ...
...
(10) MEMORY DUMP REQUESTED
ENTER VALUES AS DONE IN MEMORY INPUT (9999 FOR STARTING ADDRESS WHEN FINISHED)
STARTING S MEMORY ADDRESS = ? ...
FINAL S MEMORY ADDRESS FOR THIS BLOCK = ? ...
...

The numbers to the left of the queries correspond to the printout given in Figures 7.2 through 7.4. Each query is described in the following sections.

7.2.1 Example of Microprogram Execution

A description of the sample microprogram listed in the printout of Figure 7.2 is as follows:

> Register BR1 points to 16 fixed-point registers stored in S-memory. Fixed-point register 2 points to a linear array in S-memory with a length of three elements. (By changing the counter value, the microprogram would work for any size array. A length of 3 is used to keep down the length of the printout.) The microprogram adds the elements of the array and places the result in fixed-point register 3.

The program in reference language is listed as follows:

```
INIT: 0→BR1, LMAR
   2→LIT
   MR1, BEX, LCTR
   3→LIT
   CHK−1→AMPCR
   WHEN RDC THEN B→A1, MAR2, INC, CALL
ADD: WHEN RDC THEN BEX
   A3+B→A3
   A1+1→A1, MAR2
CHK: IF NOT COV THEN MR2, INC, JUMP
   A3→MIR, LMAR
   3→LIT
   MW1, IF SAI
   WHEN SAI THEN STEP
   END
```

In S-memory, the registers occupy the first 16 locations, so BR1 is set to 0 in the initialization routine. Register A1 is used to point to the next element of the array, and register A3 holds the running sum.

7.2.2 File Name

The name of the file containing the hexadecimal microcode is entered in response to the following query:

```
ENTER SAME FILENAME FOR HEX? ...
```

Just prior to microprogram execution, the hexadecimal microcode is loaded from the named file into MPM and nanomemory. Both types of control storage are loaded from location 0 and extend to higher-numbered addresses.

7.2.3 Output Format

During the execution of a microprogram, the values of the various machine registers can be outputted at various intervals, so the user can determine the

```
>>>>> TRANSLANG D MACHINE MICRØTRANSLATØR

ENTER FILENAME FØR HEX? F72HEX
SUPPRESS BIT PATTERNS?(1=SUPPRESS)? 1
SUPPRESS HEX LISTING?(1=SUPPRESS)? 1
IF INPUT IN FILE ENTER 1? 31
ENTER SØURCE FILENAME? FIG72

0000    INIT. 0 = BR1, LMAR $
0001        2 = LIT $
0002        MR1, BEX, LCTR $
0003        3 = LIT $
0004        CHK - 1 = AMPCR $
0005        WHEN RDC THEN B = A1, MAR2, INC, CALL $
0006    ADD. WHEN RDC THEN BEX $
0007        A3 + B = A3 $
0008        A1 + 1 = A1, MAR2 $
0009    CHK. IF NØT CØV THEN MR2, INC, JUMP $
0010        A3 = MIR, LMAR $
0011        3 = LIT $
0012        MW1, IF SAI $
0013        WHEN SAI THEN STEP $
0014        END $


THE TØTAL NUMBER ØF ERRØRS =     0

EXECUTE (Y/N)? N

2) DMACH1    (CØMPILED)  07 JAN 76  20:08


ENTER SAME FILENAME FØR HEX? F72HEX
ØUTPUT REGISTERS AND S MEMØRY IN INTEGER(1) ØR ØCTAL(2)? 1
INPUT S MEMØRY IN INTEGER(1) ØR ØCTAL IN Ø11 FØRMAT(2)? 1
STARTING ADDRESS =? 0
MAXIMUM NUMBER ØF CLØCKS TØ SIMULATE=? 30
NUMBER ØF CLØCKS BETWEEN ØUTPUT PØINTS=? 1

ENTER ØUTPUT LINES DESIRED     1-ADDRESSES AND CLØCK
2- A1,A2,A3,B    3- MIR,SAR,LIT,CTR,AMPCR    4- BR1,BR2,MAR,BMAR,GC1,GC2
 5- CØNDITIØNS
ENTER NUMBER ØF ØUTPUT LINES DESIRED? 5

BEGIN ØUTPUT AT MPM ADDRESS=? 14
END ØUTPUT AT MPM ADDRESS=? 14
ENTER 1 FØR S MEMØRY DUMP WHEN PRØGRAM TERMINATES? 1



ENTER S MEMØRY VALUES IN CØNSECUTIVE BLØCKS
ENTER 9999 FØR STARTING ADDRESS WHEN FINISHED


STARTING S MEMØRY ADDRESS=? 2
FINAL S MEMØRY ADDRESS FØR THIS BLØCK=? 3
SMEM(   2)=? 100
SMEM(   3)=? 0


STARTING S MEMØRY ADDRESS=? 100
FINAL S MEMØRY ADDRESS FØR THIS BLØCK=? 102
SMEM( 100)=? 17
SMEM( 101)=? 9
SMEM( 102)=? 24


STARTING S MEMØRY ADDRESS=? 9999
```

Figure 7.2 Sample microprogram designed to demonstrate execution of the simulator.

```
END ØF SIMULATIØN - REGISTERS CØNTAIN

P(1) ADDR. =  13      P(3) ADDR. =  13      CLØCK =   25
A1 =        103     A2 =           0     A3 =          50     B =          24
MIR =        50      SAR = 0       LIT =  3       CTR =  0      AMPCR =    5
BR1 =  0      BR2 =  0      MAR =  3      BMAR =     3      GC1=0   GC2=0
LC1=0  LC2=0  MST=0  LST=0  ABT=0  AØV=0  CØV=0  SAI=1  RDC=1  INT=0

MEMØRY DUMP REQUESTED

ENTER VALUES AS DØNE IN MEMØRY INPUT (9999 FØR STARTING ADDRESS WHEN
FINISHED)

STARTING S MEMØRY ADDRESS=? 2
FINAL S MEMØRY ADDRESS FØR THIS BLØCK=? 3

S MEMØRY(   2) TØ S MEMØRY(   3) =

      100          50
STARTING S MEMØRY ADDRESS=? 9999
```

Figure 7.2 *Continued.*

execution-time status of a microprogram. The following query allows the user to specify the type of output format that would best suit the program being executed:

OUTPUT REGISTERS AND S MEMORY IN INTEGER(1) OR OCTAL(2)? ...

D-machine data registers (that is, A1, A2, A3, B, and MIR) and S-memory locations can be printed in octal 012 format or in integer format with leading zeros suppressed. In general, octal format is preferred in dealing with nonnumeric words, such as instructions or masks. Integer format is preferred for data values because a numeric conversion is not required to verify computed results.

7.2.4 S-Memory Input

The execution of most microprograms involves the use of S-memory and a repository for S-machine instructions, S-machine registers, and data. S-memory is always preset to 0 by the simulator, and initialization, if any, is normally performed by an initialization routine of the microprogram. However, S-programs in machine-language form or large arrays must be placed in S-memory before execution. The following query permits the input format to be specified:

INPUT S MEMORY IN INTEGER(1) OR OCTAL O11 FORMAT(2)? ...

The answer to the query is intended only to specify the type of format. S-memory input is not entered at this point, but in response to a later query just prior to the initiation of microprogram execution.

7.2.5 Starting Address

The microprogram is loaded into MPM and nanomemory starting in location 0, for both types of control memories. The answer to the query

STARTING ADDRESS = ? ...

allows the MPM address of the first M-instruction to be specified. Thus, as in the case of the sample emulator, given previously, it may be desirable to initiate microprogram execution after a table of literal assignments. The starting address is specified as a decimal integer value.

7.2.6 Maximum Number of Clocks to Simulate

A time limit on the execution of a microprogram is specified in response to the next query:

MAXIMUM NUMBER OF CLOCKS TO SIMULATE = ? ...

The time limit is specified in terms of clock intervals. The value is entered as a decimal integer and should be based on the "average" number of clocks per instruction, which varies from one to two. A good rule of thumb is to use an average value of 1.5 clocks per instruction.

It is relatively easy to experience a microprogram loop, so the "maximum-clocks" value should be computed carefully, based on the algorithm being executed.

7.2.7 Number of Clocks between Output Points

It is necessary to have all the registers printed for each clock interval only when detailed debugging is required; otherwise, a lot of needless printout is generated. The query

NUMBER OF CLOCKS BETWEEN OUTPUT POINTS = ? ...

permits the interval between output points to be varied. The interval is specified as a decimal integer and controls only whether the output is printed. The simulator actually goes through each D-machine cycle, regardless of the output specifications.

7.2.8 Output Lines

The following query controls the amount of output for each print cycle:

```
ENTER OUTPUT LINES DESIRED    1- ADDRESSES AND CLOCK
2- A1, A2, A3, B    3- MIR, SAR, LIT, CTR, AMPCR
4- BR1, BR2, MAR, BMAR, GC1, GC2
5- CONDITIONS
ENTER NUMBER OF OUTPUT LINES DESIRED? ...
```

The response should be a decimal number between 1 and 5, inclusive. If the value 5 is entered, all output is generated for each print cycle, as in Figure 7.2. If a value from 2 through 4, inclusive, is entered, then a subsidiary query of the form

```
ENTER LINE NUMBERS SEPARATED BY COMMAS = ? ...
```

is generated, and the user must specify which of the lines should be printed.

7.2.9 Output Specifications

In microprogram debugging, an error can usually be isolated to exist within a specific microroutine, so that a printout of registers and conditions may be desired only within that routine. In the following query:

```
BEGIN OUTPUT AT MPM ADDRESS = ? ...
END OUTPUT AT MPM ADDRESS = ? ...
```

both values, entered as decimal integers, determine the instructions for which output will be generated—as governed by the response to preceding queries. The execution of instructions outside the specified MPM addresses, inclusive, will not trigger printed output.

The above query is followed by a query of the form

```
ENTER 1 FOR S MEMORY DUMP WHEN PROGRAM TERMINATES? ...
```

If a value of 1 is entered in response to this query, the S-memory dump mode is entered, and after execution of the microprogram has been completed, S-memory dump specifications are requested by the user. Otherwise, execution terminates automatically without the S-memory dump.

7.2.10 S-Memory Loading

S-memory is preset through the following set of interactions:

```
ENTER S MEMORY VALUES IN CONSECUTIVE BLOCKS
ENTER 9999 FOR STARTING ADDRESS WHEN FINISHED
STARTING S MEMORY ADDRESS = ? ...
FINAL S MEMORY ADDRESS FOR THIS BLOCK = ? ...
```

After the above information is entered, the simulator prompts the user to enter information for each S-memory location within the specified block, with a query of the form

SMEM(*addr*) = ?

such as in the following example:

SMEM(1234) = ? 10470000000

where the underlined information is a response by a user to the query.

When integer format is specified as the S-memory input option, then a simple decimal integer is entered in response to the query for S-memory input, such as:

SMEM(1637) = ? 163

However, when octal (011) format is selected, then precisely 11 octal digits must be entered. The 32 bits to be entered are prefixed with a 0 bit, to make the word size a multiple of 3, and the resulting 33 bits are grouped by 3 and converted to octal. Thus, the following 32 bits:

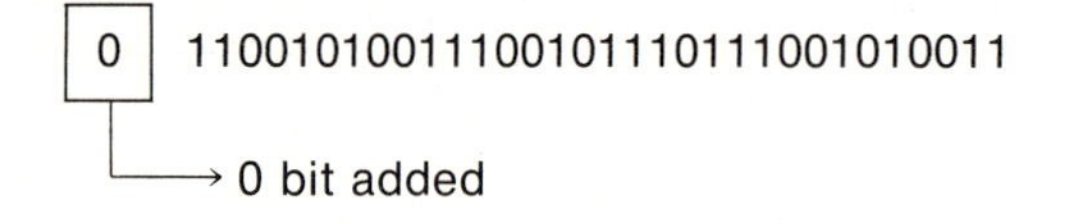

would be entered into location 75 in response to an appropriate query, as follows:

SMEM(75) = ? 31234567123

Information can be entered in blocks so that it is not necessary to enter 0 values, since all S-memory is preset to 0. The user types 9999 as the starting address when all blocks of information have been entered, and execution of the simulator commences automatically.

7.2.11 S-Memory Dump

After microprogram execution has been initiated by the simulator, it may terminate normally when the specified number of clock intervals has been executed. If no S-memory dump has been requested, execution terminates abruptly after the contents of registers and the setting of conditions has been printed. If an S-memory dump has been requested, the following query is generated:

```
MEMORY DUMP REQUESTED
ENTER VALUES AS DONE IN MEMORY INPUT (9999 FOR STARTING
  ADDRESS WHEN FINISHED)
STARTING S MEMORY ADDRESS = ? ...
FINAL S MEMORY ADDRESS FOR THIS BLOCK = ? ...
```

and a dump of S-memory is generated in the format specified in the "output format" query.

In general, the S-memory dump is the primary method of judging the correctness of a microprogram. Computed results are stored in S-memory by an emulator, as in normal S-program execution, and the S-memory dump is the only method of gaining access to this information.

7.3 PRINTED OUTPUT DURING MICROPROGRAM EXECUTION

The printed output generated by the simulator during microprogram execution is governed in type and in quantity by the parameters entered prior to execution. Figure 7.3 gives a sample set of output lines, which are printed with integer format. (The output was selected from the example of Figure 4.1.) There is a maximum of five lines that can be printed. They are referred to as the

1. Program control line
2. Logic-unit register line
3. First control register line
4. Second control register line
5. Condition line

respectively. Each line is described separately.

7.3.1 Timing—An Overview

During *each* clock interval, one instruction is going through its phase 1. For a type I instruction, this is essentially the instruction-decoding and condition-testing cycle. For a type II instruction, the entire instruction execution is completed in phase 1. During that same clock interval, another type I instruction may be in the process of being completed.

Thus far, the completion phase of a type I instruction has been referred to as "phase 3." Phase 3 is divided into two parts: the logic-unit operation part and the destination part. For example, in the statement

$$A1 + 1 \rightarrow B$$

the operation $A1 + 1 \rightarrow$ is the operation part which means "Add the contents of A1 and the value 1 in the adder." Placing the result in register B is the destination part. The logic-unit part is always performed in the next clock interval after the phase 1 clock interval. However, the destination part is not performed until the next logic-unit operation is initiated. *Phase 2* is a holding phase which occurs when a type I instruction cannot be completed, because the next instruction does not have a logic-unit operation. (This, by the way, is precisely why the LIT registers, SAR, or AMPCR can be loaded in the instruction following the type I instruction in which they are used.) The following example demonstrates the case where no holding phases are involved:

Instruction number	Microprogram	Phases	Clock
1	A1+B→A2	Phase 1 of 1	1
2	A2+1→A3	Phase 3 of 1, phase 1 of 2	2
3	A3+B→A1	Phase 3 of 2, phase 1 of 3	3

```
2) DMACH1     (CØMPILED)  07 JAN 76  19:11
ENTER SAME FILENAME FØR HEX? F41HEX
ØUTPUT REGISTERS AND S MEMØRY IN INTEGER(1) ØR ØCTAL(2)? 1
INPUT S MEMØRY IN INTEGER(1) ØR ØCTAL IN Ø11 FØRMAT(2)? 1
STARTING ADDRESS =? 0
MAXIMUM NUMBER ØF CLØCKS TØ SIMULATE=? 10
NUMBER ØF CLØCKS BETWEEN ØUTPUT PØINTS=? 1

ENTER ØUTPUT LINES DESIRED      1-ADDRESSES AND CLØCK
2- A1,A2,A3,B   3- MIR,SAR,LIT,CTR,AMPCR   4- BR1,BR2,MAR,BMAR,GC1,GC2
 5- CØNDITIØNS
ENTER NUMBER ØF ØUTPUT LINES DESIRED? 5

BEGIN ØUTPUT AT MPM ADDRESS=? 0
END ØUTPUT AT MPM ADDRESS=? 4
ENTER 1 FØR S MEMØRY DUMP WHEN PRØGRAM TERMINATES? 1


ENTER S MEMØRY VALUES IN CØNSECUTIVE BLØCKS
ENTER 9999 FØR STARTING ADDRESS WHEN FINISHED


STARTING S MEMØRY ADDRESS=? 1234
FINAL S MEMØRY ADDRESS FØR THIS BLØCK=? 1234
SMEM(1234)=? 0


STARTING S MEMØRY ADDRESS=? 9999

P(1) ADDR. =    0     P(3) ADDR. =  -1     CLØCK =     1
A1 =          0     A2 =          0     A3 =          0     B =          0
MIR =          0     SAR = 0     LIT =  0     CTR =  0     AMPCR =   0
BR1 =  0     BR2 =  0     MAR =  0     BMAR =     0     GC1=0  GC2=0
LC1=0  LC2=0  MST=0  LST=0  ABT=0  AØV=0  CØV=0  SAI=0  RDC=0  INT=0


P(1) ADDR. =    1     P(2) ADDR. =   0     CLØCK =     2
A1 =          0     A2 =          0     A3 =          0     B =          0
MIR =          0     SAR = 0     LIT =  0     CTR =  0     AMPCR =1234
BR1 =  0     BR2 =  0     MAR =  0     BMAR =     0     GC1=0  GC2=0
LC1=0  LC2=0  MST=0  LST=0  ABT=0  AØV=0  CØV=0  SAI=0  RDC=0  INT=0


P(1) ADDR. =    2     P(3) ADDR. =   0     CLØCK =     3
A1 =          0     A2 =          0     A3 =          0     B =          0
MIR =       1234     SAR = 0     LIT =  0     CTR =  0     AMPCR =1234
BR1 =  4     BR2 =  0     MAR =210     BMAR = 1234     GC1=0  GC2=0
LC1=0  LC2=0  MST=0  LST=0  ABT=0  AØV=0  CØV=0  SAI=0  RDC=0  INT=0


P(1) ADDR. =    3     P(3) ADDR. =   2     CLØCK =     4
A1 =          0     A2 =          0     A3 =          0     B =          0
MIR =       1234     SAR = 0     LIT =  0     CTR =  0     AMPCR =1234
BR1 =  4     BR2 =  0     MAR =210     BMAR = 1234     GC1=0  GC2=0
LC1=0  LC2=0  MST=0  LST=0  ABT=0  AØV=0  CØV=0  SAI=0  RDC=0  INT=0


P(1) ADDR. =    3     P(3) ADDR. =   3     CLØCK =     5
A1 =          0     A2 =          0     A3 =          0     B =          0
MIR =       1234     SAR = 0     LIT =  0     CTR =  0     AMPCR =1234
BR1 =  4     BR2 =  0     MAR =210     BMAR = 1234     GC1=0  GC2=0
LC1=0  LC2=0  MST=0  LST=0  ABT=0  AØV=0  CØV=0  SAI=1  RDC=0  INT=0
```

Figure 7.3 Sample output lines in integer format generated during microprogram execution.

```
END ØF SIMULATIØN - REGISTERS CØNTAIN

P(1) ADDR. =     3       P(3) ADDR. =     3       CLØCK =      6
A1 =            0      A2 =            0      A3 =            0      B =            0
MIR =       1234      SAR = 0      LIT =  0      CTR =  0      AMPCR =1234
BR1 =  4     BR2 =  0      MAR =210      BMAR = 1234      GC1=0   GC2=0
LC1=0  LC2=0  MST=0  LST=0  ABT=0  AØV=0  CØV=0  SAI=1  RDC=0  INT=0

MEMØRY DUMP REQUESTED

ENTER VALUES AS DØNE IN MEMØRY INPUT (9999 FØR STARTING ADDRESS WHEN
FINISHED)

STARTING S MEMØRY ADDRESS=? 1234
FINAL S MEMØRY ADDRESS FØR THIS BLØCK=? 1234


S MEMØRY(1234) TØ S MEMØRY(1234) =


      1234
STARTING S MEMØRY ADDRESS=? 9999
```

Figure 7.3 *Continued.*

However, in the next case a holding phase is required because a type I instruction cannot be completed due to the lack of a logic-unit operation caused by an intervening type II instruction:

Instruction number	Microprogram	Phases	Clock
1	A1+B R→A2	Phase 1 of 1	1
2	3→SAR, 2→LIT	Phase 2 of 1, phase 1 of 2	2
3	A2→MIR, LMAR	Phase 3 of 1, phase 1 of 3	3

In the next case, a holding phase is required because of a condition that is not true:

Instruction number	Microprogram	Phases	Clock
1	A1+1→A2	Phase 1 of 1	1
2	IF ABT THEN A2→B SKIP ELSE STEP (assume false condition)	Phase 2 of 1, phase 1 of 2	2
3	B_{TFF}→MIR	Phase 3 of 1, phase 1 of 3	3

In this case, the second instruction, that is, IF ABT THEN A2→B, does not have a phase 2 or 3 because the logic-unit operation is conditional and the condition is false. Finally, in the last case, an unconditional logic-unit operation in an IF statement causes a completion of previous operations and causes the IF statement, for either a true or a false condition, to require a phase 3:

Instruction number	Microprogram	Phases	Clock
1	A1+1→A2	Phase 1 of 1	1
2	A2→B IF ABT THEN SKIP ELSE STEP (assume false condition)	Phase 3 of 1, phase 1 of 2	2
3	B_{TFF}→MIR	Phase 3 of 2, phase 1 of 3	3

Additional information of timing is given in Chapter 10.

7.3.2 Program Control Line

The *program control line* gives the MPM addresses of microinstructions that are going through the various phases of execution. This line also gives a running count of the clock interval being executed. The meaning of the various entries is given in the following example:

P(1) = ADDR. = 23	P(3) ADDR. = 22	CLOCK = 47
The MPM address of the instruction going through *phase 1* is 23.	The *phase 3* cycle of an instruction is being executed. The MPM address of that instruction is 22.	This is the 47th clock interval executed in this run.

A holding phase is indicated in an analogous manner:

P(1) ADDR. = 75	P(2) ADDR. = 74	CLOCK = 256
The MPM address of the instruction going through *phase 1* is 75.	The *phase 2* cycle of an instruction is being executed. The MPM address of that instruction is 74.	This is the 256th clock interval executed in this run.

MPM addresses are always given as decimal integers.

To sum up, the phase 1 cycle of one microinstruction *and* either the phase 2 or the phase 3 cycle of another microinstruction are executed during each clock interval of the processor.

7.3.3 Logic-Unit Register Line

The *logic-unit register line* gives the contents of the A1-, A2-, A3-, and B-registers at the completion of the clock interval specified in the program control line. This line may be printed in integer or octal format, as specified earlier during the input part of a run. If integer format is selected, then the contents of the registers are printed in decimal with leading 0s suppressed. If octal format is selected, the contents of the registers are printed as 11 octal digits with no zero suppression. The fact that registers are 32 bits wide requires special attention. The 2 high-order bits of a register prefixed with a binary zero correspond to one octal digit. The remaining 30 bits are partitioned in groups of three to form the remaining octal digits. If for example, a register contains the following bits:

10/100/111/001/101/011/110/000/010/111/100

then the octal equivalent is printed as

24715360274

Because a binary zero is prefixed to the contents of a register to make the number of bits an even multiple of 3, the leftmost octal digit is forced to be a 0, 1, 2, or 3.

Figure 7.4 gives a sample set of output lines in which registers are printed in octal format.

7.3.4 First Control Register Line

The first control register line gives the contents of the MIR, SAR, LIT, CTR, and the AMPCR. The MIR is printed in the same format as the logic-unit register line, that is, in either octal (011) format or in integer format. The contents of the SAR, LIT, CTR, and AMPCR registers are printed in decimal. The LIT, CTR, and AMPCR registers are simply converted to decimal and printed. The SAR register is adjusted so that the bit inserted to compensate for register width is removed.

The value in the SAR is either a true value or the word-length complement, which is equivalent to the binary twos complement. The width of the SAR is 5 bits. Thus, if the following is printed for the SAR:

SAR = 8

then it may represent a true 8, as in 8→SAR or a 32 minus 24, as in the statement COMP 24→SAR.

The LIT register is 8 bits wide and can hold values in the range 0 to 255. The contents of the LIT register may represent either a true value or the word-length complement of a value, *minus* 1, that is, the ones complement. Thus, if the following value were printed for the LIT register:

LIT = 13

then the value may represent a true 13, as in 13→LIT or the value 256 − 242 − 1 in the statement COMP 242→LIT. When SLIT is used as the destination in a literal assignment statement, the interpretation of the contents of the LIT register may vary somewhat. In other words, the user has to know how the LIT is used in the microprogram. If the statement 5→SLIT is used, the translator

```
2) DMACH1    (CØMPILED)  07 JAN 76  19:19


ENTER SAME FILENAME FØR HEX? F41HEX
ØUTPUT REGISTERS AND S MEMØRY IN INTEGER(1) ØR ØCTAL(2)? 2
INPUT S MEMØRY IN INTEGER(1) ØR ØCTAL IN Ø11 FØRMAT(2)? 2
STARTING ADDRESS =? 0
MAXIMUM NUMBER ØF CLØCKS TØ SIMULATE=? 10
NUMBER ØF CLØCKS BETWEEN ØUTPUT PØINTS=? 1

ENTER ØUTPUT LINES DESIRED      1-ADDRESSES AND CLØCK
2- A1,A2,A3,B   3- MIR,SAR,LIT,CTR,AMPCR   4- BR1,BR2,MAR,BMAR,GC1,GC2
 5- CØNDITIØNS
ENTER NUMBER ØF ØUTPUT LINES DESIRED? 5

BEGIN ØUTPUT AT MPM ADDRESS=? 0
END ØUTPUT AT MPM ADDRESS=? 4
ENTER 1 FØR S MEMØRY DUMP WHEN PRØGRAM TERMINATES? 1


ENTER S MEMØRY VALUES IN CØNSECUTIVE BLØCKS
ENTER 9999 FØR STARTING ADDRESS WHEN FINISHED


STARTING S MEMØRY ADDRESS=? 1234
FINAL S MEMØRY ADDRESS FØR THIS BLØCK=? 1234
SMEM(1234)=? 00000000000


STARTING S MEMØRY ADDRESS=? 9999

P(1) ADDR. =    0      P(3) ADDR. =   -1      CLØCK =      1
A1=00000000000    A2=00000000000    A3=00000000000    B =00000000000
MIR =00000000000      SAR = 0      LIT =   0      CTR =   0      AMPCR =    0
BR1 =   0      BR2 =   0      MAR =   0      BMAR =     0      GC1=0   GC2=0
LC1=0  LC2=0  MST=0  LST=0  ABT=0  AØV=0  CØV=0  SAI=0  RDC=0  INT=0


P(1) ADDR. =    1      P(2) ADDR. =    0      CLØCK =      2
A1=00000000000    A2=00000000000    A3=00000000000    B =00000000000
MIR =00000000000      SAR = 0      LIT =   0      CTR =   0      AMPCR =1234
BR1 =   0      BR2 =   0      MAR =   0      BMAR =     0      GC1=0   GC2=0
LC1=0  LC2=0  MST=0  LST=0  ABT=0  AØV=0  CØV=0  SAI=0  RDC=0  INT=0


P(1) ADDR. =    2      P(3) ADDR. =    0      CLØCK =      3
A1=00000000000    A2=00000000000    A3=00000000000    B =00000000000
MIR =00000002322      SAR = 0      LIT =   0      CTR =   0      AMPCR =1234
BR1 =   4      BR2 =   0      MAR =210      BMAR = 1234      GC1=0   GC2=0
LC1=0  LC2=0  MST=0  LST=0  ABT=0  AØV=0  CØV=0  SAI=0  RDC=0  INT=0


P(1) ADDR. =    3      P(3) ADDR. =    2      CLØCK =      4
A1=00000000000    A2=00000000000    A3=00000000000    B =00000000000
MIR =00000002322      SAR = 0      LIT =   0      CTR =   0      AMPCR =1234
BR1 =   4      BR2 =   0      MAR =210      BMAR = 1234      GC1=0   GC2=0
LC1=0  LC2=0  MST=0  LST=0  ABT=0  AØV=0  CØV=0  SAI=0  RDC=0  INT=0


P(1) ADDR. =    3      P(3) ADDR. =    3      CLØCK =      5
A1=00000000000    A2=00000000000    A3=00000000000    B =00000000000
MIR =00000002322      SAR = 0      LIT =   0      CTR =   0      AMPCR =1234
BR1 =   4      BR2 =   0      MAR =210      BMAR = 1234      GC1=0   GC2=0
LC1=0  LC2=0  MST=0  LST=0  ABT=0  AØV=0  CØV=0  SAI=1  RDC=0  INT=0
```

Figure 7.4 Sample set of output lines demonstrating registers printed in octal format.

```
END ØF SIMULATIØN - REGISTERS CØNTAIN

P(1) ADDR. =    3      P(3) ADDR. =    3      CLØCK =      6
A1=00000000000     A2=00000000000     A3=00000000000      B =00000000000
MIR =00000002322      SAR = 0      LIT =  0      CTR =  0      AMPCR =1234
BR1 =   4      BR2 =  0      MAR =210      BMAR = 1234      GC1=0   GC2=0
LC1=0  LC2=0  MST=0  LST=0  ABT=0  AØV=0  CØV=0  SAI=1  RDC=0  INT=0

MEMØRY DUMP REQUESTED

ENTER VALUES AS DØNE IN MEMØRY INPUT (9999 FØR STARTING ADDRESS WHEN
FINISHED)

STARTING S MEMØRY ADDRESS=? 1234
FINAL S MEMØRY ADDRESS FØR THIS BLØCK=? 1234

S MEMØRY(1234) TØ S MEMØRY(1234) =

00000002322
STARTING S MEMØRY ADDRESS=? 9999
```

Figure 7.4 *Continued.*

would generate a type II statement to place the following binary value in the LIT:

```
00001001
    |
    └──→ extra bit
```

and a register printout would give

LIT = 9

On the other hand, if the statement COMP 5→SLIT were used, the translator would generate a type II statement to place the following binary value in the LIT:

```
11110011
    |
    └──→ extra bit
```

and a register printout would give

LIT = 243

If SLIT is used as the destination register in a type II statement, then it is expected that a type I statement of the form

LIT→SAR, ...

would subsequently be executed.

The value in the CTR should be interpreted as the word-length complement of a value, *minus* 1. Thus, if the following statements were executed:

LCTR
2→LIT

for example, the CTR would contain the value

11111101

and a register printout would give

CTR=253

Thus, if the CTR contained 247, then it corresponds to a value of 8 in the CTR. Recall that whenever a value is moved to the CTR, which must be performed in a type I statement, the ones complement of the source value is taken. Thus, if the value n is moved to the CTR, repeated execution of the INC command will cause the CTR to overflow in $n + 1$ incrementation operations.

The value in the AMPCR represents a true value or the word-length complement of a value, *minus* 1—that is, the ones complement of a register 12 bits wide. Thus, if the following statement were executed:

1234→AMPCR

for example, a register printout would generate the following:

AMPCR=1234

as a part of the first control register line.

7.3.5 Second Control Register Line

The second control register line gives the contents of the BR1, BR2, MAR, BMAR, GC1, and GC2 registers. The values in this line are always printed in decimal format.

The contents of the BR1- and BR2-registers are the high-order (that is, leftmost) 8 bits of a 16-bit external address. The registers can be loaded independently of the memory address register (MAR) or at the same time as the MAR with the MAR1 or MAR2 destination operand. Similarly, the memory address register (MAR), which is the low-order (that is, rightmost) 8 bits of the same 16-bit external address, can be loaded separately as the MAR operand or collectively with BR1 or BR2 with the MAR1 and MAR2 operands. Thus, for example, the statements

AMPCR→MAR1, MIR
1234→AMPCR
MW1

cause the 16-bit representation of S-memory address 1234 to be placed in the BR1/MAR registers, as follows:

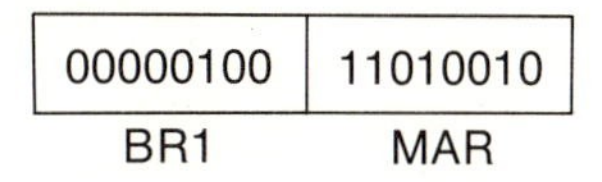

00000100	11010010
BR1	MAR

When the 8-bit values are converted to decimal, the corresponding printout of the BR1- and MAR registers would be

BR1 = 4 MAR = 210 BMAR = 1234

where BMAR is the *last* external BR*i*/MAR address used in a memory read or write operation.

The GC1 and GC2 indicators refer to global condition 1 and global condition 2, respectively. An indicator of 1 means that the condition is set; an indicator of 0 indicates that the condition is not set. Global conditions are designed for an operational environment that includes more than one D-machine, and they are not reset by listing. Thus, a global condition is set with a command of the form SET GC1 or SET GC2, and is reset with a command of the form RESET GC1 and RESET GC2. Global conditions are not covered in this primer; however, the facilities are available in the translator/simulator.

7.3.6 Condition Line

The condition line gives the status of the LC1, LC2, MST, LST, ABT, AOV, COV, SAI, RDC, and INT indicators. The LC1, LC2, COV, SAI, and RDC indicators are reset by testing. The MST, LST, ABT, and AOV indicators are set during each adder operation, which occurs for each type I instruction in which the adder operation is unconditional or conditionally true. The conditions that result from an adder operation may be tested in the next type I instruction.

In all cases, an indicator of 1 denotes that the specified condition exists, and an indicator of 0 denotes that the condition does not exist. Thus, for example, a printout with the following expression:

AOV = 1

denotes that an adder overflow occurred during the last adder operation, and a printout that includes

LST = 0

indicates that upon completion of the last adder operation, the value of the least significant bit was 0. The other conditions should be interpreted accordingly.

The INT condition is an interruption facility for systems with multiple processing units. The SET INT command interrupts all processing units and causes the INT indicator to be set. This condition may be tested with the INT condition, of the form IF INT THEN . . . . As with global conditions, the interruption facility is not covered in this primer but is supported by the translator/simulator.

VOCABULARY

The reader should be familiar with the following terms in the context in which they were used in the chapter:

File name
Integer format
Octal format
Starting address
Maximum number of clocks to simulate
Clocks between output points
Output lines
Starting S-memory address
Final S-memory address
Block
Phase 1
Phase 2
Phase 3

QUESTION SET

The following questions are intended to test your comprehension of the subject matter. All questions can be answered from the text directly or possibly through a logical extension of the subjects presented. Some questions would be suitable for discussion sessions.

1 What purpose does the "file name" query serve?
2 What is the range of values the starting address can assume?
3 What numerical address does MPM memory start with? Nanomemory? S-memory?
4 What is a "holding phase"?
5 What output line gives the M-instruction being executed?
6 Why is a dump of MPM and nanomemory not required? How would one determine the contents of either of these memories?
7 What is BMAR? Be specific.
8 Which conditions are reset by testing? Which are reset in other ways? How?
9 In COMP 5→SAR, is the ones or twos complement taken? In COMP 5→LIT, is the ones or twos complement taken?
10 What special function does the value 9999 serve?

EXERCISES

1 In the following microprogram segment:

```
LIT+1 R→B
5→LIT, 1→SAR
IF LST THEN ...
```

does LST test true or false? Why?

2 Given the following output:

BR2 = 5   MAR = 326

what external address does this represent?

3 Given the following output:

CTR = 237

what information does this value represent?

4 Given the following microprogram segment:

```
1→A1
IF LST THEN LIT→SAR
9→SAR, 17→SLIT
```

after the segment is executed, give the following:

A1 = ______   LIT = ______   SAR = ______

5 Execute the following microprogram segments by hand or by using the simulator and give the output lines during *each* clock interval. Interpret the results.

a
```
AMPCR→A1
4032→AMPCR
A1 + LIT C→A2
2→LIT, 2→SAR
IF LST THEN A2 + 1→A3 SKIP ELSE STEP
B100→A3
STEP
```

b
```
AMPCR→A2
75→AMPCR
A2 − LIT L→MIR
3→LIT, COMP 1→SAR
A2 + 1→A2, IF LST THEN SKIP ELSE STEP
B100→MIR
STEP
```

6 Write, execute, and show results for a microprogram that places the value 6379 in S-memory location 238. Show that the value is actually placed in location 238 with an S-memory dump.

7 Write, execute, and show results for a microprogram that reads the contents of S-memory location 123 and places them in S-memory location 321. Using S-memory input options, initially place the value 10450000000 in S-memory location 123.

8 Write, execute, and show complete results for a microprogram that generates the even integers between 10 and 20, inclusive, and places them in consecutive S-memory locations starting with 1002.

9 Write, execute, and show complete results for a microprogram segment that generates the first 10 Fibonacci numbers and places them in consecutive S-memory locations beginning with location 75.

10 Write, execute, and show complete results for a microprogram that places the integers 10, 9, 8, 7, 6, and 5 in S-memory locations 3150, 3151, 3152, 3153, 3154, and 3155 respectively. Do not preset S-memory to these values but generate them in the microprogram.

Chapter 8

Principles of Emulation I: Arithmetic Operations

8.1 OVERVIEW

This chapter presents an introduction to emulation through the microprogrammed implementation of arithmetic operations in the fixed-point or the floating-point mode. Other than possibly load, store, and input/output operations, the class of arithmetic operations is the most widely executed set of computer operations and requires special attention. The efficiency of microprogrammed arithmetic operation is a prime contributor to good overall system performance, and as a result, the corresponding microroutines are reworked until every extra clock interval is ''squeezed'' out of them. This fact is also evident to some degree by comparing the sample microroutines for arithmetic operations in this chapter and the sample emulators in Chapter 9. Actually, the emulators were simplified to clarify the concepts for pedagogical reasons, but the arithmetic operations are inherently more efficient. Another consideration, however, is that arithmetic operations deal almost exclusively with the bits in a word and there is more opportunity to optimize. By its very nature, an emulator involves a certain amount of branching between microroutines, and control functions are more difficult to optimize.

8.2 FIXED-POINT OPERATIONS—COMPLEMENT ARITHMETIC

With complement arithmetic, positive values are stored in true form, and negative values are stored in twos complement form. The most significant bit can be regarded as a sign bit—0 for plus and 1 for minus—even though complement arithmetic does not explicitly utilize a sign bit.

8.2.1 Addition and Subtraction

Fixed-point addition and subtraction in twos complement form are straightforward to implement. For addition, the operands are simply added; for subtraction, the minuend is added to the twos complement of the subtrahend. Both operations are demonstrated in the following example:

```
SETUP:  LIT→MAR2
    2→LIT
    MR2, BEX, LMAR          %  READ FIRST OPERAND
    3→LIT
    WHEN RDC THEN B→A1, MR2        %  READ SECOND OPERAND
    ADD-1→AMPCR          %  READ SECOND OPERAND
    WHEN RDC THEN BEX, CALL
    A3→MIR, LMAR         %  RESULT IN A3
    4→LIT
    MW2, IF SAI       %  WRITE SUM TO S-MEM
    WHEN SAI THEN STEP
    SUB-1→AMPCR
    CALL       %  TO SUB AND RETURN
    A3→MIR, LMAR         %  RESULT IN A3
    5→LIT
    MW2, IF SAI
    FINI-1→AMPCR
    WHEN SAI THEN JUMP

 ADD:  A1+B→A3, JUMP                 Addition and
 SUB:  A1+NOT B+1→A3, JUMP           subtraction
 FINI:  END                          microroutines
```

The microprogram reads the first and second operands from S-memory locations 2 and 3, respectively, and writes the sum and difference to S-memory locations 4 and 5, respectively. The addition and subtraction operations are implemented as one-statement routines that accept the first operand (that is, the addend or the minuend) in register A1 and the second operand (that is, the augend or subtrahend) in register B. The result (that is, the sum or difference) is returned in register A3. The complete microprogram is given only because the routines are short. For subsequent algorithms, only the microroutine for the respective operation is given. The printouts for translator/simulator runs for

```
>>>>> TRANSLANG D MACHINE MICRØTRANSLATØR

ENTER FILENAME FØR HEX? BADSBHEX
SUPPRESS BIT PATTERNS?(1=SUPPRESS)? 1
SUPPRESS HEX LISTING?(1=SUPPRESS)? 1
IF INPUT IN FILE ENTER 1? 31
ENTER SØURCE FILENAME? BINADSB

0000    SETUP. LIT = MAR2 $
0001       2 = LIT $
0002       MR2, BEX, LMAR $ READ FIRST ØPERAND
0003       3 = LIT $
0004       WHEN RDC THEN B = A1, MR2 $ READ SECØND ØPERAND
0005       ADD - 1 = AMPCR $
0006       WHEN RDC THEN BEX, CALL $ TØ ADD AND RETURN
0007       A3 = MIR, LMAR $ RESULT IN A3
0008       4 = LIT $
0009       MW2, IF SAI $ WRITE SUM TØ S MEMØRY
0010       SUB - 1 = AMPCR $
0011       CALL $ TØ SUB AND RETURN
0012       A3 = MIR, LMAR $ RESULT IN A3
0013       5 = LIT $
0014       MW2, IF SAI $
0015       FINI - 1 = AMPCR $
0016       WHEN SAI THEN JUMP $
0017    ADD. A1 + B = A3, JUMP $
0018    SUB. A1 + NØT B + 1 = A3, JUMP $
0019    FINI. STEP $
0020       END $

THE TØTAL NUMBER ØF ERRØRS =     0

EXECUTE (Y/N)? N
```

Figure 8.1 Microprogram to demonstrate fixed-point addition and subtraction in twos complement form. The first and second operands are in S-memory locations 2 and 3; the sum and difference are placed in S-memory locations 4 and 5. (Execution is in Figures 8.2 and 8.3.)

addition and subtraction are given in Figures 8.1 through 8.3. The translator listing is given in Figure 8.1, and Figures 8.2 and 8.3 give simulator runs for values 15 and 8 and for values 15 and -8, respectively.

Fixed-point subtraction incorporates the following expression:

$$\text{A1} + \text{NOT B} + 1$$

which is equivalent to $\text{A1} - \text{B}$ when complement arithmetic is used.

8.2.2 Multiplication

Binary multiplication is performed by repeated addition and shifting and generates a double-length product. In the following examples, a double-length (64-bit) product is computed, but only the rightmost 32 bits are retained. The operation uses a double-length accumulator (the AC and MQ) and an auxiliary register as follows:[1]

[1] MQ is an acronym for multiplier-quotient.

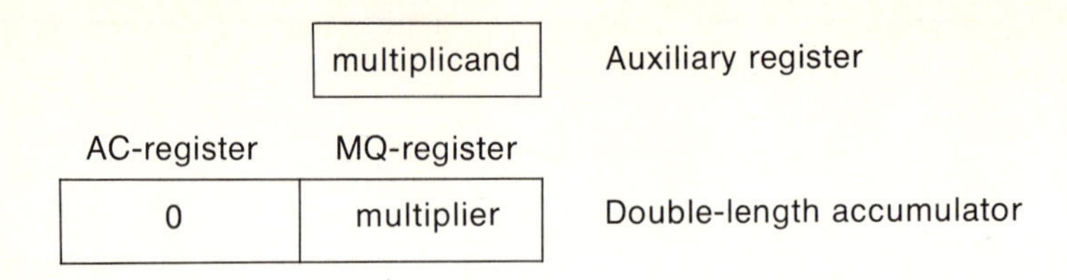

The double-length accumulator is implemented as two machine registers that are used in such a way that a bit that is right-shifted out of the AC-register enters the MQ register, as though the two registers were actually one double-length register. The process of binary multiplication operates as follows:

1 The multiplicand, multiplier, and a zero are moved to the auxiliary MQ- and AC-registers, respectively.

2 If the rightmost bit of the MQ-register is 1, then the multiplicand is added to the AC-register. The combined ⟨AC,MQ⟩ registers are shifted one place to the right, regardless of whether the addition was performed. A count is made of the number of shift operations.

3 When the number of shifts is equal to the number of digits in the multiplier, then the multiplication operation is complete. Otherwise, the process continues with step 2.

4 The result is in the combined ⟨AC,MQ⟩ registers. If a single-length product is generated, then it is contained completely in the MQ-register.

As an example of the technique, assume 4-bit registers, a multiplier of 0011 (in binary), and a multiplicand of 0010 (in binary). Initially, the multiplicand of 0010 is placed in the auxiliary register, and the multiplier of 0011 is placed in the MQ-register. The AC-register is set to 0, so that the registers are pictured as follows:

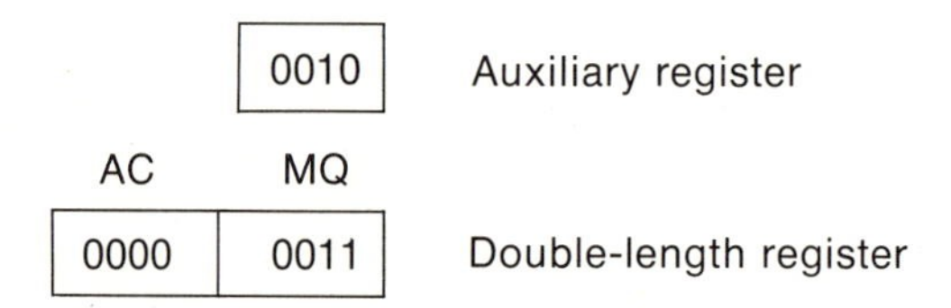

The contents of the auxiliary register are not changed during the multiplication operation.

During the first add/shift cycle, the multiplicand is added to the AC-register because the rightmost bit of the MQ-register is 1, so that the AC- and MQ-registers would look as follows:

```
2) DMACH1     (COMPILED)  05 JAN 76   13:43


ENTER SAME FILENAME FØR HEX? BADSBHEX
ØUTPUT REGISTERS AND S MEMØRY IN INTEGER(1) ØR ØCTAL(2)? 1
INPUT S MEMØRY IN INTEGER(1) ØR ØCTAL IN Ø11 FØRMAT(2)? 1
STARTING ADDRESS =? 0
MAXIMUM NUMBER ØF CLØCKS TØ SIMULATE=? 25
NUMBER ØF CLØCKS BETWEEN ØUTPUT PØINTS=? 1

ENTER ØUTPUT LINES DESIRED      1-ADDRESSES AND CLØCK
2- A1,A2,A3,B    3- MIR,SAR,LIT,CTR,AMPCR     4- BR1,BR2,MAR,BMAR,GC1,GC2
 5- CØNDITIØNS
ENTER NUMBER ØF ØUTPUT LINES DESIRED? 5

BEGIN ØUTPUT AT MPM ADDRESS=? 20
END ØUTPUT AT MPM ADDRESS=? 20
ENTER 1 FØR S MEMØRY DUMP WHEN PRØGRAM TERMINATES? 1



ENTER S MEMØRY VALUES IN CØNSECUTIVE BLØCKS
ENTER 9999 FØR STARTING ADDRESS WHEN FINISHED


STARTING S MEMØRY ADDRESS=? 2
FINAL S MEMØRY ADDRESS FØR THIS BLØCK=? 3
SMEM(    2)=? 15
SMEM(    3)=? 8

STARTING S MEMØRY ADDRESS=? 9999


END ØF SIMULATIØN - REGISTERS CØNTAIN


P(1) ADDR. =   19      P(3) ADDR. =   19      CLØCK =    21
A1 =          15       A2 =          0       A3 =          7      B =          8
MIR =          7       SAR = 0       LIT =  5      CTR =  0      AMPCR =  18
BR1 =  0      BR2 =  0       MAR =  5       BMAR =    5    GC1=0  GC2=0
LC1=0  LC2=0  MST=0  LST=0  ABT=0  AØV=0  CØV=0  SAI=1  RDC=1  INT=0


MEMØRY DUMP REQUESTED

ENTER VALUES AS DØNE IN MEMØRY INPUT (9999 FØR STARTING ADDRESS WHEN
FINISHED)

STARTING S MEMØRY ADDRESS=? 2
FINAL S MEMØRY ADDRESS FØR THIS BLØCK=? 5


S MEMØRY(    2) TØ S MEMØRY(    5) =

        15            8             23             7
STARTING S MEMØRY ADDRESS=? 9999
```

Figure 8.2 Execution of fixed-point addition and subtraction in twos complement form. Printout demonstrates 15+8→23 and 15−8→7.

```
2) DMACH1     (COMPILED)  05 JAN 76  13:49


ENTER SAME FILENAME FOR HEX? BADSBHEX
OUTPUT REGISTERS AND S MEMORY IN INTEGER(1) OR OCTAL(2)? 2
INPUT S MEMORY IN INTEGER(1) OR OCTAL IN O11 FORMAT(2)? 2
STARTING ADDRESS =? 0
MAXIMUM NUMBER OF CLOCKS TO SIMULATE=? 25
NUMBER OF CLOCKS BETWEEN OUTPUT POINTS=? 1

ENTER OUTPUT LINES DESIRED       1-ADDRESSES AND CLOCK
2- A1,A2,A3,B    3- MIR,SAR,LIT,CTR,AMPCR    4- BR1,BR2,MAR,BMAR,GC1,GC2
 5- CONDITIONS
ENTER NUMBER OF OUTPUT LINES DESIRED? 5

BEGIN OUTPUT AT MPM ADDRESS=? 20
END OUTPUT AT MPM ADDRESS=? 20
ENTER 1 FOR S MEMORY DUMP WHEN PROGRAM TERMINATES? 1



ENTER S MEMORY VALUES IN CONSECUTIVE BLOCKS
ENTER 9999 FOR STARTING ADDRESS WHEN FINISHED


STARTING S MEMORY ADDRESS=? 2
FINAL S MEMORY ADDRESS FOR THIS BLOCK=? 3
SMEM(    2)=? 00000000017
SMEM(    3)=? 37777777770


STARTING S MEMORY ADDRESS=? 9999


END OF SIMULATION - REGISTERS CONTAIN


P(1) ADDR. =  19      P(3) ADDR. =  19      CLOCK =    21
A1=00000000017     A2=00000000000     A3=00000000027     B =37777777770
MIR =00000000027     SAR = 0     LIT =  5     CTR =  0     AMPCR =  18
BR1 =  0     BR2 =  0     MAR =  5     BMAR =    5     GC1=0   GC2=0
LC1=0  LC2=0  MST=0  LST=0  ABT=0  AOV=0  COV=0  SAI=1  RDC=1  INT=0


MEMORY DUMP REQUESTED

ENTER VALUES AS DONE IN MEMORY INPUT (9999 FOR STARTING ADDRESS WHEN
FINISHED)

STARTING S MEMORY ADDRESS=? 2
FINAL S MEMORY ADDRESS FOR THIS BLOCK=? 5


S MEMORY(    2) TO S MEMORY(    5) =


00000000017  37777777770  00000000007  00000000027
STARTING S MEMORY ADDRESS=? 9999
```

Figure 8.3 Execution of fixed-point addition and subtraction in twos complement form. Printout demonstrates $15+(-8)\rightarrow 7$ and $15-(-8)\rightarrow 23$.

The combined contents of the AC and MQ are shifted one place to the right as follows:

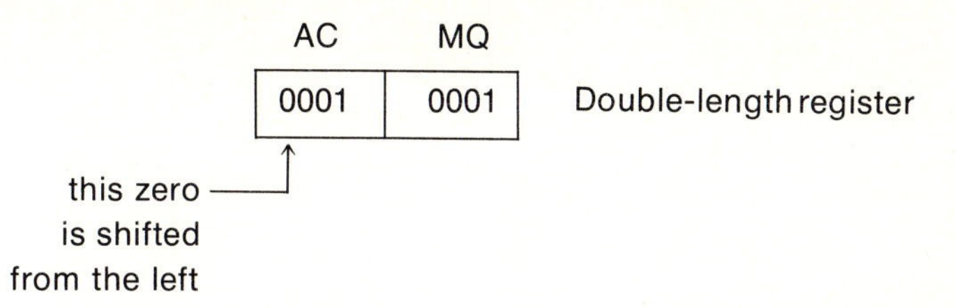

This completes the first add/shift cycle. During the second add/shift cycle, the multiplicand is again added to the AC-register because the rightmost bit of the MQ-register again is a 1, so that the AC- and MQ-registers would be as follows:

The combined contents of the AC and MQ are shifted one place to the right as follows:

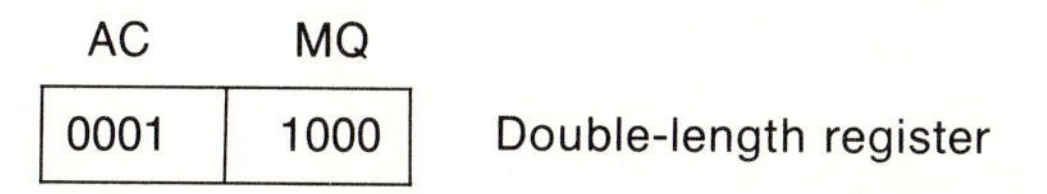

This completes the second add/shift cycle. During the third and fourth add/shift cycles, the multiplicand is *not* added to the AC-register because the rightmost bits of the MQ-register are 0s. After two right shifts, for the cycles not requiring addition, the combined AC- and MQ-registers would be as follows:

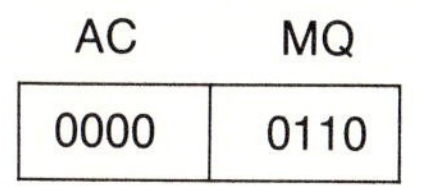

The double-length product is in the AC- and MQ-registers; the AC-register contains the high-order part, and the MQ-register contains the low-order part. When the product is expected to be of a single length, then the high-order part can be ignored.

Fixed-point multiplication is microprogrammed in most modern computers. In the following example, the combined ⟨A1,A2⟩ registers are used as the AC- and MQ-registers, respectively, so that repeated additions are made to the A1-register. The multiplier is placed in the A2-register, and the multiplicand is placed in the B-register.

When the multiply microroutine is entered, the operands have already been placed in their respective registers by a setup routine. The binary multiply routine, listed as follows, returns the double-length product in the ⟨A1,A2⟩ isters as indicated above:

```
BMULT:  AMPCR→MIR          % SAVE RETURN ADDRESS
    0→A1, LCTR
    32→LIT, 1→SAR
    BMTEST−1→AMPCR
    INC, CALL
          ┌─────────────────────────────────────────────────┐
          │ IF NOT LST THEN A1 R→A1, SKIP ELSE STEP         │
          │ A1+B R→A1                                       │
Main loop │ IF NOT LST THEN A2 R→A2, SKIP ELSE STEP         │
          │ A2 OR 1 C→A2                                    │
          │BMTEST: IF NOT COV THEN A2→, INC, JUMP ELSE STEP │
          └─────────────────────────────────────────────────┘
    BMI     % RESTORE RETURN ADDRESS
    B→AMPCR
    JUMP
```

A printout of the translation of the microprogram for binary multiplication to hexadecimal microcode is given in Figure 8.4, and a sample run on the simulator is given as Figure 8.5. The multiply routine is called by a setup routine that reads the multiplier from S-memory location 100 and places it in register A2 and reads the multiplicand from S-memory location 101 and places it in register B, prior to the call. After the multiply operation, the setup routine places the product in S-memory location 103.

The binary multiplication microroutine demonstrates two techniques other than multiplication:

1 The method of leading decisions
2 The technique of storing a return address in the MIR

Clearly, the program can be made slightly more efficient by not using the method of leading decisions and by using register A3 to store the return address, as follows:

```
BMULT:  AMPCR→A3, LCTR        % SAVE RETURN ADDRESS
    31→LIT, 1→SAR
    A2→, SAVE
          ┌──────────────────────────────────────────┐
          │ IF NOT LST THEN A1 R→A1 SKIP ELSE STEP   │
          │ A1+B R→A1                                │
Main loop │ IF NOT LST THEN A2 R→A2 SKIP ELSE STEP   │
          │ A2 OR 1 C→A2, INC                        │
          │ A2→, IF COV THEN STEP ELSE JUMP          │
          └──────────────────────────────────────────┘
    A3→AMPCR      % RESTORE RETURN ADDRESS
    JUMP
```

```
>>>>> TRANSLANG D MACHINE MICRØTRANSLATØR

ENTER FILENAME FØR HEX? BMHEX
SUPPRESS BIT PATTERNS?(1=SUPPRESS)? 1
SUPPRESS HEX LISTING?(1=SUPPRESS)? 1
IF INPUT IN FILE ENTER 1? 31
ENTER SØURCE FILENAME? BINMLT

0000   SETUP. LMAR $
0001      100 = LIT $
0002      MR2, BEX, LMAR $
0003      101 = LIT $
0004      WHEN RDC THEN B = A2, MR2 $
0005      BMULT - 1 = AMPCR $
0006      WHEN RDC THEN BEX, CALL $
0007      A2 = MIR, LMAR $
0008      102 = LIT $
0009      MW2, IF SAI $
0010      FINI - 1 = AMPCR $
0011      WHEN SAI THEN JUMP $
0012   BMULT. AMPCR = MIR $ SAVE RETURN ADDRESS
0013      0 = A1, LCTR $
0014      32 = LIT, 1 = SAR $
0015      BMTEST - 1 = AMPCR $
0016      INC, CALL $
0017      IF NØT LST THEN A1 R = A1, SKIP ELSE STEP $
0018      A1 + B R = A1 $
0019      IF NØT LST THEN A2 R = A2, SKIP ELSE STEP $
0020      A2 ØR 1 C = A2 $
0021   BMTEST. IF NØT CØV THEN A2 =, INC, JUMP ELSE STEP $
0022      BMI $ RESTØRE RETURN ADDRESS
0023      B = AMPCR $
0024      JUMP $
0025   FINI. STEP $
0026     END $

THE TOTAL NUMBER ØF ERRØRS =    0

EXECUTE (Y/N)? N
```

Figure 8.4 Printout of the translation of the microprogram for binary multiplication to hexadecimal microcode.

The return from the binary multiplication microroutine can also be made to a fixed location in the microprogram, such as a fetch routine, which is usually the method of implementation in an emulator. The main loop of the binary multiplication routine is five type I statements, which is fairly efficient for a computation of this type.

8.2.3 Division

Binary division is performed by repeated subtraction and shifting, and it generates a single-length quotient from a double-length dividend and a single-length divisor. In the following examples, a double-length dividend is obtained from a single-length dividend by prefixing it with a zero word. The operation uses a double-length accumulator and an auxiliary register, as follows:

divisor — Auxiliary register

AC-register | MQ-register

high-order part of dividend | low-order part of dividend — Double-length accumulator

The double-length accumulator is implemented as two machine registers that are used in such a way that a bit that is left shifted out of the MQ-register enters the AC-register, as though the two registers were actually one double-length register. The binary division procedure operates as follows:

1 The double-length dividend is moved to the combined ⟨AC,MQ⟩ registers. The divisor is moved to the auxiliary register. If the contents of the AC-register (above) are greater than or equal to the divisor, then the division halts because an overflow condition would result.

2 The combined ⟨AC,MQ⟩ registers are shifted left one place. A count is made of the number of shift operations.

3 If the contents of the AC-register are greater than or equal to the contents of the auxiliary register, then the contents of the auxiliary register are subtracted from the AC-register, and a 1 bit is placed in the low-order (that is, rightmost) position of the MQ-register. Otherwise, the process continues with step 4.

4 When the number of shift operations is equal to the number of digits in the divisor, then the division operation is complete. Otherwise, the process continues with step 2.

5 The quotient is left in MQ-register; the remainder is in the AC-register.

As an example of the technique, assume 4-bit registers, a dividend of 00001100 (in binary), and a divisor of 0100 (in binary). Initially, the dividend and the divisor are placed in the combined ⟨AC,MQ⟩ registers and the auxiliary register, respectively, as follows:

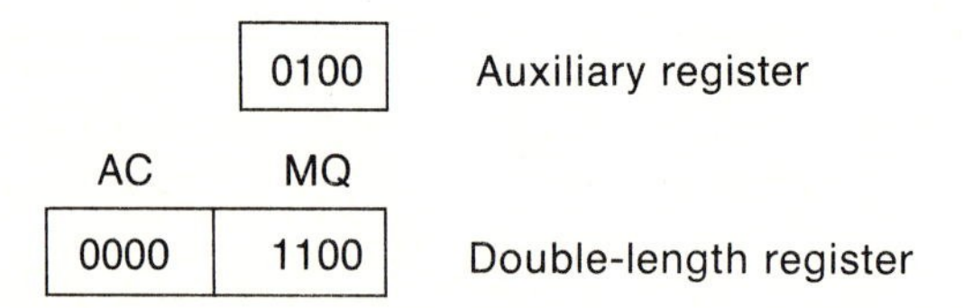

The contents of the auxiliary register are not changed during the division operation.

During the first shift/subtract cycle, the ⟨AC,MQ⟩ registers are left-shifted one place, but no subtraction is performed because the contents of the auxiliary register are greater than the contents of AC; the ⟨AC,MQ⟩ registers are pictured

```
2) DMACHI     (CØMPILED)  05 JAN 76   14:08

ENTER SAME FILENAME FØR HEX? BMHEX
ØUTPUT REGISTERS AND S MEMØRY IN INTEGER(1) ØR ØCTAL(2)? 1
INPUT S MEMØRY IN INTEGER(1) ØR ØCTAL IN Ø11 FØRMAT(2)? 1
STARTING ADDRESS =? 0
MAXIMUM NUMBER ØF CLØCKS TØ SIMULATE=? 150
NUMBER ØF CLØCKS BETWEEN ØUTPUT PØINTS=? 1

ENTER ØUTPUT LINES DESIRED      1-ADDRESSES AND CLØCK
2- A1,A2,A3,B    3- MIR,SAR,LIT,CTR,AMPCR     4- BR1,BR2,MAR,BMAR,GC1,GC2
 5- CØNDITIØNS
ENTER NUMBER ØF ØUTPUT LINES DESIRED? 5

BEGIN ØUTPUT AT MPM ADDRESS=? 26
END ØUTPUT AT MPM ADDRESS=? 26
ENTER 1 FØR S MEMØRY DUMP WHEN PRØGRAM TERMINATES? 1



ENTER S MEMØRY VALUES IN CØNSECUTIVE BLØCKS
ENTER 9999 FØR STARTING ADDRESS WHEN FINISHED


STARTING S MEMØRY ADDRESS=? 100
FINAL S MEMØRY ADDRESS FØR THIS BLØCK=? 101
SMEM( 100)=? 37
SMEM( 101)=? 15


STARTING S MEMØRY ADDRESS=? 9999



END ØF SIMULATIØN - REGISTERS CØNTAIN


P(1) ADDR. =  25      P(3) ADDR. =  25      CLØCK =  127
A1 =          0     A2 =         555      A3 =          0      B =          6
MIR =        555       SAR = 1      LIT =102       CTR =  0       AMPCR =  24
BR1 =  0       BR2 =  0      MAR =102      BMAR =  102       GC1=0  GC2=0
LC1=0  LC2=0  MST=0  LST=0  ABT=0  AØV=0  CØV=0  SAI=1  RDC=1  INT=0


MEMØRY DUMP REQUESTED

ENTER VALUES AS DØNE IN MEMØRY INPUT (9999 FØR STARTING ADDRESS WHEN
FINISHED)

STARTING S MEMØRY ADDRESS=? 100
FINAL S MEMØRY ADDRESS FØR THIS BLØCK=? 102


S MEMØRY( 100) TØ S MEMØRY( 102) =


         37          15          555
STARTING S MEMØRY ADDRESS=? 9999
```

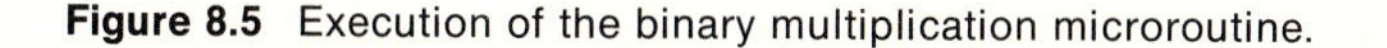

Figure 8.5 Execution of the binary multiplication microroutine.

as follows:

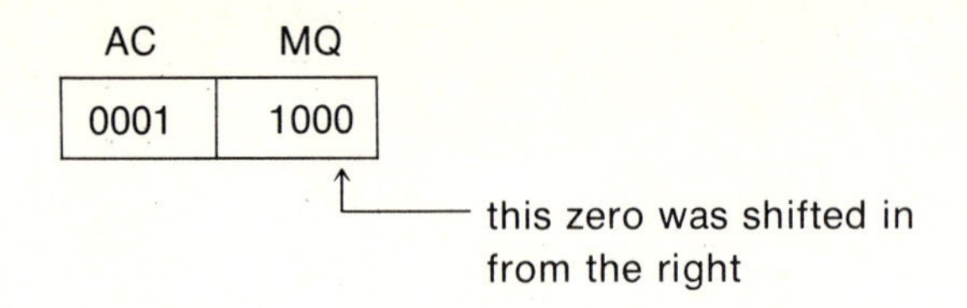

During the second shift/subtract cycle, the left shift is again performed, but no subtraction takes place for the same reason; the ⟨AC,MQ⟩ registers are pictured as follows:

AC	MQ
0011	0000

During the third shift/subtract cycle, the left shift is performed, with the following result:

AC	MQ
0110	0000

The subtraction is performed, and a 1 bit is placed in the low-order position of the MQ-register as follows:

AC	MQ
0010	0001

During the fourth and final shift/subtract cycle, the left shift is performed, with the following result:

AC	MQ
0100	0010

and the final subtraction completes operation:

AC	MQ
0000	0011

The quotient of 0011 (in binary) is in the MQ-register, and the remainder, of 0 in this case, is in the AC-register.

As was the case with fixed-point multiplication, fixed-point division is microprogrammed in most modern computers. In the following example, the combined ⟨A1,A2⟩ registers are used as the AC- and MQ-registers, respectively, so that subtractions are made to the A1-register. The divisor is placed in the B-register. When the divide microroutine is entered, the operands have already been placed in their respective registers by a setup routine. The binary divide routine, listed as follows, returns a single-length quotient in register A2 and the remainder in register A1:

```
BDIV:  LCTR
       32→ LIT, COMP 1→SAR
       BDTEST−1→AMPCR
       INC, CALL
           ┌──────────────────────────────────────────────────────┐
           │ IF NOT MST THEN A1 L→A1, SKIP ELSE STEP               │
           │ A1 OR B100 C→A1                                       │
Main loop  │ A1−B→                                                 │
           │ IF AOV THEN A1−B→A1, STEP ELSE SKIP                   │
           │ A2 OR 1→A2                                            │
           │BDTEST: IF NOT COV THEN A2 L→A2, INC JUMP ELSE STEP    │
           └──────────────────────────────────────────────────────┘
       RET−1→AMPCR
       JUMP
```

A printout of the translation of the microprogram for binary division to hexadecimal microcode is given in Figure 8.6, and a sample run on the simulator is given in Figure 8.7. The divide routine is called by a setup routine that reads the dividend from S-memory location 100 and places it in register A2 and then reads the divisor from S-memory location 101 and places it in register B. Also, register A1 is set to 0 prior to the call. After the divide operation, the setup routine places the quotient in S-memory location 102.

The binary division routine uses the same general techniques as binary multiplication for controlled looping and the saving of the return address. Binary division additionally demonstrates the following:

1 A "greater than or equal to" test of the form:

```
A1 − B→
IF AOV
```

to test if the contents of register A1 are greater than or equal to the contents of register B

2 A circular left shift of 1—that is,

```
A1 OR B100 C→A1
```

where the SAR contains COMP 1.

The main loop of the binary division routine is six type I statements, which is comparable in efficiency to binary multiplication.

```
>>>>> TRANSLANG D MACHINE MICRØTRANSLATØR

ENTER FILENAME FØR HEX? BDHEX
SUPPRESS BIT PATTERNS?(1=SUPPRESS)? 1
SUPPRESS HEX LISTING?(1=SUPPRESS)? 1
IF INPUT IN FILE ENTER 1? 31
ENTER SØURCE FILENAME? BINDIV

0000    SETUP. 0 = A1, LMAR $
0001       100 = LIT $
0002       MR2, BEX, LMAR $
0003       101 = LIT $
0004       WHEN RDC THEN B = A2, MR2 $
0005       BDIV - 1 = AMPCR $
0006       WHEN RDC THEN BEX, JUMP $
0007    RET. A2 = MIR, LMAR $
0008       102 = LIT $
0009       MW2, IF SAI $
0010       FINI - 1 = AMPCR $
0011       WHEN SAI THEN JUMP $
0012    BDIV. LCTR $
0013       32 = LIT, CØMP 1 = SAR $
0014       BDTEST - 1 = AMPCR $
0015       INC, CALL $
0016       IF NØT MST THEN A1 L = A1, SKIP ELSE STEP $
0017       A1 ØR B100 C = A1 $
0018       A1 - B = $
0019       IF AØV THEN A1 - B = A1, STEP ELSE SKIP $
0020       A2 ØR 1 = A2 $
0021    BDTEST. IF NØT CØV THEN A2 L = A2, INC, JUMP ELSE STEP $
0022       RET - 1 = AMPCR $
0023       JUMP $
0024    FINI. STEP $
0025       END $

THE TØTAL NUMBER ØF ERRØRS =     0

EXECUTE (Y/N)? N
```

Figure 8.6 Printout of the translation of the microprogram for binary division to hexadecimal microcode.

8.3 FIXED-POINT ARITHMETIC OPERATIONS—SIGNED-MAGNITUDE REPRESENTATION

Signed-magnitude representation of fixed-point numbers is introduced in Chapter 4, where procedures for addition and subtraction are given. A summary of those procedures and a combined addition/subtraction microprogram are given here. Multiplication and division of fixed-point values in signed-magnitude representation are also introduced, and procedures are given so that appropriate microroutines can be developed as an exercise.

8.3.1 Addition and Subtraction

Addition and subtraction are precisely the same except that for subtraction, the sign of the subtrahend must be changed prior to the add operation. The method corresponds to the school-book algorithm for subtraction which reads,

```
2) DMACH1     (CØMPILED)  05 JAN 76  14:26
                                                      Katzan  Page 8-12b
ENTER SAME FILENAME FØR HEX? BDHEX
ØUTPUT REGISTERS AND S MEMØRY IN INTEGER(1) ØR ØCTAL(2)? 1
INPUT S MEMØRY IN INTEGER(1) ØR ØCTAL IN Ø11 FØRMAT(2)? 1
STARTING ADDRESS =? 0
MAXIMUM NUMBER ØF CLØCKS TØ SIMULATE=? 175
NUMBER ØF CLØCKS BETWEEN ØUTPUT PØINTS=? 1

ENTER ØUTPUT LINES DESIRED      1-ADDRESSES AND CLØCK
2- A1,A2,A3,B    3- MIR,SAR,LIT,CTR,AMPCR    4- BR1,BR2,MAR,BMAR,GC1,GC2
 5- CØNDITIØNS
ENTER NUMBER ØF ØUTPUT LINES DESIRED? 5

BEGIN ØUTPUT AT MPM ADDRESS=? 25
END ØUTPUT AT MPM ADDRESS=? 25
ENTER 1 FØR S MEMØRY DUMP WHEN PRØGRAM TERMINATES? 1



ENTER S MEMØRY VALUES IN CØNSECUTIVE BLØCKS
ENTER 9999 FØR STARTING ADDRESS WHEN FINISHED


STARTING S MEMØRY ADDRESS=? 100
FINAL S MEMØRY ADDRESS FØR THIS BLØCK=? 101
SMEM( 100)=? 180
SMEM( 101)=? 12


STARTING S MEMØRY ADDRESS=? 9999



END ØF SIMULATIØN - REGISTERS CØNTAIN


P(1) ADDR. =  24      P(3) ADDR. =  24      CLØCK =  157
A1 =          0      A2 =          15      A3 =          0      B =          12
MIR =         15      SAR =31      LIT =102      CTR =  0      AMPCR =  23
BR1 =  0      BR2 =  0      MAR =102      BMAR =  102      GC1=0  GC2=0
LC1=0  LC2=0  MST=0  LST=0  ABT=0  AØV=0  CØV=0  SAI=1  RDC=1  INT=0


MEMØRY DUMP REQUESTED

ENTER VALUES AS DØNE IN MEMØRY INPUT (9999 FØR STARTING ADDRESS WHEN
FINISHED)

STARTING S MEMØRY ADDRESS=? 100
FINAL S MEMØRY ADDRESS FØR THIS BLØCK=? 102


S MEMØRY( 100) TØ S MEMØRY( 102) =


        180          12          15
STARTING S MEMØRY ADDRESS=? 9999
```

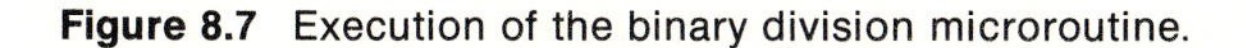

Figure 8.7 Execution of the binary division microroutine.

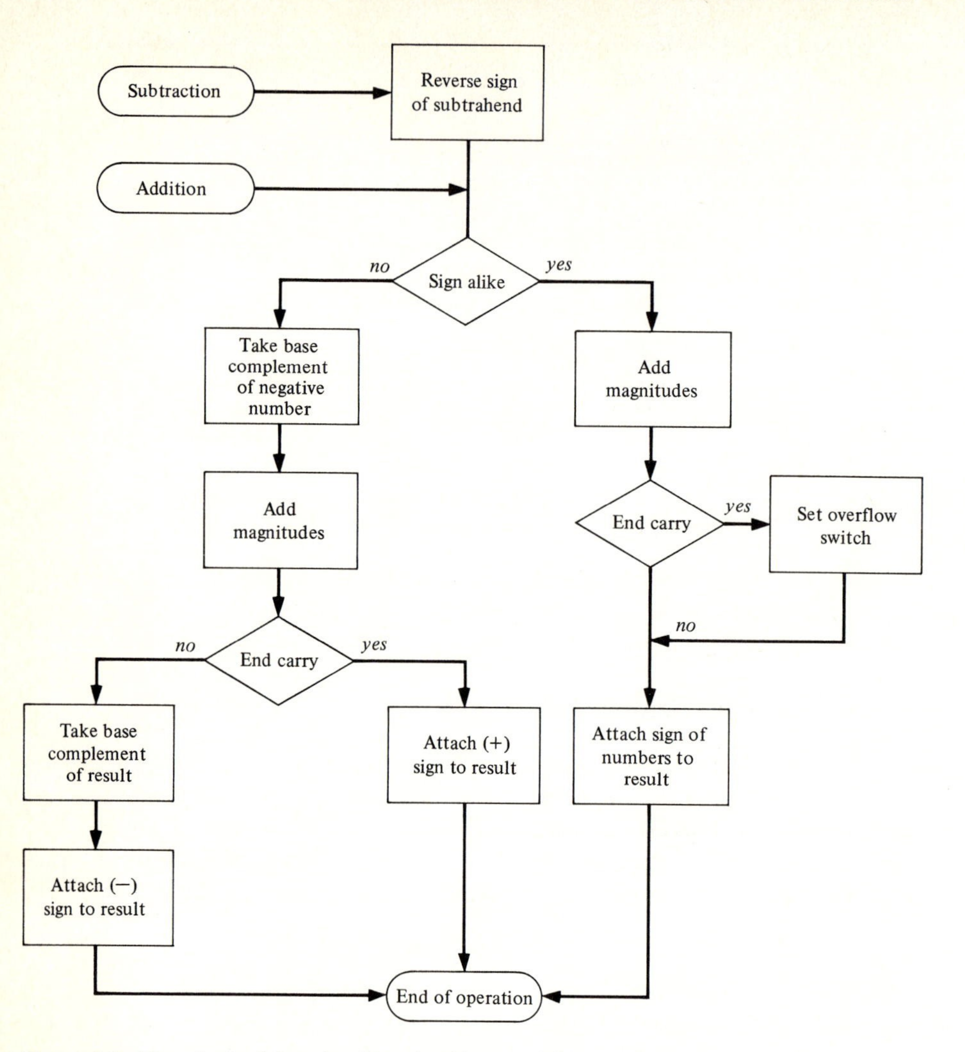

Figure 8.8 Flowchart of the algorithm for binary addition and subtraction of values with signed-magnitude representation.

"Change the sign of the subtrahend and add the numbers." Therefore, the addition and subtraction routines are normally implemented as a single routine with two entry points. The algorithm is summarized by a flow diagram in Figure 8.8.

The microprogram for addition and subtraction of binary values in signed-magnitude representation expects the first operand (that is, the addend or the minuend) to be in register A1 and the second operand (that is, the augend or the subtrahend) in register B. The result (that is, the sum or the difference) is returned to register A3. The main loop of the routine is given as follows:

```
SUB:  B_FTT→B
ADD:  AMPCR→MIR             %  SAVE RETURN
    A1 XOR B→, IF LC1          %  RESET OVERFLOW INDICATOR
    SDIF−1→AMPCR           %  BRANCH ADDR FOR DIFF SIGNS
    IF NOT MST THEN A1+B→A3, STEP ELSE JUMP
    IF MST THEN A3 AND B_011→A3, SET LC1
    A3 OR B_T00→A3, BMI
    B→AMPCR          %  RESTORE RETURN ADDRESS
    JUMP        %  RETURN−RESULT IN A3
SDIF:  B→A3
    IF NOT MST THEN A1→B, STEP ELSE SKIP
    A3→A1        %  B ALWAYS CONTAINS NEG NUM
    B_OFF→B
    A1+B+1→B
    OVR−1→AMPCR
    IF MST THEN B_0TT→A3, BMI, JUMP
    B_1FF→B
    0+B+1→A3, BMI
OVR:  B→AMPCR          %  RESTORE RETURN ADDRESS
    JUMP        %  RETURN−RESULT IN A3
```

The routine effectively masks off the high-order bit of the operands and then performs the add operation, taking the sign of the respective operands into consideration. After the add operation, the high-order bit of the result (that is, the MST bit) is used to check for operational overflow. In the microroutine, the LC1 condition is used to indicate the presence of an overflow condition.

A printout of the translation of the signed-magnitude addition and subtraction microroutine, along with an appropriate calling routine, is given in Figure 8.9. Sample runs are given in Figures 8.10 and 8.11.

8.3.2 Multiplication and Division

The multiplication and division of binary values in signed-magnitude form require the use of the microroutines for twos complement operations and some straightforward procedures for sign control. For multiplication, the sign bits of the operands are interrogated, possibly with the exclusive-or (XOR) condition, and a switch is set, possibly LC1, LC2, or LC3, if the signs are the same. Then binary multiplication is performed with positive values, which is indeed the case. A plus sign is affixed to the result if the operands had the same sign, and a minus sign is affixed if the signs of the operands were different. It should be noted that the size of operands is 1 bit shorter after the algebraic signs are removed.

The same method for sign control is normally used with division, with additional consideration given to determining the sign of the remainder. If m and n are the dividend and divisor, respectively, then division is defined as follows:

$$m = q \times n + r$$

```
>>>>> TRANSLANG D MACHINE MICRØTRANSLATØR

ENTER FILENAME FØR HEX? SMHEX
SUPPRESS BIT PATTERNS?(1=SUPPRESS)? 1
SUPPRESS HEX LISTING?(1=SUPPRESS)? 1
IF INPUT IN FILE ENTER 1? 31
ENTER SØURCE FILENAME? SMAG

0000    SETUP. LMAR $
0001       2 = LIT $
0002       MR2, BEX, LMAR $ READ FIRST ØPERAND
0003       3 = LIT $
0004       WHEN RDC THEN B = A1, MR2 $ READ SECØND ØPERAND
0005       ADD - 1 = AMPCR $
0006       WHEN RDC THEN BEX, CALL $ TØ ADD
0007       A3 = MIR, LMAR $ RETURN SUM IN A3
0008       4 = LIT $
0009       MW2, LMAR, IF SAI $ WRITE SUM TØ S MEM
0010       3 = LIT $
0011       WHEN SAI THEN MR2, STEP $
0012       SUB - 1 = AMPCR $
0013       WHEN RDC THEN BEX, CALL $ TØ SUB
0014       A3 = MIR, LMAR $ RETURN DIFF IN A3
0015       5 = LIT $
0016       MW2, IF SAI $ WRITE DIFF TØ S MEM
0017       FINI - 1 = AMPCR $
0018       WHEN SAI THEN JUMP $
0019    SUB. BFTT = B $
0020    ADD. AMPCR = MIR $ SAVE RETURN
0021       A1 XØR B =, IF LC1 $ RESET ØVRFLW (LC1)
0022       SDIF - 1 = AMPCR $
0023       IF NØT MST THEN A1 + B = A3, STEP ELSE JUMP $
0024       IF MST THEN A3 AND B011 = A3, SET LC1 $
0025       A3 ØR BT00 = A3, BMI $
0026       B = AMPCR $
0027       JUMP $ RETURN RESULT IN A3
0028    SDIF. B = A3 $
0029       IF NØT MST THEN A1 = B, STEP ELSE SKIP $
0030       A3 = A1 $ B CØNTAINS NEG NUM
0031       BOFF = B $
0032       A1 + B + 1 = B $
0033       ØVR - 1 = AMPCR $
0034       IF MST THEN BOTT = A3, BMI, JUMP $
0035       B1FF = B $
0036       0 + B + 1 = A3, BMI $
0037    ØVR. B = AMPCR $ RESTØRE RETURN
0038       JUMP $ RETURN RESULT IN A3
0039    FINI. STEP $
0040       END $

THE TØTAL NUMBER ØF ERRØRS =     0

EXECUTE (Y/N)? N
```

Figure 8.9 Printout of the translation of the microprogram for signed-magnitude binary addition and subtraction to hexadecimal microcode.

where q is the quotient, r is the remainder, and the absolute value of r is less than the absolute value of n. The signs of the quotient and remainder are determined from the signs of the dividend and divisor. If the algebraic signs of m and n are alike, then the sign of q is positive; otherwise, it is negative. The sign of r is the same as the sign of m.

```
2) DMACH1     (COMPILED)  05 JAN 76   14:42


ENTER SAME FILENAME FØR HEX? SMHEX
ØUTPUT REGISTERS AND S MEMØRY IN INTEGER(1) ØR ØCTAL(2)? 1
INPUT S MEMØRY IN INTEGER(1) ØR ØCTAL IN Ø11 FØRMAT(2)? 1
STARTING ADDRESS =? 0
MAXIMUM NUMBER ØF CLØCKS TØ SIMULATE=? 50
NUMBER ØF CLØCKS BETWEEN ØUTPUT PØINTS=? 1

ENTER ØUTPUT LINES DESIRED      1-ADDRESSES AND CLØCK
2- A1,A2,A3,B    3- MIR,SAR,LIT,CTR,AMPCR    4- BR1,BR2,MAR,BMAR,GC1,GC2
 5- CØNDITIØNS
ENTER NUMBER ØF ØUTPUT LINES DESIRED? 5

BEGIN ØUTPUT AT MPM ADDRESS=? 40
END ØUTPUT AT MPM ADDRESS=? 40
ENTER 1 FØR S MEMØRY DUMP WHEN PRØGRAM TERMINATES? 1



ENTER S MEMØRY VALUES IN CØNSECUTIVE BLØCKS
ENTER 9999 FØR STARTING ADDRESS WHEN FINISHED


STARTING S MEMØRY ADDRESS=? 2
FINAL S MEMØRY ADDRESS FØR THIS BLØCK=? 3
SMEM(    2)=? 15
SMEM(    3)=? 8


STARTING S MEMØRY ADDRESS=? 9999



END ØF SIMULATIØN - REGISTERS CØNTAIN


P(1) ADDR. =   39      P(3) ADDR. =   39        CLØCK =     42
A1 =          15      A2 =           0       A3 =          7      B =          13
MIR =          7      SAR = 0      LIT =  5       CTR =  0       AMPCR =  38
BR1 =  0      BR2 =  0      MAR =  5       BMAR =     5        GC1=0   GC2=0
LC1=0  LC2=0  MST=0  LST=0  ABT=0  AØV=0  CØV=0  SAI=1  RDC=1  INT=0


MEMØRY DUMP REQUESTED

ENTER VALUES AS DØNE IN MEMØRY INPUT (9999 FØR STARTING ADDRESS WHEN
FINISHED)

STARTING S MEMØRY ADDRESS=? 2
FINAL S MEMØRY ADDRESS FØR THIS BLØCK=? 5


S MEMØRY(    2) TØ S MEMØRY(    5) =


         15            8            23              7
STARTING S MEMØRY ADDRESS=? 9999
```

Figure 8.10 Execution of fixed-point addition and subtraction in signed-magnitude form. Printout demonstrates 15+8=23 and 15−8=7. (Output is displayed in integer format.)

```
2) DMACH10    05 JAN 76   15:01


ENTER SAME FILENAME FØR HEX? SMHEX
ØUTPUT REGISTERS AND S MEMØRY IN INTEGER(1) ØR ØCTAL(2)? 2
INPUT S MEMØRY IN INTEGER(1) ØR ØCTAL IN Ø11 FØRMAT(2)? 2
STARTING ADDRESS =? 0
MAXIMUM NUMBER ØF CLØCKS TØ SIMULATE=? 50
NUMBER ØF CLØCKS BETWEEN ØUTPUT PØINTS=? 1

ENTER ØUTPUT LINES DESIRED      1-ADDRESSES AND CLØCK
2- A1,A2,A3,B    3- MIR,SAR,LIT,CTR,AMPCR    4- BR1,BR2,MAR,BMAR,GC1,GC2
 5- CØNDITIØNS
ENTER NUMBER ØF ØUTPUT LINES DESIRED? 5

BEGIN ØUTPUT AT MPM ADDRESS=? 40
END ØUTPUT AT MPM ADDRESS=? 40
ENTER 1 FØR S MEMØRY DUMP WHEN PRØGRAM TERMINATES? 1



ENTER S MEMØRY VALUES IN CØNSECUTIVE BLØCKS
ENTER 9999 FØR STARTING ADDRESS WHEN FINISHED


STARTING S MEMØRY ADDRESS=? 2
FINAL S MEMØRY ADDRESS FØR THIS BLØCK=? 3
SMEM(    2)=? 00000000017
SMEM(    3)=? 20000000010


STARTING S MEMØRY ADDRESS=? 9999



END ØF SIMULATIØN - REGISTERS CØNTAIN


P(1) ADDR. =   39       P(3) ADDR. =   39       CLØCK =    42
A1=00000000017     A2=00000000000     A3=00000000027     B =00000000015
MIR =00000000027       SAR = 0      LIT =  5      CTR =  0      AMPCR =  38
BR1 =   0      BR2 =   0      MAR =   5      BMAR =    5      GC1=0  GC2=0
LC1=0  LC2=0  MST=0  LST=0  ABT=0  AØV=0  CØV=0  SAI=1  RDC=1  INT=0


MEMØRY DUMP REQUESTED

ENTER VALUES AS DØNE IN MEMØRY INPUT (9999 FØR STARTING ADDRESS WHEN
FINISHED)

STARTING S MEMØRY ADDRESS=? 2
FINAL S MEMØRY ADDRESS FØR THIS BLØCK=? 5


S MEMØRY(    2) TØ S MEMØRY(    5) =


00000000017  20000000010  00000000007  00000000027
STARTING S MEMØRY ADDRESS=? 9999
```

Figure 8.11 Execution of fixed-point addition and subtraction in signed-magnitude form. Printout demonstrates 15+(−8)=7 and 15−(−8)=23. (Output is displayed in octal format.)

8.4 FLOATING-POINT OPERATIONS

Floating-point operations are defined in most modern medium- to large-scale computers as part of the computer architecture and are either hard-wired or implemented through microprogramming. In small-scale computers or in mini- or microcomputers, floating-point operations frequently are not defined in the computer architecture and are implemented as S-machine subroutines. In either case, the floating-point algorithms are essentially the same, and the difference is solely the level of implementation.

8.4.1 Representation

The representation of a floating-point number requires a special format since the exponent and fraction fields must be handled independently during floating-point operations. The general format is given as follows:

The exponent implicitly determines the range of the numbers that can be represented, and the fraction implicitly determines their accuracy. The leftmost bit is used as the algebraic sign of the value—consistent with common usage.

The exponent field is *biased* to allow for a negative exponent, and the most common method of implementation is to use the leftmost bit of the exponent as the bias. Thus, if a 7-bit exponent is used, then a zero exponent would exist as follows:

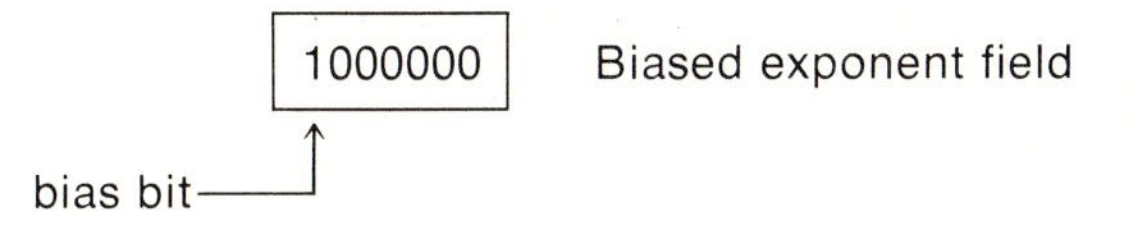

where the leftmost bit corresponds to a bias of 64. A binary exponent of +101 would be represented as

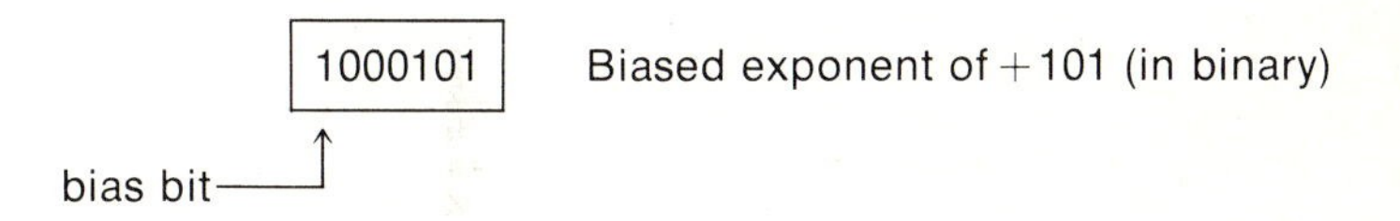

Similarly, a binary exponent of −100 would be represented as

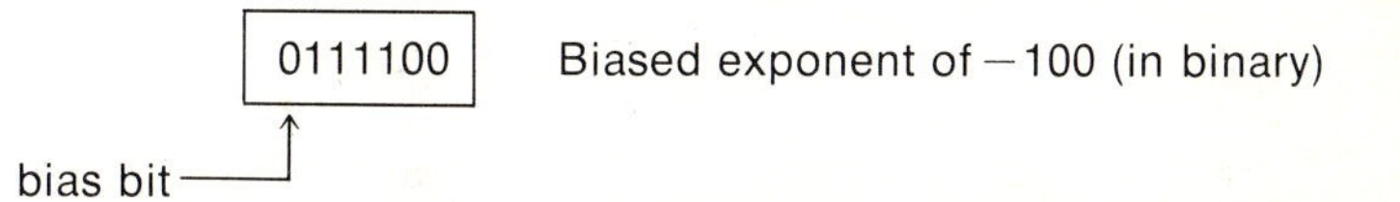

The binary exponent denotes a power of 2, as in scientific mathematical notation. For example, consider the following 32-bit floating-point format, which is used for the remainder of this chapter:

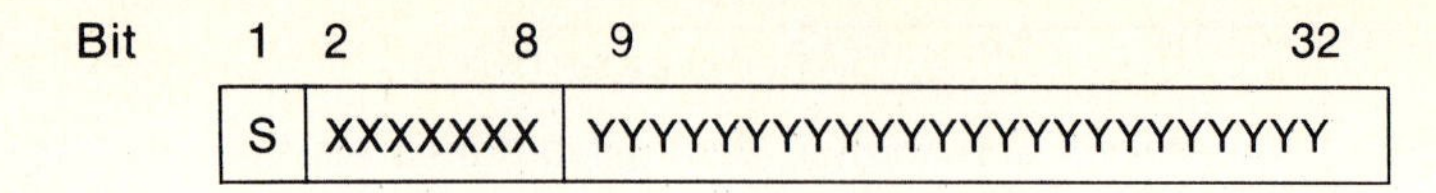

The decimal value 5 is expressed in decimal and binary scientific notation as follows:

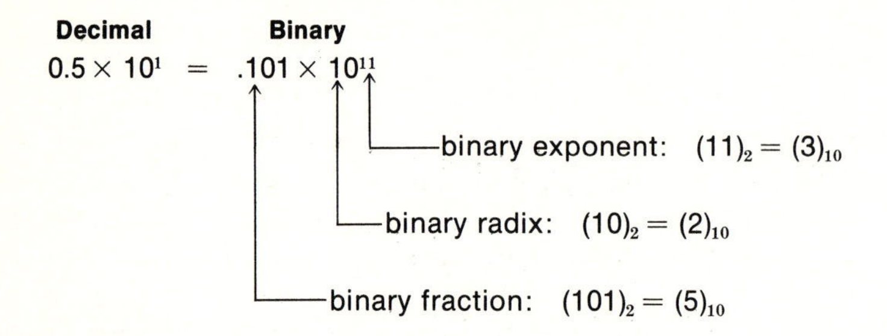

which corresponds to the following floating-point word:

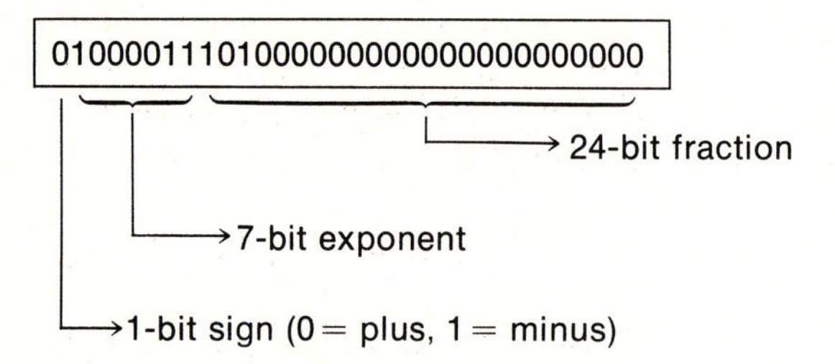

where the binary exponent of $(11)_2 = (3)_{10}$ means an interpretation of the binary point as being three places to the right, as follows:

$$.101000000000000000000000$$

Thus, the binary point is understood to be just to the left of the leftmost digit of the fraction. In a similar manner, a decimal value of 0.25 is expressed in decimal and binary scientific notation as follows:

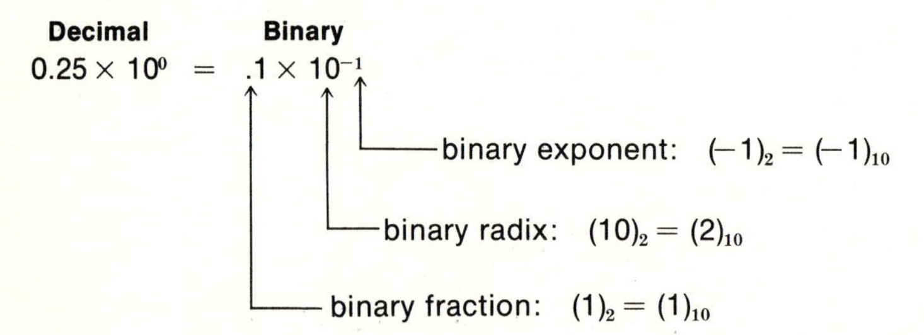

Clearly, $(0.25)_{10} = (.01)_2$, which corresponds to the following floating-point word:

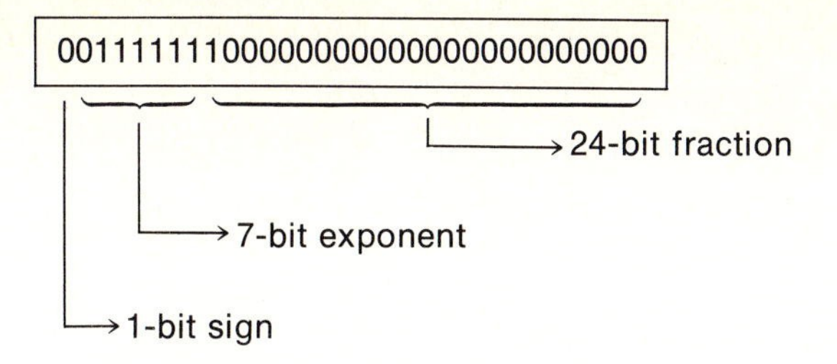

It is important to point out that a binary exponent does not always represent powers of 2. Since the exponent implicitly determines the range of a floating-point number, the practice of allowing the exponent to represent powers of 8 (that is, groups of 3 bits) or powers of 16 (that is, groups of 4 bits) is frequently used. On the IBM 360/370 computers, for example, a 7-bit biased binary exponent represents powers of 16—that is, hexadecimal digits—which gives an exponent range of -64 bits to $+63$, permitting decimal numbers in the range 10^{-78} to 10^{75} to be stored.

Since the fraction of a floating-point number determines its precision, it is important that leading zeros be eliminated to maximize the number of significant digits. A floating-point number in which the leftmost digit of the fraction is nonzero is said to be *normalized,* which is the most desirable form because it gives the greatest accuracy. Therefore, even though the unnormalized floating-point number

0	1000110	001101010000000000000000

is equivalent to the following normalized number

0	1000100	110101000000000000000000

the latter form would always be used for the reasons cited above. An arithmetic operation on floating-point numbers always generates a normalized result.

The exponent and fraction fields of floating-point numbers are exclusively stored in true form—as in signed-magnitude representation—and complement arithmetic is rarely, if ever, used. However, there does not appear to be any a priori reason why complement arithmetic cannot be applied, except that possibly it would complicate the equalizing of exponents during additive operations.

8.4.2 Basic Floating-Point Algorithms

This section gives basic algorithms for performing floating-point operations. In order to facilitate the exposition, a decimal form is used. In this form, the excess -64 exponent represents powers of 10, so that the value 23.84 would be stored as

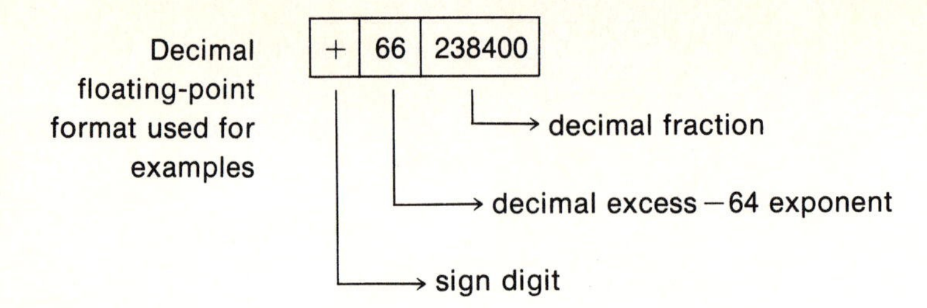

The exponent of (66 − 64) = 2 specifies, in this case, that the decimal point is located two positions from the left in the fraction. Knowledge of the precise location of the decimal point is required in floating-point addition and subtraction operations.

8.4.2.1 Addition and Subtraction For floating-point addition and subtraction, the operation can be performed only if the radix point of the two operands is in the same relative position, which occurs when the exponents are equal. When necessary, therefore, the exponent and fraction of a floating-point number can be adjusted using the following procedure: "For every digit position that the fraction is shifted to the right, the value of the exponent is increased by 1. For every digit position that the fraction is shifted to the left, the value of the exponent is decreased by 1." Employing this procedure, the execution of floating-point addition and subtraction operations is summarized as follows:

1 The exponents are compared.
2 If the exponents are not equal, the fraction part of the number with the smaller exponent is shifted right until the exponents are equal.
3 The functions are added or subtracted.
4 The result is normalized by shifting the fraction to the left, and adjusting the exponent accordingly, until the leftmost bit of the fraction is nonzero.

The algebraic sign of the result is managed as in fixed-point operations on signed-magnitude operands.

As an example of the algorithm, consider the following values in simplified decimal floating-point form:

Variable	Floating-point value		
X	+	68	123456
Y	+	67	789012

Computation of the expression X − Y is performed as follows:

1 The exponents are equalized:

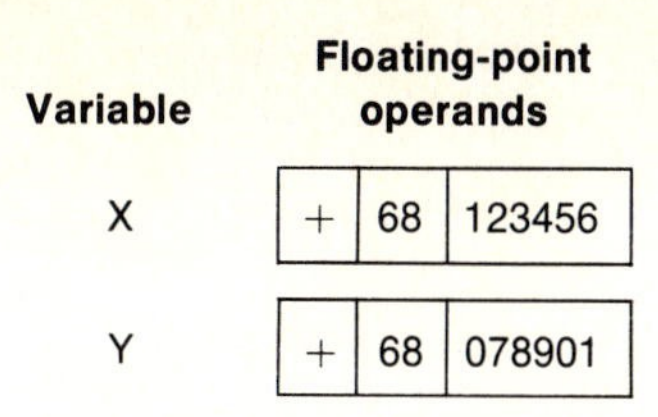

2 The subtraction operation is performed:

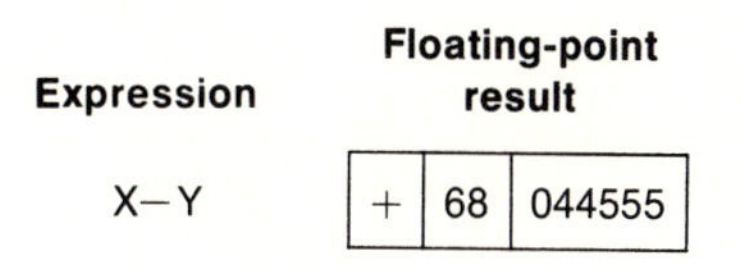

3 The result is normalized:

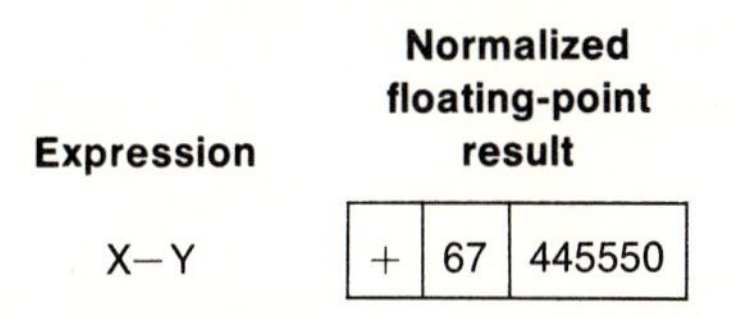

Floating-point addition is performed in a similar manner.

It is also possible that the result of the floating-point addition or subtraction operation will generate an overflow out of the high-order digit position. In this case, the fraction is shifted to the right—the opposite of normalization—and the exponent is increased accordingly.

8.4.2.2 Multiplication and Division The multiplication and division of floating-point numbers employ the following mathematical relations:

$$(f_1 \times b^{e_1}) \times (f_2 \times b^{e_2}) = (f_1 \times f_2) \times b^{e_1 + e_2}$$
$$(f_1 \times b^{e_1}) \div (f_2 \times b^{e_2}) = (f_1 \div f_2) \times b^{e_1 + e_2}$$

Where b is the base, f_1 and f_2 are the fractions, and e_1 and e_2 are the exponents. Thus, the operations are reduced to an addition or subtraction of exponents and a multiplication or division of binary fractions, respectively.

As an example of the algorithms, consider the following values in simplified decimal floating-point form:

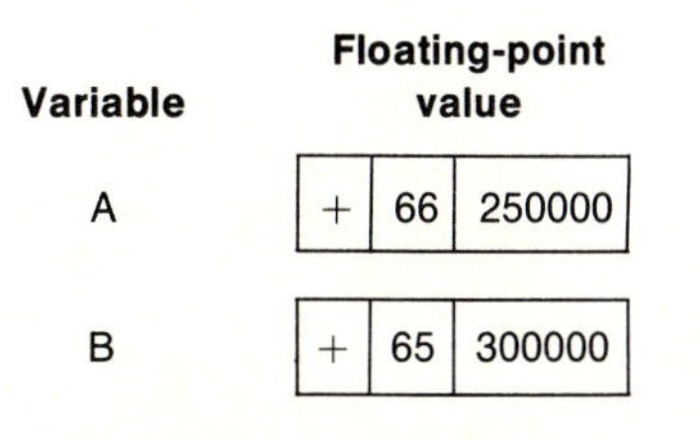

Computation of the expression A × B is performed as follows:

1 The exponents and fractions are isolated.

Variable	Exponent	Fraction
A	02	25000
B	01	300000

2 The exponents are added, and the fractions are multiplied.

Expression	Exponent	Fraction
A×B	03	075000

3 The result is normalized, if necessary.

Expression	Exponent	Fraction
A×B	02	750000

4 The computed exponent and fraction are combined.

Expression	Normalized floating-point result		
A×B	+	66	750000

Floating-point division is performed in a similar manner.

One of the primary advantages of using the leftmost bit of a binary exponent as a bias is that it is a relatively straightforward process to isolate the value of the exponent by masking. Another obvious technique is to leave the bias intact and adjust the computed exponent by subtracting the bias when the exponents are added and by adding the bias when the exponents are subtracted.

8.4.3 Addition Microprogram

Even though a single microinstruction is all that is needed to perform a binary add operation, the housekeeping functions required for floating-point operations largely obscure the actual addition operation. This section describes a microprogram that does floating-point addition. A translator listing of the microprogram is given in Figure 8.12. The operands are read from S-memory locations 100 and 101 by a setup routine that places the operands in registers A1 and B, respectively, and calls the floating-add microroutine. The sum is returned in register A3. The microprogram is annotated to describe how the add operation is performed, and the reader should relate the statements given here to Figure 8.12 to obtain an overview of the overall procedure.

```
>>>>> TRANSLANG D MACHINE MICRØTRANSLATØR

ENTER FILENAME FØR HEX? FAHEX
SUPPRESS BIT PATTERNS?(1=SUPPRESS)? 1
SUPPRESS HEX LISTING?(1=SUPPRESS)? 1
IF INPUT IN FILE ENTER 1? 31
ENTER SØURCE FILENAME? FLTADD

0000    SETUP. LMAR $
0001        100 = LIT $
0002        MR2, BEX, LMAR $
0003        101 = LIT $
0004        WHEN RDC THEN B = A1, MR2 $
0005        FLADD - 1 = AMPCR $
0006        WHEN RDC THEN BEX, CALL $
0007        A3 = MIR, LMAR $ SUM IN A3
0008        102 = LIT $
0009        MW2, IF SAI $
0010        FINI - 1 = AMPCR $
0011        WHEN SAI THEN JUMP $
0012    FLADD. AMPCR = MIR $
0013        B = A2 $ ØPERAND 2 TØ A2
0014        A1 AND B011 R = A3 $ EXP ØF ØPND 1 TØ A3
0015        24 = SAR $
0016        A2 AND B011 R = B $ EXP ØF ØPND 2 TØ B
0017        A1 L = A1 $
0018        CØMP 8 = SAR $
0019        A2 L = A2 $
0020        A1 R = A1 $ FRACTIØN ØF ØPND 1
0021        8 = SAR $
0022        A2 R = A2 $ FRACTIØN ØF ØPND 2
0023    TEST. A3 EQV B = $
0024        EQUAL - 1 = AMPCR $
0025        IF ABT THEN JUMP ELSE STEP $
0026        A3 - B = $
0027        LESS - 1 = AMPCR $
0028        IF NØT AØV THEN JUMP ELSE STEP $
0029        A2 R = A2 $
0030        1 = SAR $
0031        TEST - 1 = AMPCR $
0032        0 + B + 1 = B, JUMP $
0033    LESS. A1 R = A1 $
0034        1 = SAR $
0035        TEST - 1 = AMPCR $
0036        A3 + 1 = A3, JUMP $
0037    EQUAL. A2 = B $
0038        A1 + B R = A1 $ SUM IN A1
0039        1 = SAR $
0040        A3 + 1 = A3 $
0041    NØRM. A1 R = A2 $
0042        23 = SAR $
0043        ØK - 1 = AMPCR $
0044        A2 = $
0045        IF LST THEN JUMP ELSE STEP $
0046        A1 L = A1 $
0047        CØMP 1 = SAR $
0048        A3 - 1 = A3 $
0049    ØK. A3 L = B $
0050        CØMP 24 = SAR $
0051        A1 ØR B = A3, BMI $ RESTØRE RETURN
0052        B = AMPCR $
0053        JUMP $
0054    FINI. STEP $
0055        END $

THE TØTAL NUMBER ØF ERRØRS =     0

EXECUTE (Y/N)? N
```

Figure 8.12 Printout of the translation of the microprogram for floating-point addition to hexadecimal microcode.

The microroutine is entered at symbolic location FLADD and the following statements prepare the operands:

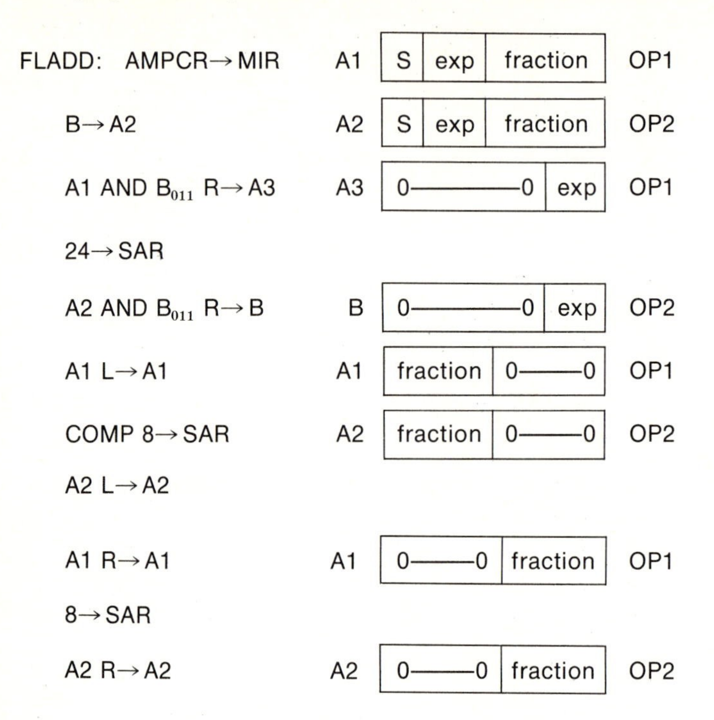

The statements simply isolate the exponents and fractions, as indicated in the preceding algorithm.

At symbolic location TEST, the exponents are compared and the comparison techniques, given in an earlier chapter, are employed. The exponents and fractions are adjusted accordingly until the two exponents are equal, which means that the radix points are aligned:

```
TEST:  A3 EQV B→
    EQUAL − 1→AMPCR
    IF ABT THEN JUMP ELSE STEP
    A3 − B→
    LESS − 1→AMPCR
    IF NOT AOV THEN JUMP ELSE STEP
    A2 R→A2
    1→SAR
    TEST − 1→AMPCR
    0 + B + 1→B, JUMP
LESS:  A1 R→A1
    1→SAR
    TEST − 1→AMPCR
    A3 + 1→A3, JUMP
```

When the exponents have been equalized through the adjustment procedure, the fractions are added and shifted one place to the right to allow for overflow:

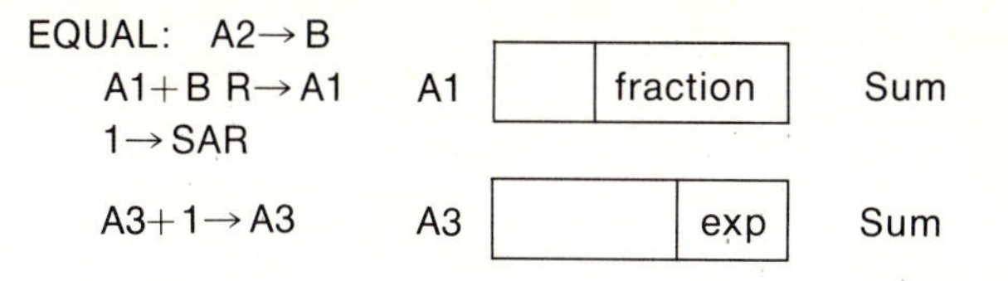

The result is then normalized by inspecting the leftmost bit of the fraction:

```
NORM:  A1 R→A2
   23→SAR
   OK−1→AMPCR
   A2→
   IF LST THEN JUMP ELSE STEP
   A1 L→A1
   COMP 1→SAR
   A3−1→A3
```

After normalization, the exponent and fraction are combined, and control returns to the setup routine:

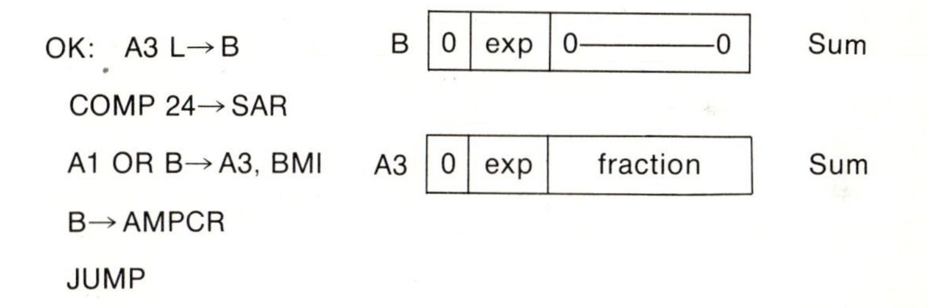

In this case, the sign has been ignored to clarify the presentation and emphasize the housekeeping functions that are involved with floating-point operations. When the algebraic signs of the operands are taken into consideration, only the addition of the fractions is affected, and the methodology applied to signed-magnitude representation would be used.

A sample run of floating-point addition is given in Figure 8.13.

8.4.4 Multiplication Microprogram

The microroutine for floating-point multiplication uses the microroutine for fixed-point multiplication as a subroutine to multiply the fractions. A translator listing of a microprogram that performs floating-point multiplication is given in Figure 8.14. The operands are read from S-memory locations 100 and 101 by a setup routine that places the operands in registers A1 and B, respectively, and calls the floating-multiply microroutine. The product is returned in register A3.

The microroutine is entered at symbolic location FLMLT, and the follow-

```
2) DMACH1     (COMPILED)  02 JAN 76   14:10


ENTER SAME FILENAME FOR HEX? FAHEX
OUTPUT REGISTERS AND S MEMORY IN INTEGER(1) OR OCTAL(2)? 2
INPUT S MEMORY IN INTEGER(1) OR OCTAL IN O11 FORMAT(2)? 2
STARTING ADDRESS =? 0
MAXIMUM NUMBER OF CLOCKS TO SIMULATE=? 100
NUMBER OF CLOCKS BETWEEN OUTPUT POINTS=? 1

ENTER OUTPUT LINES DESIRED      1-ADDRESSES AND CLOCK
2- A1,A2,A3,B    3- MIR,SAR,LIT,CTR,AMPCR    4- BR1,BR2,MAR,BMAR,GC1,GC2
 5- CONDITIONS
ENTER NUMBER OF OUTPUT LINES DESIRED? 5

BEGIN OUTPUT AT MPM ADDRESS=? 55
END OUTPUT AT MPM ADDRESS=? 55
ENTER 1 FOR S MEMORY DUMP WHEN PROGRAM TERMINATES? 1



ENTER S MEMORY VALUES IN CONSECUTIVE BLOCKS
ENTER 9999 FOR STARTING ADDRESS WHEN FINISHED


STARTING S MEMORY ADDRESS=? 100
FINAL S MEMORY ADDRESS FOR THIS BLOCK=? 101
SMEM( 100)=? 10454000000
SMEM( 101)=? 10260000000


STARTING S MEMORY ADDRESS=? 9999



END OF SIMULATION - REGISTERS CONTAIN


P(1) ADDR. =   54     P(3) ADDR. =   54      CLOCK =    65
A1=00070000000     A2=00000000000     A3=10470000000      B =00000000006
MIR =10470000000      SAR = 8      LIT =102       CTR =   0       AMPCR =   53
BR1 =   0       BR2 =   0       MAR =102        BMAR =   102        GC1=0   GC2=0
LC1=0  LC2=0  MST=0  LST=0  ABT=0  AOV=0  COV=0  SAI=1   RDC=1   INT=0


MEMORY DUMP REQUESTED

ENTER VALUES AS DONE IN MEMORY INPUT (9999 FOR STARTING ADDRESS WHEN
FINISHED)

STARTING S MEMORY ADDRESS=? 100
FINAL S MEMORY ADDRESS FOR THIS BLOCK=? 102


S MEMORY( 100) TO S MEMORY( 102) =


10454000000  10260000000  10470000000
STARTING S MEMORY ADDRESS=? 9999
```

Figure 8.13 Execution of floating-point addition with input and output displayed displayed in octal format.

```
>>>>> TRANSLANG D MACHINE MICRØTRANSLATØR

ENTER FILENAME FØR HEX? FMHEX
SUPPRESS BIT PATTERNS?(1=SUPPRESS)? 1
SUPPRESS HEX LISTING?(1=SUPPRESS)? 1
IF INPUT IN FILE ENTER 1? 31
ENTER SØURCE FILENAME? FLTMLT

0000    SETUP. LMAR $
0001       100 = LIT $
0002       MR2, BEX, LMAR $
0003       101 = LIT $
0004       WHEN RDC THEN B = A1, MR2 $
0005       FLMLT - 1 = AMPCR $
0006       WHEN RDC THEN BEX, JUMP $
0007    DØNE. A3 = MIR, LMAR $
0008       102 = LIT $
0009       MW2, IF SAI $
0010       FINI - 1 = AMPCR $
0011       WHEN SAI THEN JUMP $
0012    FLMLT. B = A2 $ ØPND 2 TØ A2 $
0013       A1 AND B011 R = A3 $ EXP ØF ØPND 1 TØ A3
0014       24 = SAR $
0015       A2 AND B011 R = B $ EXP ØF ØPND 2 TØ B
0016       A1 L = A1 $
0017       CØMP 8 = SAR $
0018       A2 L = A2 $
0019       A1 R = A1 $ FRACTIØN ØF ØPND 1
0020       8 = SAR $
0021       A2 R = A2 $ FRACTIØN ØF ØPND 2
0022       A3 + B = A3 $
0023       64 = LIT $
0024       A3 - LIT = A3 $ NEW EXPØNENT
0025       FXMLT - 1 = AMPCR $
0026       A1 = B, JUMP $
0027    RET. A2 = B $ PRØDUCT IN <A1,A2>
0028       B R = MIR $
0029       24 = SAR $
0030       A1 L = BBI $ FRACTIØN IN B
0031    NØRM. B R = A1 $
0032       23 = SAR $
0033       ØK - 1 = AMPCR $
0034       A1 = $
0035       IF LST THEN JUMP ELSE STEP $
0036       B L = B $
0037       CØMP 1 = SAR $
0038       A3 - 1 = A3 $
0039    ØK. A3 L = A3 $
0040       CØMP 24 = SAR $
0041       DØNE - 1 = AMPCR $
0042       A3 ØR B = A3, JUMP $
0043    FXMLT. 0 = A1, LCTR $
0044       32 = LIT, 1 = SAR $
0045       XTEST - 1 = AMPCR $
0046       INC, CALL $
0047       IF NØT LST THEN A1 R = A1, SKIP ELSE STEP $
0048       A1 + B R = A1 $
0049       IF NØT LST THEN A2 R = A2, SKIP ELSE STEP $
0050       A2 ØR 1 C = A2 $
0051    XTEST. IF NØT CØV THEN A2 =, INC, JUMP ELSE STEP $
0052       RET - 1 = AMPCR $
0053       JUMP $
0054    FINI. STEP $
0055       END $
THE TØTAL NUMBER ØF ERRØRS =     0

EXECUTE (Y/N)? N
```

Figure 8.14 Printout of the translation of the microprogram for floating-point multiplication to hexadecimal microcode.

ing statements prepare the operands and the exponents and call the fixed-multiply microroutine:

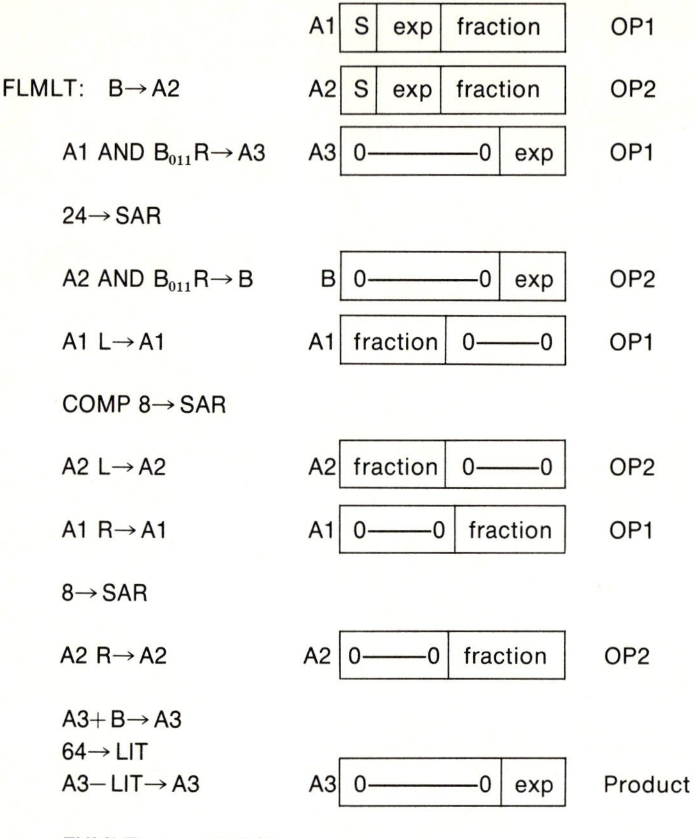


```
FXMLT−1→AMPCR
A1→B, JUMP
```

The fixed-point multiply microroutine, FXMLT, expects operands in the A2 and B registers, and returns a double-length product in the combined ⟨A1,A2⟩ registers. In this case, the product is 48 bits long:

```
FXMLT:  0→A1, LCTR
     32→LIT, 1→SAR
     XTEST−1→AMPCR
     INC, CALL
     IF NOT LST THEN A1 R→A1, SKIP ELSE STEP
     A1+B R→A1
     IF NOT LST THEN A2 R→A2, SKIP ELSE STEP
     A2 OR 1 C→A2
XTEST: IF NOT COV THEN A2→, INC, JUMP ELSE STEP
     RET−1→AMPCR
     JUMP
```

```
2) DMACH1     (COMPILED)  02 JAN 76  14:30


ENTER SAME FILENAME FOR HEX? FMHEX
OUTPUT REGISTERS AND S MEMORY IN INTEGER(1) OR OCTAL(2)? 2
INPUT S MEMORY IN INTEGER(1) OR OCTAL IN O11 FORMAT(2)? 2
STARTING ADDRESS =? 0
MAXIMUM NUMBER OF CLOCKS TO SIMULATE=? 250
NUMBER OF CLOCKS BETWEEN OUTPUT POINTS=? 1

ENTER OUTPUT LINES DESIRED      1-ADDRESSES AND CLOCK
2- A1,A2,A3,B   3- MIR,SAR,LIT,CTR,AMPCR    4- BR1,BR2,MAR,BMAR,GC1,GC2
 5- CONDITIONS
ENTER NUMBER OF OUTPUT LINES DESIRED? 5

BEGIN OUTPUT AT MPM ADDRESS=? 55
END OUTPUT AT MPM ADDRESS=? 55
ENTER 1 FOR S MEMORY DUMP WHEN PROGRAM TERMINATES? 1



ENTER S MEMORY VALUES IN CONSECUTIVE BLOCKS
ENTER 9999 FOR STARTING ADDRESS WHEN FINISHED


STARTING S MEMORY ADDRESS=? 100
FINAL S MEMORY ADDRESS FOR THIS BLOCK=? 101
SMEM( 100)=? 10360000000
SMEM( 101)=? 10250000000


STARTING S MEMORY ADDRESS=? 9999



END OF SIMULATION - REGISTERS CONTAIN


P(1) ADDR. =  54      P(3) ADDR. =  54      CLOCK =  150
A1=00000000000    A2=00000000000    A3=10474000000     B =00074000000
MIR =10474000000     SAR = 8     LIT =102     CTR =  0     AMPCR =  53
BR1 =  0    BR2 =  0     MAR =102     BMAR =  102      GC1=0  GC2=0
LC1=0  LC2=0  MST=0  LST=0  ABT=0  AOV=0  COV=0  SAI=1  RDC=1  INT=0


MEMORY DUMP REQUESTED

ENTER VALUES AS DONE IN MEMORY INPUT (9999 FOR STARTING ADDRESS WHEN
FINISHED)

STARTING S MEMORY ADDRESS=? 100
FINAL S MEMORY ADDRESS FOR THIS BLOCK=? 102


S MEMORY( 100) TO S MEMORY( 102) =


10360000000  10250000000  10474000000
STARTING S MEMORY ADDRESS=? 9999
```

Figure 8.15 Execution of floating-point multiplication with input and output displayed in octal format.

After the fractions are multiplied and a 48-bit product is obtained, only the high-order 24 bits are retained, and the low-order 24 bits are shifted off. The double-register shift uses the technique given earlier with the contents of the rightmost register of the product in the B-register:

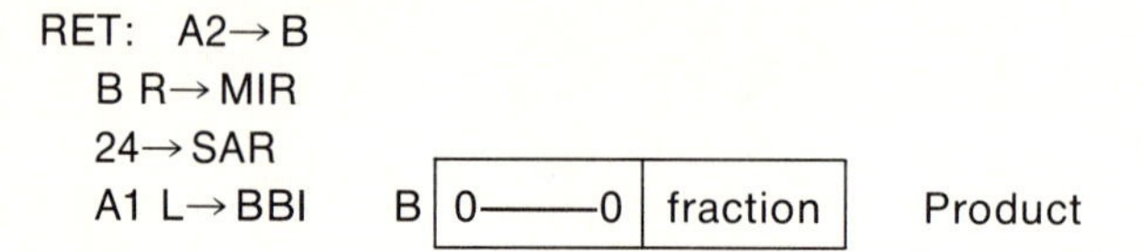

Lastly, the floating-point product is normalized, the exponent and fraction are combined, and a return is made to other calling microroutine with the product in register A3:

```
NORM:  B R→A1
       23→SAR
       OK−1→AMPCR
       A1→, IF LST THEN JUMP ELSE STEP
       B L→B
       COMP 1→SAR
       A3−1→A3
  OK:  A3 L→A3
       COMP 24→SAR
       DONE−1→AMPCR
       A3 OR B→A3, JUMP
```

A sample run of the floating-multiply microroutine is given in Figure 8.15.

In this case, the algebraic sign has again been ignored. However, taking the sign into consideration is relatively straightforward. First, the sign bits are compared, and the LC1 condition is set if the sign bits are different, as follows:

```
A1 XOR B→, IF LC1
IF MST THEN SET LC1
```

Then, just prior to the exit from the floating-multiply microroutine, a statement of the form

IF LC1 THEN A3 OR B_{100}→A3

would be added to insert the negative sign if the product were negative. Actual implementation is left as an exercise.

VOCABULARY

The reader should be familiar with the following terms in the context in which they were used in the chapter:

Complement arithmetic
Sign bit
Minuend
Subtrahend
Addend
Augend
Multiplicand
Multiplier
Double-length accumulator
Auxiliary register
Signed-magnitude representation
Remainder
Biased exponent
Fraction
Exponent
Normalized number
Normalization

QUESTION SET

The following questions are intended to test your comprehension of the subject matter. All questions can be answered from the text directly or through a logical extension of the subjects presented. Some questions would be suitable for discussion sessions.

1 Why is a double-length product always generated for binary multiplication? Considering significant digits, when is the product actually of double length?
2 Why is a zero moved to the A1-register prior to the binary multiplication operation?
3 Why would an overflow result from binary division if the initial contents of the AC-register were greater than the contents of the auxiliary register?
4 How does the statement $B_{FTT} \rightarrow B$ change the sign of the subtrahend? Consider the statement $B_{1FF} \rightarrow B$. Does it take the ones or twos complement?
5 What is the major advantage in floating-point format of locating the implicit radix point to the left of the high-order digit of the fraction instead of to the right of the rightmost digit of the fraction? Is there any advantage at all?
6 Consider the microprogram for floating-point multiplication. What would be an advantage of normalizing the fraction before the rightmost 24 bits are truncated?
7 In what obvious way can the fixed-point multiply routine used with floating-point multiply be speeded up?
8 In the floating-point multiply microroutine, what basic function does the statement $A3 - LIT \rightarrow A3$ serve?

EXERCISES

1 Summarize, in as few words as possible, the process of doing binary fixed-point twos complement multiplication. Do the same for division.
2 Show why $A1 - B$ is equivalent to $A1 + \text{NOT } B + 1$.
3 In an earlier chapter, a technique for shifting two "combined" registers *n* places to the right or left was given. Show *how* the technique works.
4 Write a microprogram segment to mask off the low-order bit of register B and place the result in register A1.
5 Modify the floating-point addition routine to include algebraic sign control.
6 Modify the floating-point multiplication routine to include algebraic sign control.

PROBLEMS

1 When doing fixed-point multiplication, the microprogram goes through unnecessary machine cycles when the multiplier contains several leading zeros. Modify the

binary multiply microroutine, therefore, to "kick out" when the remainder of the multiplier is zero. (*Hint:* Place the multiplier in another register—in addition to A2. Shift it along with A2 and test for zero accordingly.)

2 Write microroutine to implement the following operations using signed-magnitude representation:
  a Fixed-point multiplication
  b Fixed-point division

3 Write microroutines to implement the following floating-point operations:
  a Floating-point subtraction
  b Floating-point division

4 Double-precision floating operations use double-word operands as follows:

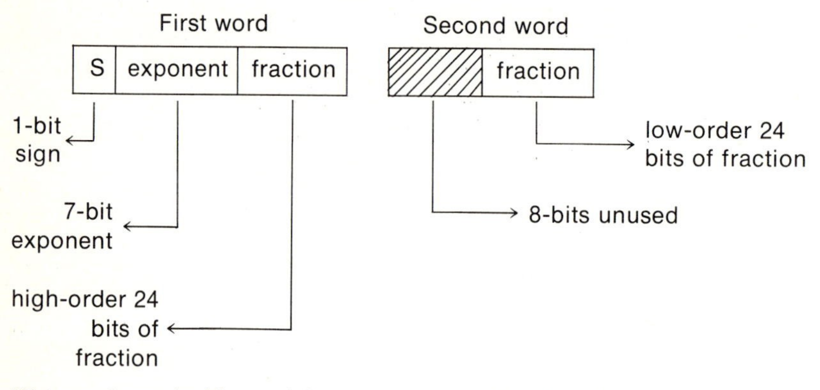

Write and test double-precision microroutines for the following operations:
  a Floating-point addition
  b Floating-point subtraction
  c Floating-point multiplication
  d Floating-point division

5 Develop a microroutine that computes the absolute value of a floating-point argument. The microroutine should accept the argument in register A2 and return the absolute value of the contents of A2 in the same register.

6 Develop a microroutine that computes the integer function of a floating-point argument X, that is, INT(X) in BASIC or AINT(X) in FORTRAN. The microroutine should accept the argument in register A2 and return the integral part of the argument in the same register. (The result should also be in floating-point format.)

7 Develop a microutine that computes the square root (R) of floating-point argument X, that is, SQR(X) in BASIC or SQRT(X) in FORTRAN, using the following algorithm:

```
      E=.01
      R=1.0
2     R=.5*(X/R+R)
      IF (ABS(R**2-X).GE.E) GO TO 2
      ...
```

The microroutine should accept the argument in register A2 and return the square root of the contents of register A2 in the same register.

Chapter 9

Principles of Emulation II: Design of an Interpreter

9.1 OVERVIEW

Within the confines of microprogramming, an *interpreter* is a microprogram that fetches, decodes, and executes S-instructions on a controlled basis. From a slightly different viewpoint, an interpreter is the set of microprograms that occupy control storage of a microprogrammed computer and control its operation. The terms *interpreter* and *emulator* are synonymous.

Several factors must be considered in the design of an interpreter:

1. The operational philosophy of the computer
2. The implementation of machine registers
3. The S-instruction format
4. The set of usable S-machine operations

The method of presentation will include a brief discussion of each topic and examples of the concepts presented in the implementation of an actual interpreter.

9.2 DESIGN CONSIDERATIONS

The design of an interpreter involves the interplay of the four factors mentioned above. Essentially, this means that the computer architect must explicitly or implicitly make a design decision regarding each of the factors, and collectively the decisions give the computer system its operational characteristics.

9.2.1 Operational Philosophy of the Computer

The operational philosophy of the computer affects the instruction formats, the machine registers needed, and to some extent the available operations. Two basic designs are considered here: the stack machine and a multiple-register machine. The stack machine, sometimes known as a "Polish notation machine," uses a stack of machine registers as accumulators and accepts an S-machine program in a form that resembles Polish notation. The multiple-register machine uses a set of addressable registers for arithmetic/logic operations and addressing and accepts an S-machine program in a form similar to conventional machine language.

9.2.2 Machine Registers

Three considerations apply to the design and implementation of machine registers: the number of registers, how they are accessed, and how they are implemented. Register access refers to whether a register is addressed directly, as in

```
L   1,XPL
```

which can be interpreted to mean, "load the contents of XPL into register one," or indirectly, as when the registers are implemented as a stack and loading a value into the stack causes the other values in the stack to be pushed down. The number of registers obviously refers to the number of physical or logical components; however, in a stack machine, the register system is frequently designed so that entries go to S-memory when the stack is full. Machine registers can be implemented as hardware components, as locations in control storage, or as locations in S-memory. The use of hardware registers and control storage is normally designed into the host computer. The use of S-memory for machine registers is implemented through microprogramming alone. In the interpreters described here, S-memory is used for the implementation of machine registers.

9.2.3 S-Instruction Format

The S-instruction format reflects the operational philosophy of the computer and indirectly determines the range of operation codes, the operand registers, and the addressing structure. Since the instructions of an S-program are held in S-memory, instruction length is also of importance, and the relationship between instructions and computer words must be specified before the interpreter can be developed. The width of the operation-code field gives an upper limit on the number of different operation codes that are permitted—that is, unless a special field or word is used to augment the operation code. For example, if the operation-code field includes n bits, then the maximum number of different operation codes is $2^n - 1$. However, as shown in Chapter 2, the operation-code field sometimes includes instruction length and type-of-operation indicators, as in the System 360/370, so that the operation-code field is structured to provide useful information in addition to a simple operation-code specification.

When machine registers participate in the execution of an instruction, then the corresponding instruction format includes fields for register specifications. The width of each register field effectively determines the range of registers that can be used. The address field of an instruction is related to the range of S-memory locations that can be accessed. However, the total range of S-memory addresses that can be accessed is determined by the addressing structure, which may incorporate the base/index/displacement method, the index/address method, or another similar technique. A base register specification field is usually included in the instruction format when base/index/displacement addressing is used. It is also possible that a base register could be used in effective-address computation without allowing the specification and loading of the base register to be under programmer control. In other words, the base register could be loaded by the operating system when a user program is given control of the processing unit.

Thus, a larger number of factors affect the operational characteristics of a computer, and it is the computer architect's responsibility to put the pieces together to be an operationally effective combination.

9.2.4 S-Machine Operations

The choice of S-machine operations is ultimately dependent upon the design objectives of the computer system. Housekeeping operations, such as load, store, etc., are always needed, and very little more can be said about them. The choice, for example, of whether to include floating-point operations requires a close look at the intended applications. If a minicomputer to be used for control applications is being designed, for example, then there is very little need for floating-point, or even decimal, arithmetic to be designed into the computer architecture—provided that the basic facility is available for programming the same functions using S-instructions. Also, other factors may, in part, determine the set of S-machine operations. Some of these are word size, amount of control storage for microprograms, cost of the computer system, and the relationship between the S-machine and the host microprogrammed computer.

9.3 DESIGN AND IMPLEMENTATION OF A STACK MACHINE

This section describes the design and implementation of a stack machine. The term *stack machine* implies the following:

1 Machine registers are implemented as a stack, and information enters and leaves the stack on a last-in-first-out (LIFO) basis.

2 S-instructions are designed to utilize the stack and are interpreted as Polish postfix notation.

Presentation of the basic concepts is considered to be of more importance than efficiency. Therefore, there are several instances in the design where improvement could be made. The instruction formats, for example, include unused fields in some cases. If an actual machine were being constructed, a means would be developed of eliminating the unused fields. Overall, however, the interpreter actually functions, and a stack machine is emulated. This is the primary objective.

9.3.1 Polish Notation

Polish notation is a parenthesis-free notation used to represent arithmetic/logic expressions in an unambiguous manner. Polish postfix notation is used here. Consider the mathematical expression $A+B$. In postfix notation, it is written $AB+$. The operands precede the operator. Similarly, the expression $(A+B)*(C-D)$ would be expressed in postfix notation as $AB+CD-*$. Parentheses are not needed.

The execution of postfix notation uses an operand stack. An expression in postfix notation is scanned from left to right. If an operand is encountered, it is pushed into the stack. If an operator is encountered, it is performed on the top elements of the stack, and the result is pushed back into the stack. As an example, the statement

$$A=(B+C)*(D-E)$$

would exist in postfix as

$$ABC+DE-*=$$

The postfix string would be executed as follows:

Instruction	Postfix	Operation
1	A	Push address of A into stack.
2	B	Push value of B into stack.
3	C	Push value of C into stack.
4	+	Pop top two entries in stack. Add them and push sum into stack.
5	D	Push value of D into stack.
6	E	Push value of E into stack.
7	−	Pop top two entries in stack. Subtract them and push difference into stack.
8	*	Pop top two entries in stack. Multiply them and push product into stack.
9	=	Pop value and address. Place value in address.

S-instructions based on Polish postfix notation are interpreted in a similar manner.

9.3.2 Instruction Format and Machine Operations

The instruction format for the stack machine is defined as follows:

1 — 6	7 — 32
operation code	operand field

where the operation code is a binary number and the operand field is an address or a value or is unused.

The following instructions are defined:

Instruction	Format		Definition
Name call	000001	*address*	Place *address* in the stack.
Value call	000010	*address*	Place the contents of *address* in the stack.
Literal call	000011	*value*	Place *value* in the stack.
Store	000100	(unused)	Pop first element in stack (V). Pop second element in stack (A). V→(A).
Add	000101	(unused)	Pop first element in stack (X). Pop second element in stack (Y). X+Y→STACK
Subtract	000110	(unused)	Pop first element in stack (X). Pop second element in stack (Y). Y−X→STACK
Branch	000111	*address*	Branch to *address* in S-memory.
Branch on zero	001000	*address*	Pop first element in stack (X). Branch to *address* if X ⩽ 0.
Halt	001001	(unused)	Halt S-machine.

The instruction repertoire is minimal, but it can easily be extended. Enhancements are defined as exercises and problems.

9.3.3 Implementation of Machine Registers

The stack resides in S-memory starting with location 1, and values are loaded into ascending addresses. A pointer to the top of the stack exists. When a value is pushed into the stack, the value of the pointer is incremented by 1, and the value is placed in that S-memory location. When a value is popped from the stack, the value at the top-of-the-stack pointer is retrieved. Then, the pointer is decremented by 1. In short, instead of values being pushed down, the top of the stack moves up.

9.3.4 Operational Conventions

The following operational conventions are adopted in the implementation of the interpreter:

Register A1 points to the current instruction address.
Register A2 points to the top of the stack.
Register B holds the instruction being decoded.
S-memory location 1 is the base of the stack.
S-memory location 64 (decimal) is the load point for the S-program.
Register A3 is used as a temporary accumulator.
S-memory location 50 is used as an error indicator: 0 denotes a success exit; all 1s denote an error exit.

9.3.5 Stack Machine Interpreter

A listing of the stack machine interpreter is given in Figure 9.1, and the various routines are described in the following paragraphs. The interpreter utilizes the emulation techniques given in Chapter 5.

The directory serves as a jump table to the microroutines used to execute the S-machine instructions: it is listed as follows:

```
DIR:  PERR-1→AMPCR
      PERR-1→AMPCR
      PNAM-1→AMPCR
      PVAL-1→AMPCR
      PLIT-1→AMPCR
      PST-1→AMPCR
      PADD-1→AMPCR
      PSUB-1→AMPCR
      PBR-1→AMPCR
      PBRZ-1→AMPCR
      PHLT-1→AMPCR
      PERR-1→AMPCR
```

The directory has to be structured carefully because it is loaded into microprogram memory (MPM) location 0 and because it is referenced in the fetch routine through the EXEC command with the operation code—the AMPCR. Since the EXEC command executes the instruction at (AMPCR) + 1, the literal assignment statement for an operation must be located at an MPM address of one higher than the operation code. For example, the name call operation has an operation code of 000001. The corresponding literal assignment statement, that is, PNAM − 1→AMPCR, must be located at MPM address 2, which it is.

The initialization routine initializes the stack pointer to 0 and the current address pointer to 64 (decimal) as follows:

```
INIT:  0→A2
       LIT→A1
       64→LIT
```

The stack pointer always points to the top of the stack.

The fetch routine reads an S-instruction, increases the contents of the current-address register by 1, isolates the operation code, places the MPM address of the corresponding microroutine in the AMPCR (with the EXEC command), and passes control to a microroutine to have the S-instruction executed. It is listed as follows:

```
FETCH:  A1→MAR1
  MR1, A1+1→A1
  WHEN RDC THEN BEX
  B R→A3
  26→SAR,15→LIT
  A3 AND LIT→AMPCR
  EXEC
  JUMP
```

The fetch routine leaves the S-instruction in the B-register.

The address routine performs a utility function and serves to isolate the address field, right-justified, in register A3. It is listed as follows:

```
ADDR:  B L→B
  COMP 6→SAR
  B R→A3
  6→SAR
  JUMP
```

The address routine always returns to the calling program at (AMPCR)+1.

The stack routine increases the stack pointer by 1 and writes the value to be pushed into the stack as S-memory. It is listed as follows:

```
STACK:  A2+1→A2, MAR1
  A3→MIR
  MW1, IF SAI
  FETCH−1→AMPCR
  WHEN SAI THEN JUMP
```

The stack routine always exits to the fetch routine to execute the next instruction.

The unstack routine pops the top value in the stack and places it in register

```
>>>>> TRANSLANG D MACHINE MICRØTRANSLATØR

ENTER FILENAME FØR HEX? PMHEX
SUPPRESS BIT PATTERNS?(1=SUPPRESS)? 1
SUPPRESS HEX LISTING?(1=SUPPRESS)? 1
IF INPUT IN FILE ENTER 1? 31
ENTER SØURCE FILENAME? PMACH

0000    DIR. PERR - 1 = AMPCR $
0001       PERR - 1 = AMPCR $
0002       PNAM - 1 = AMPCR $
0003       PVAL - 1 = AMPCR $
0004       PLIT - 1 = AMPCR $
0005       PST - 1 = AMPCR $
0006       PADD - 1 = AMPCR $
0007       PSUB - 1 = AMPCR $
0008       PBR - 1 = AMPCR $
0009       PBRZ - 1 = AMPCR $
0010       PHLT - 1 = AMPCR $
0011       PERR - 1 = AMPCR $
0012    INIT. 0 = A2 $ STACK PTR
0013       LIT = A1 $ CURRENT ADDR REGISTER
0014       64 = LIT $ PRØG STARTS AT LØC 100 ØCTAL
0015    FETCH. A1 = MAR1 $
0016       MR1, A1 + 1 = A1 $
0017       WHEN RDC THEN BEX $
0018       B R = A3 $
0019       26 = SAR, 15 = LIT $
0020       A3 AND LIT = AMPCR $
0021       EXEC $
0022       JUMP $
0023    ADDR. B L = B $
0024       CØMP 6 = SAR $
0025       B R = A3 $
0026       6 = SAR $
0027       JUMP $
0028    STACK. A2 + 1 = A2, MAR1 $
0029       A3 = MIR $
0030       MW1, IF SAI $
0031       FETCH - 1 = AMPCR $
0032       WHEN SAI THEN JUMP $
0033    UNST. NØT A2 = $
0034       IF ABT THEN EXEC ELSE SKIP $
0035       JUMP $
0036       A2 = MAR1 $
0037       MR1, A2 + B111 = A2 $
0038       WHEN RDC THEN BEX $
0039       B = A3, RETN $
0040    PNAM. ADDR - 1 = AMPCR $
0041       CALL $
0042       STACK - 1 = AMPCR $
0043       JUMP $
0044    PVAL. ADDR - 1 = AMPCR $
0045       CALL $
0046       A3 = MAR1 $
0047       MR1 $
0048       WHEN RDC THEN BEX $
0049       STACK - 1 = AMPCR $
0050       B = A3, JUMP $
0051    PLIT. ADDR - 1 = AMPCR $
0052       CALL $
0053       STACK - 1 = AMPCR $
0054       JUMP $
0055    PST. UNST - 1 = AMPCR $
0056       CALL $
0057       PERR - 1 = AMPCR $
0058       A3 = MIR $
```

Figure 9.1 Translator listing of the stack machine interpreter.

```
0059       UNST - 1 = AMPCR $
0060       CALL $
0061       PERR - 1 = AMPCR $
0062       A3 = MAR1 $
0063       MW1, IF SAI $
0064       FETCH - 1 = AMPCR $
0065       WHEN SAI THEN JUMP $
0066    PADD. UNST - 1 = AMPCR $
0067       CALL $
0068       PERR - 1 = AMPCR $
0069       A3 = MIR $
0070       UNST - 1 = AMPCR $
0071       CALL $
0072       PERR - 1 = AMPCR $
0073       BMI $
0074       STACK - 1 = AMPCR $
0075       A3 + B = A3, JUMP $
0076    PSUB. UNST - 1 = AMPCR $
0077       CALL $
0078       PERR - 1 = AMPCR $
0079       A3 = MIR $
0080       UNST - 1 = AMPCR $
0081       CALL $
0082       PERR - 1 = AMPCR $
0083       BMI $
0084       STACK - 1 = AMPCR $
0085       A3 - B = A3, JUMP $
0086    PBR. ADDR - 1 = AMPCR $
0087       CALL $
0088       FETCH - 1 = AMPCR $
0089       A3 = A1, JUMP $
0090    PBRZ. ADDR - 1 = AMPCR $
0091       CALL $
0092       A3 = MIR $
0093       UNST - 1 = AMPCR $
0094       CALL $
0095       PERR - 1 = AMPCR $
0096       PBRZ1 - 1 = AMPCR $
0097       NØT A3 = $
0098       IF ABT THEN JUMP ELSE STEP $
0099       NØT A3 = $
0100       IF NØT MST THEN JUMP ELSE STEP $
0101       FETCH - 1 = AMPCR $
0102       JUMP $
0103    PBRZ1. BMI $
0104       FETCH - 1 = AMPCR $
0105       B = A1, JUMP $
0106    PHLT. 0 = MIR, LMAR, SKIP $
0107    PERR. NØT 0 = MIR, LMAR $
0108       50 = LIT $
0109       MW2, IF SAI $
0110       WHEN SAI THEN STEP $
0111       END $


THE TØTAL NUMBER ØF ERRØRS =     0

EXECUTE (Y/N)? N
```

Figure 9.1 *Continued.*

A3. It is listed as follows:

```
UNST: NOT A2→
  IF ABT THEN EXEC ELSE SKIP
  JUMP
  A2→MAR1
  MR1, A2+B111→A2
  WHEN RDC THEN BEX
  B→A3, RETN
```

If the stack is empty, then the unstack routine branches to an error exit. Otherwise, the topmost value of the stack is placed in register A3, and the value of the stack pointer is decreased by 1. The routine returns to the calling program at (AMPCR) + 2.

The name call routine places the contents of the instruction address field of the S-instruction in the stack and exits, by way of the stack routine, to the fetch routine:

```
PNAM: ADDR-1→AMPCR
  CALL
  STACK-1→AMPCR
  JUMP
```

The value call routine places the contents of the address specified in the S-instruction in the stack and exits, by way of the stack routine, to the fetch routine:

```
PVAL: ADDR-1→AMPCR
  CALL
  A3→MAR1
  MR1
  WHEN RDC THEN BEX
  STACK-1→AMPCR
  B→A3, JUMP
```

The literal call routine places the contents of the value field in the S-instruction in the stack and exits, by way of the stack routine, to the fetch routine to execute the next S-instruction. It is listed as follows:

```
PLIT: ADDR-1→AMPCR
  CALL
  STACK-1→AMPCR
  JUMP
```

The store routine places the value at the top of the stack into the address specified by the next entry in the stack:

```
PST:  UNST − 1→AMPCR
      CALL
      PERR − 1→AMPCR
      A3→MIR
      UNST − 1→AMPCR
      CALL
      PERR − 1→AMPCR
      A3→MAR1
      MW1, IF SAI
      FETCH − 1→AMPCR
      WHEN SAI THEN JUMP
```

The store routine exits to the fetch routine directly.

The add routine pops the top two values in the stack, adds them, and places the sum back in the stack, as follows:

```
PADD: UNST − 1→AMPCR
      CALL
      PERR − 1→AMPCR
      A3→MIR
      UNST − 1→AMPCR
      CALL
      PERR − 1→AMPCR
      BMI
      STACK − 1→AMPCR
      A3 + B→A3, JUMP
```

The add routine exits, by way of the stack routine, to the fetch routine to execute the next S-instruction.

The subtract routine is identical to the add routine except that the subtraction operation is performed, as follows:

```
PSUB: UNST − 1→AMPCR
      CALL
      PERR − 1→AMPCR
      A3→MIR
      UNST − 1→AMPCR
      CALL
      PERR − 1→AMPCR
      BMI
      STACK − 1→AMPCR
      A3 − B→A3, JUMP
```

The branch routine places the effective address into the current-address register and exits to the fetch routine:

```
PBR:    ADDR-1→AMPCR
        CALL
        FETCH-1→AMPCR
        A3→A1, JUMP
```

The branch-on-zero routine places the effective address into the current-address register if the value at the top of the stack is less than or equal to 0. The value at the top of the stack is popped and is lost for subsequent operation:

```
PBRZ:   ADDR-1→AMPCR
        CALL
        A3→MIR
        UNST-1→AMPCR
        CALL
        PERR-1→AMPCR
        PBRZ1-1→AMPCR
        NOT A3→
        IF ABT THEN JUMP ELSE STEP
        NOT A3→
        IF NOT MST THEN JUMP ELSE STEP
        FETCH-1→AMPCR
        JUMP
PBRZ1:  BMI
        FETCH-1→AMPCR
        B→A1, JUMP
```

The branch-on-zero routine always exits to the fetch routine.

The halt routine places a 0 in S-memory location 50 and terminates microprogram execution. The error routine places all 1s in S-memory location 50 and also terminates microprogram execution. The routines are combined as follows:

```
PHLT:   0→MIR, LMAR, SKIP
PERR:   NOT 0→MIR, LMAR
        50→LIT
        MW2, IF SAI
        WHEN SAI THEN STEP
        END
```

Using the above microroutines as a model, additional instructions can be added to the stack machine. Several suggestions are given as exercises.

9.3.6 Sample Runs

In preparing a sample run, a set of S-instructions must be developed, converted to octal format, and placed in S-memory—prior to execution. The first example

```
2) DMACH1     (COMPILED)  02 JAN 76   15:12


ENTER SAME FILENAME FOR HEX? PMHEX
OUTPUT REGISTERS AND S MEMORY IN INTEGER(1) OR OCTAL(2)? 2
INPUT S MEMORY IN INTEGER(1) OR OCTAL IN O11 FORMAT(2)? 2
STARTING ADDRESS =? 12
MAXIMUM NUMBER OF CLOCKS TO SIMULATE=? 100
NUMBER OF CLOCKS BETWEEN OUTPUT POINTS=? 1

ENTER OUTPUT LINES DESIRED      1-ADDRESSES AND CLOCK
2- A1,A2,A3,B    3- MIR,SAR,LIT,CTR,AMPCR    4- BR1,BR2,MAR,BMAR,GC1,GC2
 5- CONDITIONS
ENTER NUMBER OF OUTPUT LINES DESIRED? 5

BEGIN OUTPUT AT MPM ADDRESS=? 111
END OUTPUT AT MPM ADDRESS=? 111
ENTER 1 FOR S MEMORY DUMP WHEN PROGRAM TERMINATES? 1


ENTER S MEMORY VALUES IN CONSECUTIVE BLOCKS
ENTER 9999 FOR STARTING ADDRESS WHEN FINISHED


STARTING S MEMORY ADDRESS=? 64
FINAL S MEMORY ADDRESS FOR THIS BLOCK=? 68
SMEM(   64)=? 00400000104
SMEM(   65)=? 01400000002
SMEM(   66)=? 02000000000
SMEM(   67)=? 04400000000
SMEM(   68)=? 00000000000

STARTING S MEMORY ADDRESS=? 9999

END OF SIMULATION - REGISTERS CONTAIN

P(1) ADDR. = 110       P(3) ADDR. = 110       CLOCK =    95
A1=00000000104     A2=00000000000     A3=00000000011      B =04400000000
MIR =00000000000       SAR =26      LIT = 50      CTR =   0      AMPCR = 105
BR1 =   0      BR2 =   0       MAR = 50       BMAR =    50       GC1=0   GC2=0
LC1=0  LC2=0  MST=0  LST=0  ABT=0  AOV=0  COV=0  SAI=1  RDC=1  INT=0


MEMORY DUMP REQUESTED

ENTER VALUES AS DONE IN MEMORY INPUT (9999 FOR STARTING ADDRESS WHEN
FINISHED)

STARTING S MEMORY ADDRESS=? 50
FINAL S MEMORY ADDRESS FOR THIS BLOCK=? 50


S MEMORY(   50) TO S MEMORY(   50) =


00000000000
STARTING S MEMORY ADDRESS=? 64
FINAL S MEMORY ADDRESS FOR THIS BLOCK=? 68


S MEMORY(   64) TO S MEMORY(   68) =


00400000104  01400000002  02000000000  04400000000  00000000002

STARTING S MEMORY ADDRESS=? 9999
```

Figure 9.2 Sample run of the stack machine for the execution of the statement A = 2, translated into S-language.

executes the statement A = 2, which is expressed in postfix notation as A2 =. A set of corresponding S-instructions in symbolic and octal format is:

Decimal location	Octal location	Symbolic instruction	Octal instruction
64	100	*name* A	00400000104
65	101	*literal* 2	01400000002
66	102	*store*	02000000000
67	103	*halt*	04400000000
68	104	(A) (storage location)	00000000000

A printout of the sample run is given in Figure 9.2 in which the S-memory dump shows that the replacement operation has been performed successfully.

The second example executes the statements

A = 2
B = 3
C = A + B − 1

The prefix form of the statements is

A2 = B3 = CAB + 1 − =

A set of corresponding S-instructions in symbolic and octal format is:

Decimal location	Octal location	Symbolic instruction	Octal instruction
64	100	*name* A	00400000116
65	101	*literal* 2	01400000002
66	102	*store*	02000000000
67	103	*name* B	00400000117
68	104	*literal* 3	01400000003
69	105	*store*	02000000000
70	106	*name* C	00400000120
71	107	*value* A	01000000116
72	110	*value* B	01000000117
73	111	*add*	02400000000
74	112	*literal* 1	01400000001
75	113	*subtract*	03000000000
76	114	*store*	02000000000
77	115	*halt*	04400000000
78	116	(A)	00000000000
79	117	(B)	00000000000
80	120	(C)	00000000000

A printout of the sample run is given in Figure 9.3 in which the S-memory dump shows that the computations have been performed successfully.

As a final example, consider a simulated multiply operation that computes R = M × N. In symbolic form, the program segment is written as follows:

```
      M=5
      N=4
      T=0
α     IF N=0 THEN GO TO β
      T=T+M
      N=N-1
      GO TO α
β     R=T
      HLT
```

A set of symbolic S-instructions for this program is given as follows:

Decimal location	Symbolic S-instructions
64	*name* M
65	*literal* 5
66	*store*
67	*name* N
68	*literal* 4
69	*store*
70	*name* T
71	*literal* 0
72	*store*
73	*value* N
74	*bzero* 86
75	*name* T
76	*value* T
77	*value* M
78	*add*
79	*store*
80	*name* N
81	*value* N
82	*literal* 1
83	*subtract*
84	*store*
85	*branch* 73
86	*name* R
87	*value* T
88	*store*
89	*halt*
90	(M)
91	(N)
92	(T)
93	(R)

Translation of this S-program to octal format and running it on the simulator are left as an exercise. The program does not appear to be efficient—at least as far as the number of S-instructions is concerned. This is partially the case because the topmost register in the stack is effectively the only one that is accessed and real S-memory must be used for temporary storage, resulting in a relatively high number of value call and store operations.

```
2) DMACH1     (COMPILED)  02 JAN 76   15:20


ENTER SAME FILENAME FØR HEX? PMHEX
ØUTPUT REGISTERS AND S MEMØRY IN INTEGER(1) ØR ØCTAL(2)? 2
INPUT S MEMØRY IN INTEGER(1) ØR ØCTAL IN Ø11 FØRMAT(2)? 2
STARTING ADDRESS =? 12
MAXIMUM NUMBER ØF CLØCKS TØ SIMULATE=? 400
NUMBER ØF CLØCKS BETWEEN ØUTPUT PØINTS=? 1

ENTER ØUTPUT LINES DESIRED      1-ADDRESSES AND CLØCK
2- A1,A2,A3,B   3- MIR,SAR,LIT,CTR,AMPCR    4- BR1,BR2,MAR,BMAR,GC1,GC2
 5- CØNDITIØNS
ENTER NUMBER ØF ØUTPUT LINES DESIRED? 5

BEGIN ØUTPUT AT MPM ADDRESS=? 111
END ØUTPUT AT MPM ADDRESS=? 111
ENTER 1 FØR S MEMØRY DUMP WHEN PRØGRAM TERMINATES? 1



ENTER S MEMØRY VALUES IN CØNSECUTIVE BLØCKS
ENTER 9999 FØR STARTING ADDRESS WHEN FINISHED


STARTING S MEMØRY ADDRESS=? 64
FINAL S MEMØRY ADDRESS FØR THIS BLØCK=? 80
SMEM(   64)=? 00400000116
SMEM(   65)=? 01400000002
SMEM(   66)=? 02000000000
SMEM(   67)=? 00400000117
SMEM(   68)=? 01400000003
SMEM(   69)=? 02000000000
SMEM(   70)=? 00400000120
SMEM(   71)=? 01000000116
SMEM(   72)=? 01000000117
SMEM(   73)=? 02400000000
SMEM(   74)=? 01400000001
SMEM(   75)=? 03000000000
SMEM(   76)=? 02000000000
SMEM(   77)=? 04400000000
SMEM(   78)=? 00000000000
SMEM(   79)=? 00000000000
SMEM(   80)=? 00000000000

STARTING S MEMØRY ADDRESS=? 9999

END ØF SIMULATIØN - REGISTERS CØNTAIN


P(1) ADDR. = 110      P(3) ADDR. = 110      CLØCK =   367
A1=00000000116    A2=00000000000     A3=00000000011      B =04400000000
MIR =00000000000      SAR =26      LIT = 50     CTR =  0      AMPCR = 105
BR1 =   0     BR2 =   0      MAR = 50      BMAR =    50      GC1=0   GC2=0
LC1=0   LC2=0   MST=0   LST=0   ABT=0   AØV=0   CØV=0   SAI=1   RDC=1   INT=0


MEMØRY DUMP REQUESTED

ENTER VALUES AS DØNE IN MEMØRY INPUT (9999 FØR STARTING ADDRESS WHEN
FINISHED)

STARTING S MEMØRY ADDRESS=? 50
FINAL S MEMØRY ADDRESS FØR THIS BLØCK=? 50

S MEMØRY(   50) TØ S MEMØRY(   50) =
```

Figure 9.3 Sample run of the stack machine for the execution of the S-instructions for the statements A = 2, B = 3, and C = A + B − 1.

```
00000000000
STARTING S MEMØRY ADDRESS=? 64
FINAL S MEMØRY ADDRESS FØR THIS BLØCK=? 80


S MEMØRY(   64) TØ S MEMØRY(   80) =

00400000116  01400000002  02000000000  00400000117  01400000003

02000000000  00400000120  01000000116  01000000117  02400000000

01400000001  03000000000  02000000000  04400000000  00000000002

00000000003  00000000004
STARTING S MEMØRY ADDRESS=? 9999
```

Figure 9.3 *Continued.*

9.4 DESIGN AND IMPLEMENTATION OF A MULTIPLE-REGISTER MACHINE

This section describes a multiple-register machine that is similar to the hypothetical 16-bit computer that was emulated in Chapter 5. This machine is characterized by a set of 16 general-purpose registers that are used for arithmetic/logic operations and for addressing. This machine is a conventional load/add/store computer similar to well-known computers such as the System 360/370 or the PDP 11.

9.4.1 Instruction Format and Machine Operations

The instruction format for the multiple-register machine is defined as follows:

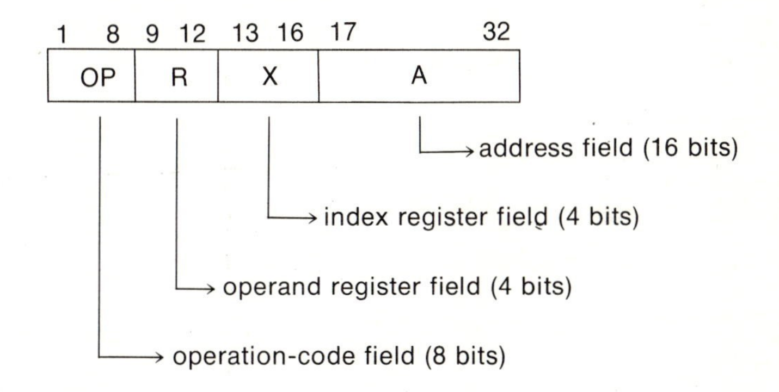

The 8-bit operation-code field permits 255 distinct operation codes, and each of the register fields permits the specification of any of 16 general-purpose registers. Each register in the machine is 32 bits wide, so that a 32-bit effective address can be generated. The 16-bit address field can be interpreted as an address or a displacement. Similarly, the 4-bit index register field can serve as an index register or a base register. The 4-bit operand register always serves as an accumulator.

The following instructions are defined:

Instruction	Format				Definition
Load	00000001	R	X	A	(A+(X))→(R)
Store	00000010	R	X	A	(R)→(A+(X))
Add	00000011	R	X	A	(R)+(A+(X))→(R)
Subtract	00000100	R	X	A	(R)−(A+(X))→(R)
Branch	00000101	R	X	A	Branch to A+(X)
Branch on zero	00000110	R	X	A	Branch to A+(X) if (R)≤0
Halt	00000111	R	X	A	Halt S-machine

As with the stack machine, the instruction repertoire of the multiple-register machine can easily be extended.

9.4.2 Implementation of Machine Registers

The 16 general-purpose registers are stored in S-memory starting at location 256. The advantage of placing the registers on a 256-word block boundary is that the rightmost 8 bits of the binary address are 0s—corresponding to register 0. Similarly, the binary address of word 257—corresponding to register 1—includes a binary 1 as the rightmost bit. The S-memory address of the 16 general-purpose registers is partitioned as follows:

00000001	0000 XXXX

so that the left half can be placed in the BR1-register and the right half can be moved to the MAR when a register reference must be made.

9.4.3 Operational Conventions

The following operational conventions are adopted in the implementation of the interpreter:

Register A1 points to the current-instruction address.
Register A2 holds the instruction currently being executed.
Register BR1 holds the high-order 8 bits of the S-memory address of general-purpose registers.

S-memory location 1024 (decimal) is the load point for the S-program.

S-memory location 256 is the starting location of the 16 general-purpose registers placed consecutively in S-memory.

S-memory location 50 is used as an error indicator: 0 denotes a success exit; all 1s denotes an error exit.

Register A3 is used as a temporary accumulator.

9.4.4 Multiple-Register Machine Interpreter

A listing of the multiple-register machine interpreter is given in Figure 9.4, and the various routines are described in the following paragraphs. The interpreter uses the emulation techniques given in Chapter 5.

The directory serves as a jump table to the microroutines used to execute the S-machine instructions; it is listed as follows:

```
DIR:  VERR−1→AMPCR
      VERR−1→AMPCR
      VLD−1→AMPCR
      VST−1→AMPCR
      VADD−1→AMPCR
      VSUB−1→AMPCR
      VBR−1→AMPCR
      VBRZ−1→AMPCR
      VHLT−1→AMPCR
      VERR−1→AMPCR
```

The directory is structured in the same manner as the directory for the stack machine. The jump table entry for instruction with operation code n must be placed at MPM location $n+1$.

The initialization routine sets BR1 to point to the general-purpose registers implemented in S-memory and initializes the current-address pointer to 1024 (decimal) as follows:

```
INIT:  AMPCR→BR1
       256→AMPCR
       AMPCR→A1
       1024→AMPCR
```

The fetch routine reads the next S-instruction, increases the contents of the current-address register by 1, isolates the index register field and fetches its contents from S-memory, isolates the operation code and places the MPM address of the corresponding microroutine in the AMPCR, forms the effective address and places it in register A3, right-justifies the operand register field in register A2, and passes control to a microroutine to have the S-instruction exe-

```
>>>>> TRANSLANG D MACHINE MICR0TRANSLAT0R

ENTER FILENAME F0R HEX? MRHEX
SUPPRESS BIT PATTERNS?(1=SUPPRESS)? 1
SUPPRESS HEX LISTING?(1=SUPPRESS)? 1
IF INPUT IN FILE ENTER 1? 31
ENTER S0URCE FILENAME? MRMACH

0000   DIR. VERR - 1 = AMPCR $
0001      VERR - 1 = AMPCR $
0002      VLD - 1 = AMPCR $
0003      VST - 1 = AMPCR $
0004      VADD - 1 = AMPCR $
0005      VSUB - 1 = AMPCR $
0006      VBR - 1 = AMPCR $
0007      VBRZ - 1 = AMPCR $
0008      VHLT - 1 = AMPCR $
0009      VERR - 1 = AMPCR $
0010   INIT. AMPCR = BR1 $
0011      256 = AMPCR $
0012      AMPCR = A1 $
0013      1024 = AMPCR $
0014   FETCH. A1 = MAR2 $
0015      MR2, A1 + 1 = A1 $
0016      WHEN RDC THEN BEX $
0017      B C = A2 $
0018      16 = SAR, 15 = LIT $
0019      A2 AND LIT = MAR $
0020      MR1, B R = AMPCR $ READ INDEX, 0P C0DE T0 AMPCR
0021      24 = SAR $
0022      A2 R = A3, EXEC $ ADDR FIELD T0 A3
0023      16 = SAR $
0024      WHEN RDC THEN A2 C = A2, BEX $ RT JUSTIFY R IN A2
0025      4 = SAR $
0026      A3 + B = A3, MAR2, JUMP $ EFF ADDR IN A3
0027   VLD. MR2 $
0028      WHEN RDC THEN A2 AND LIT = MAR, BEX $
0029      15 = LIT $
0030      B = MIR $
0031      MW1, IF SAI $
0032      FETCH - 1 = AMPCR $
0033      WHEN SAI THEN JUMP $
0034   VST. A2 AND LIT = MAR $
0035      15 = LIT $
0036      MR1 $
0037      WHEN RDC THEN A3 = MAR2, BEX $
0038      B = MIR $
0039      MW2, IF SAI $
0040      FETCH - 1 = AMPCR $
0041      WHEN SAI THEN JUMP $
0042   VADD. A2 AND LIT = A2, MAR $
0043      15 = LIT $
0044      MR1 $
0045      WHEN RDC THEN A3 = MAR2, BEX $
0046      B = A3, MR2 $
0047      WHEN RDC THEN A2 = MAR, BEX $
0048      A3 + B = MIR $
0049      MW1, IF SAI $
0050      FETCH - 1 = AMPCR $
0051      WHEN SAI THEN JUMP $
0052   VSUB. A2 AND LIT = A2, MAR $
0053      15 = LIT $
0054      MR1 $
0055      WHEN RDC THEN A3 = MAR2, BEX $
0056      B = A3, MR2 $
0057      WHEN RDC THEN A2 = MAR, BEX $
0058      A3 - B = MIR $
```

Figure 9.4 Translator listing of the multiple-register machine interpreter.

```
0059       MW1, IF SAI $
0060       FETCH - 1 = AMPCR $
0061       WHEN SAI THEN JUMP $
0062    VBR. FETCH - 1 = AMPCR $
0063       A3 = A1, RETN $
0064    VBRZ. A2 AND LIT = MAR $
0065       15 = LIT $
0066       MR1 $
0067       WHEN RDC THEN BEX $
0068       FETCH - 1 = AMPCR $
0069       NØT B = $
0070       IF ABT THEN A3 = A1, JUMP ELSE STEP $
0071       B = $
0072       IF MST THEN A3 = A1, JUMP ELSE JUMP $
0073    VHLT. 0 = MIR, LMAR, SKIP $
0074    VERR. NØT 0 = MIR, LMAR $
0075       50 = LIT $
0076       MW2, IF SAI $
0077       WHEN SAI THEN STEP $
0078       END $

THE TØTAL NUMBER ØF ERRØRS =     0

EXECUTE (Y/N)? N
```

Figure 9.4 *Continued.*

cuted. It is listed as follows:

```
FETCH:  A1→MAR2
  MR2, A1+1→A1
  WHEN RDC THEN BEX
  B C→A2
  16→SAR, 15→LIT
  A2 AND LIT→MAR
  MR1, B R→AMPCR      %  READ INDEX, OP CODE TO AMPCR
  24→SAR
  A2 R→A3, EXEC      %  ADDR FIELD TO A3
  16→SAR
  WHEN RDC THEN BEX, A2 C→A2      %  RT JUSTIFY IN A2
  4→SAR
  A3+B→A3, MAR2, JUMP      %  EFF ADDR IN A3
```

The fetch routine leaves the S-instruction in register A2 and the effective address in register A3.

The load routine reads the operand (to be loaded into the specified register) from S-memory and places it in the MIR for a subsequent write to the S-memory location of the specified operand register. After the operand is placed in the specified general-purpose register, the load routine exits to the fetch routine, as follows:

```
VLD: MR2
  WHEN RDC THEN A2 AND LIT→MAR, BEX
  15→LIT
  B→MIR
  MW1, IF SAI
  FETCH−1→AMPCR
  WHEN SAI THEN JUMP
```

It should be noted here that because machine registers are implemented in S-memory, the contents of a register used during the execution of an instruction is always written to S-memory after the execution of that instruction has been completed.

The store routine reads the contents of the specified register and places it in the MIR. The effective address, held in register A3, is then used as the S-memory address in the subsequent write operation. The store routine exits to the fetch routine, as follows:

```
VST: A2 AND LIT→MAR
  15→LIT
  MR1
  WHEN RDC THEN BEX, A3→MAR2
  B→MIR
  MW2, IF SAI
  FETCH−1→AMPCR
  WHEN SAI THEN JUMP
```

The add and subtract routines read the contents of the effective address and the specified register, perform the respective operation, and write the sum or difference to the register address in S-memory. The add and store routines exit to the fetch routine, as follows:

```
VADD: A2 AND LIT→A2, MAR
  15→LIT
  MR1
  WHEN RDC THEN BEX, A3→MAR2
  B→A3, MR2
  WHEN RDC THEN BEX, A2→MAR
  A3+B→MIR
  MW1, IF SAI
  FETCH−1→AMPCR
  WHEN SAI THEN JUMP
```

```
VSUB: A2 AND LIT→A2, MAR
  15→LIT
  MR1
  WHEN RDC THEN BEX, A3→MAR2
  B→A3, MR2
  WHEN RDC THEN BEX, A2→MAR
  A3−B→MIR
  MW1, IF SAI
  FETCH−1→AMPCR
  WHEN SAI THEN JUMP
```

The simplicity of the add and subtract routines suggests that complement arithmetic is assumed, which is definitely the case. The routines given earlier for signed-magnitude arithmetic could easily be substituted for the VADD and VSUB routines, given here.

The branch routine, listed as follows,

```
VBR:  FETCH-1→AMPCR
  A3→A1, RETN
```

moves the effective address to the current-address register and returns to the fetch routine. When the fetch routine receives control from the branch routine, the first instruction is not executed because the last statement in the fetch routine, that is, A3 + B→A3, MAR2, JUMP, also loads the MAR2. The MAR2 is loaded in the fetch routine specifically for the branch routine, and it is not used elsewhere. However, because a horizontal machine is used, the register is effectively loaded at no operational cost.

The branch-on-zero routine moves the effective address to the current-address register if the contents of the specified register are less than or equal to 0. The routine reads the contents of the register location in S-memory, before it can make the conditional test, as follows:

```
VBRZ:  A2 AND LIT→MAR
  15→LIT
  MR1
  WHEN RDC THEN BEX
  FETCH-1→AMPCR
  NOT B→
  IF ABT THEN A3→A1, JUMP ELSE STEP
  B→
  IF MST THEN A3→A1, JUMP ELSE JUMP
```

Regardless of the outcome of the less-than-or-equal-to-zero test, the branch-on-zero routine always exits to the fetch routine.

The halt routine places a 0 in S-memory location 50 and terminates microprogram execution. The error routine places all 1s in S-memory location 50 and also terminates microprogram execution. The routines are combined as follows:

```
VHLT:  0→MIR, LMAR, SKIP
VERR:  NOT 0→MIR, LMAR
  50→LIT
  MW2, IF SAI
  WHEN SAI THEN STEP
  END
```

One of the characteristics of an interpreter is that it is almost totally created. The operational philosophy, instruction format, machine operations, and operational conventions are synthesized to collectively form a complete computer architecture in which each design factor is complemented by the other design factors. The effectiveness and efficiency of the interpreter, however, are ob-

```
2) DMACH1    (CØMPILED)  02 JAN 76   16:53


ENTER SAME FILENAME FØR HEX? MRHEX
ØUTPUT REGISTERS AND S MEMØRY IN INTEGER(1) ØR ØCTAL(2)? 2
INPUT S MEMØRY IN INTEGER(1) ØR ØCTAL IN Ø11 FØRMAT(2)? 2
STARTING ADDRESS =? 10
MAXIMUM NUMBER ØF CLØCKS TØ SIMULATE=? 100
NUMBER ØF CLØCKS BETWEEN ØUTPUT PØINTS=? 1

ENTER ØUTPUT LINES DESIRED      1-ADDRESSES AND CLØCK
2- A1,A2,A3,B    3- MIR,SAR,LIT,CTR,AMPCR    4- BR1,BR2,MAR,BMAR, GC1, GC2
 5- CØNDITIØNS
ENTER NUMBER ØF ØUTPUT LINES DESIRED? 5

BEGIN ØUTPUT AT MPM ADDRESS=? 78
END ØUTPUT AT MPM ADDRESS=? 78
ENTER 1 FØR S MEMØRY DUMP WHEN PRØGRAM TERMINATES? 1


ENTER S MEMØRY VALUES IN CØNSECUTIVE BLØCKS
ENTER 9999 FØR STARTING ADDRESS WHEN FINISHED


STARTING S MEMØRY ADDRESS=? 1024
FINAL S MEMØRY ADDRESS FØR THIS BLØCK=? 1028
SMEM(1024)=? 00110002003
SMEM(1025)=? 00210002004
SMEM(1026)=? 00700000000
SMEM(1027)=? 00000000002
SMEM(1028)=? 00000000000

STARTING S MEMØRY ADDRESS=? 9999

END ØF SIMULATIØN - REGISTERS CØNTAIN


P(1) ADDR. =   77      P(3) ADDR. =   77      CLØCK =     68
A1=00000002003     A2=00000000160      A3=00000000000      B =00000000000
MIR =00000000000     SAR = 4      LIT = 50      CTR =   0      AMPCR =   72
BR1 =   1     BR2 =   0     MAR = 50     BMAR =    50     GC1=0  GC2=0
LC1=0  LC2=0  MST=0  LST=0  ABT=0  AØV=0  CØV=0  SAI=1  RDC=1  INT=0


MEMØRY DUMP REQUESTED

ENTER VALUES AS DØNE IN MEMØRY INPUT (9999 FØR STARTING ADDRESS WHEN
FINISHED)

STARTING S MEMØRY ADDRESS=? 50
FINAL S MEMØRY ADDRESS FØR THIS BLØCK=? 50


S MEMØRY(   50) TØ S MEMØRY(   50) =


00000000000
STARTING S MEMØRY ADDRESS=? 1024
FINAL S MEMØRY ADDRESS FØR THIS BLØCK=? 1028


S MEMØRY(1024) TØ S MEMØRY(1028) =


00110002003   00210002004   00700000000   00000000002   00000000002

STARTING S MEMØRY ADDRESS=? 9999
```

Figure 9.5 Sample run of the multiple-register machine for the execution of the statement A = 2, translated into S-language.

```
2) DMACH1    (COMPILED)  02 JAN 76   17:18


ENTER SAME FILENAME FOR HEX? MRHEX
OUTPUT REGISTERS AND S MEMORY IN INTEGER(1) OR OCTAL(2)? 2
INPUT S MEMORY IN INTEGER(1) OR OCTAL IN 011 FORMAT(2)? 2
STARTING ADDRESS =? 10
MAXIMUM NUMBER OF CLOCKS TO SIMULATE=? 750
NUMBER OF CLOCKS BETWEEN OUTPUT POINTS=? 1

ENTER OUTPUT LINES DESIRED      1-ADDRESSES AND CLOCK
2- A1,A2,A3,B    3- MIR,SAR,LIT,CTR,AMPCR    4- BR1,BR2,MAR,BMAR,GC1,GC2
 5- CONDITIONS
ENTER NUMBER OF OUTPUT LINES DESIRED? 5

BEGIN OUTPUT AT MPM ADDRESS=? 78
END OUTPUT AT MPM ADDRESS=? 78
ENTER 1 FOR S MEMORY DUMP WHEN PROGRAM TERMINATES? 1



ENTER S MEMORY VALUES IN CONSECUTIVE BLOCKS
ENTER 9999 FOR STARTING ADDRESS WHEN FINISHED


STARTING S MEMORY ADDRESS=? 1024
FINAL S MEMORY ADDRESS FOR THIS BLOCK=? 1042
SMEM(1024)=? 00110002022
SMEM(1025)=? 00210002014
SMEM(1026)=? 00110002021
SMEM(1027)=? 00210002015
SMEM(1028)=? 00110002017
SMEM(1029)=? 00114002015
SMEM(1030)=? 00614002012
SMEM(1031)=? 00310002014
SMEM(1032)=? 00414002020
SMEM(1033)=? 00500002006
SMEM(1034)=? 00210002016
SMEM(1035)=? 00700000000
SMEM(1036)=? 00000000000
SMEM(1037)=? 00000000000
SMEM(1038)=? 00000000000
SMEM(1039)=? 00000000000
SMEM(1040)=? 00000000001
SMEM(1041)=? 00000000004
SMEM(1042)=? 00000000005


STARTING S MEMORY ADDRESS=? 9999

END OF SIMULATION - REGISTERS CONTAIN


P(1) ADDR. =   77     P(3) ADDR. =   77     CLOCK =   540
A1=00000002014    A2=00000000160    A3=00000000000      B =00000000000
MIR =00000000000      SAR = 4      LIT = 50      CTR =   0       AMPCR =   72
BR1 =   1     BR2 =   0      MAR = 50       BMAR =    50       GC1=0   GC2=0
LC1=0  LC2=0  MST=0  LST=0  ABT=0  AOV=0  COV=0  SAI=1  RDC=1  INT=0


MEMORY DUMP REQUESTED

ENTER VALUES AS DONE IN MEMORY INPUT (9999 FOR STARTING ADDRESS WHEN
FINISHED)

STARTING S MEMORY ADDRESS=? 50
FINAL S MEMORY ADDRESS FOR THIS BLOCK=? 50
```

Figure 9.6 Sample run of the multiple-register machine interpreter for a series of S-instructions that multiply two integers. (See text.)

```
S MEMØRY(   50) TØ S MEMØRY(   50) =


00000000000
STARTING S MEMØRY ADDRESS=? 1024
FINAL S MEMØRY ADDRESS FØR THIS BLØCK=? 1042


S MEMØRY(1024) TØ S MEMØRY(1042) =


00110002022  00210002014  00110002021  00210002015  00110002017

00114002015  00614002012  00310002014  00414002020  00500002006

00210002016  00700000000  00000000005  00000000004  00000000024

00000000000  00000000001  00000000004  00000000005
STARTING S MEMØRY ADDRESS=? 9999
```

Figure 9.6 *Continued.*

viously dependent upon how closely the computer architecture matches the host microprogrammed processing unit and the main storage (that is, S-memory) unit.

9.4.5 Sample Runs

The first sample run of the interpreter for a multiple-register machine executes the statement A = 2, which is translated into S-instructions in symbolic and octal format as:

Decimal location	Octal location	Symbolic instruction	Octal instruction
1024	2000	LD 2,TWO	00110002003
1025	2001	ST 2,A	00210002004
1026	2002	HLT	00700000000
1027	2003	(TWO)	00000000002
1028	2004	(A)	00000000000

A printout of the sample run is given in Figure 9.5 in which the S-memory dump shows that the replacement operation has been performed successfully.

The second example executes the simulated multiply operation of the form R = M × N, given previously. In symbolic form, the program segment is written as:

```
   M=5
   N=4
   T=0
α  IF N=0 THEN GO TO β
   T=T+M
   N=N-1
   GO TO α
β  R=T
   HLT
```

The program is coded in machine language, and the S-instructions in symbolic and octal format are given as:

Decimal location	Octal location	Symbolic instruction	Octal instruction
1024	2000	LD 2,FIVE	00110002022
1025	2001	ST 2,M	00210002014
1026	2002	LD 2,FOUR	00110002021
1027	2003	ST 2,N	00210002015
1028	2004	LD 2,ZERO	00110002017
1029	2005	LD 3,N	00114002015
1030	2006	BZERO 3,1034	00614002012
1031	2007	A 2,M	00310002014
1032	2010	S 3,ONE	00414002020
1033	2011	BR 1030	00500002006
1034	2012	ST 2,R	00210002016
1035	2013	HLT	00700000000
1036	2014	(M)	00000000000
1037	2015	(N)	00000000000
1038	2016	(R)	00000000000
1039	2017	(ZERO)	00000000000
1040	2020	(ONE)	00000000001
1041	2021	(FOUR)	00000000004
1042	2022	(FIVE)	00000000005

A printout of the sample run is given in Figure 9.6, in which the S-memory dump shows that the product of $M \times N$ has been performed successfully.

The multiple-register machine version of the S-language program appears to be more efficient than the stack machine version—as far as the number of S-instructions is concerned. Each of the general-purpose registers can be accessed so that registers can be used for temporary storage.

VOCABULARY

The reader should be familiar with the following terms in the context in which they were used in the chapter:

Interpreter
Stack machine
Polish postfix notation
Instruction format
Name call
Value call
Instruction fetch
Directory
Jump table
Multiple-register machine
Current-instruction address

QUESTION SET

The following questions are intended to test your comprehension of the subject matter. All questions can be answered from the text directly or through a logical extension of the subjects presented. Some questions would be suitable for discussion sessions.

1 In what manner does the design and use of machine registers influence the design of the instruction format?
2 Name three methods of implementing machine registers.
3 What is the relationship between Polish postfix notation and the use of an operand stack?
4 Describe verbally the operation-code format for the System 360/370 computers. (See Chapter 2.)
5 How could unused fields be eliminated in an S-instruction format?
6 What function does the EXEC statement play in the interpreter for the stack machine?
7 The name call and literal call instructions are implemented in precisely the same manner. In a real computer, explain how they might be implemented differently.
8 How many clocks are needed to execute A = 2 in the stack machine? In the multiple-register machine? Can you explain the difference?
9 Consider the multiple-register machine interpreter. Why does the branch routine use RETN instead of JUMP?

EXERCISES

1 List the operational advantages and disadvantages of the stack machine and the multiple-register machine.
2 Run the stack machine interpreter on the translator/simulator for the R = M × N multiplication example given in the chapter. Compare the number of clocks required with the number required for the multiple-register machine.
3 Code and execute S-instructions for the following statements on the stack machine and the multiple-register machine:

A = 10
B = 5
C = 2
D = A − B + C − 4

4 Code the square root algorithm given in Chapter 8 into S-instructions for the stack and multiple-register machines. Compute the square root of the same value, for example, 25, on each interpreter. Compare the number of clocks used.

PROBLEMS

1 Add a shift instruction to the multiple-register machine. Use the following format:

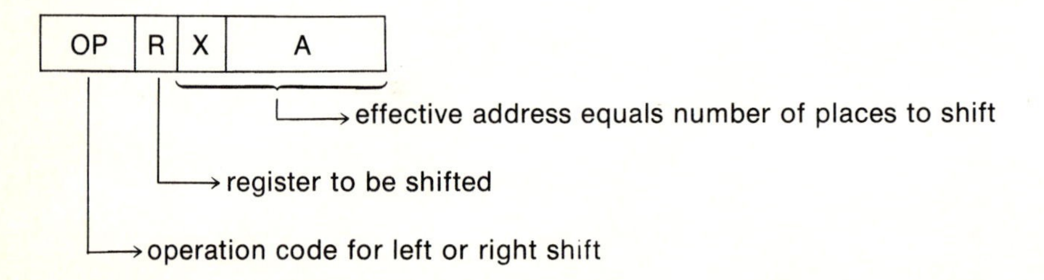

2 Add floating-point arithmetic to the stack machine and test it for the square root algorithm. Implement addition, subtraction, multiplication, and division.

3 Add signed-magnitude arithmetic to the multiple-register machine. Implement addition and subtraction.

4 Add fixed-point multiplication and division to the multiple-register machine. Use an odd/even pair of registers as the AC/MQ registers.

5 Add register-to-register operations to the multiple-register machine. Implement the following operations: load, add, subtract, and load positive. Use the following instruction format:

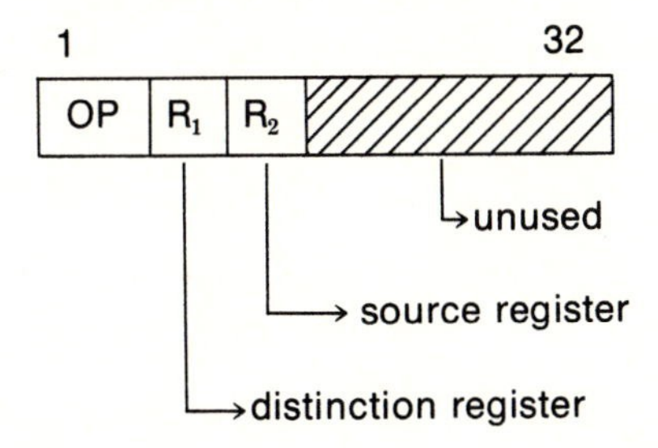

Chapter 10

Microprogramming Miscellanea

10.1 OVERVIEW

This chapter completes the primer by providing additional information on timing and by giving a set of microprogramming superproblems that can be used for longer-term projects. The superproblems are analogous to the interpreters given in Chapter 9 in the sense that a fairly detailed analysis of the problem is required before the desired microprogram can be written.

10.2 TIMING

A computer operates continuously by generating clock pulses and by moving information from one place to another. Because a computer is deterministic, events always take place in a prescribed sequence. Therefore, the task of microprogramming is to plan the instruction sequence so that the desired results are obtained.

10.2.1 Clock Pulses

A convenient way of conceptualizing the operation of the D-machine is to regard the clock pulse as a means of moving information from one place to an-

Clock Pulse		Clock Pulse		Clock Pulse	
	⟵ One phase of microprogram execution (one clock interval) ⟶		⟵ One phase of microprogram execution (one clock interval) ⟶		⟵

Figure 10.1 Microinstruction timing.

other. In other words, information is moved during a clock pulse. Figure 10.1 gives a conceptual view of microinstruction timing. It is important to recognize that during each clock interval, the phase 1 cycle of one instruction *and* the phase 2 or 3 cycle of another instruction are being executed.

10.2.2 Description of Instruction Phases

For a type II instruction, one clock interval provides enough time to complete the literal assignment and to establish the successor control, which is always a step to the next instruction in microprogram memory.

For a type I instruction, the following basic functions are performed during and after phases 1 and 3:

During Phase 1
Select condition (AOV, ABT, MST, etc.).
Establish whether a true condition or a complement condition is to be tested.

At End of Phase 1
Determine successor (true or false successor).
Update command register (conditional).
Initiate external operation (for example, MW1).
Adjust condition (for example, SET LC1).

During Phase 2 (holding phase)
Previous logic operation applies continuously for testing in next phase 1 cycle.

During Phase 3
Select adder X input.
Select adder Y input.
Perform adder or logic operation (dynamic conditions are available for testing in a concurrent phase 1).
Shift operation.

At End of Phase 3
Change destination register.

The process is summarized in Figure 10.2 and should be interpreted as follows:

1 The phase 3 cycle for a type I instruction always follows the phase 1 cycle, except when the condition fails and the logic-unit operation is condi-

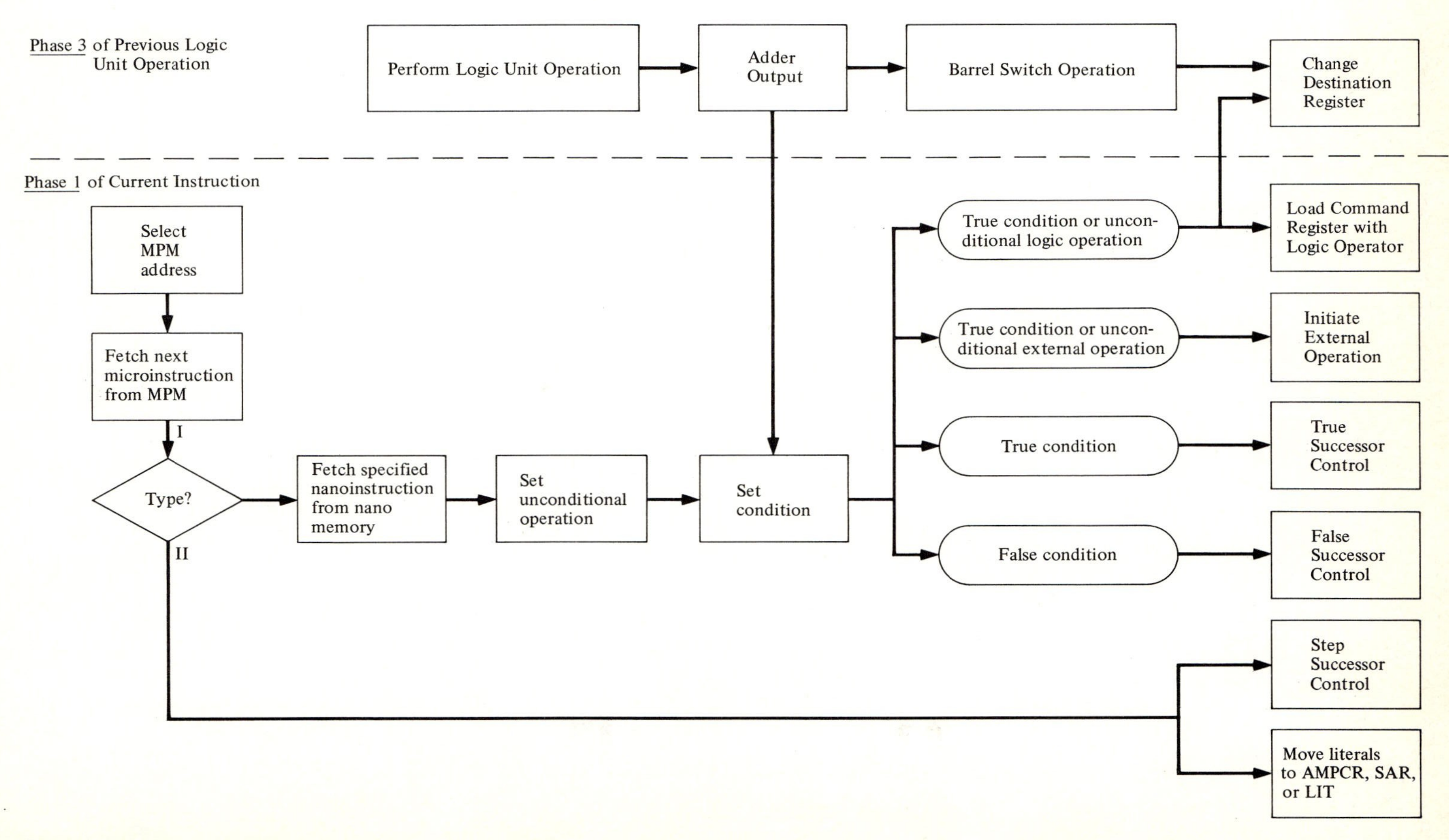

Figure 10.2 Synchronization of machine operations.

tional. If no logic-unit operation is specified, then a null operation of the form $0 + B_{000} \rightarrow$ is executed.

2 Registers change state during a clock pulse. Thus, a destination register is replaced at the same time the command register for a new logic-unit operation is loaded. Therefore, replacement is performed only when a new logic-unit operation is initiated.

3 A holding phase 2 is created when a type I instruction, with a logic operation, is followed by either a type II instruction or by a type I instruction in which the logic-unit operation is conditional and the condition fails. During a phase 2 cycle, the logic-unit command continues to apply so that the corresponding condition can be tested in the next type I instruction.

4 A register successfully replaced in a type I instruction can be used in the type I instruction that immediately follows it. Thus, for example, the microprogram segment

```
0→A1
A1 + 1→A1
A1 + 1→MIR
MW1, IF SAI
```

causes a value of 2 to be written to S-memory.

It is relatively easy to generate incorrect results from a microprogram due to timing and the sequence in which events take place. This is particularly true when several type I and II instructions are intermixed. The next section gives several examples that will help point out the pitfalls that can occur.

10.2.3 Timing Examples

The timing examples give three short microprogram segments. The objective is to show *when* the various events take place during the execution of a sequence of instructions.

The first example is a repetition of the example in the preceding section and consists of four unconditional type I instructions executed in succession, as follows:

```
0→A1
A1 + 1→A1
A1 + 1→MIR
MW1, IF SAI
```

A timing diagram of this microprogram segment is given in Figure 10.3. At clock 1, instruction 1 is fetched. At clock 2, a logic-unit operation of $0 + B_{000}$ is loaded into the command register (for instruction 1), and instruction 2 is fetched. At clock 3, register A1 is replaced with 0 (for instruction 1), a logic-unit operation of $A1 + B_{001}$ is loaded into the command register (for instruction 2), and instruction 3 is fetched. At clock 4, register A1 is replaced with 1 (for in-

Clock	1	2	3	4	5	6
1 0→A1	Ph. 1	Ph. 3				
2 A1+1→A1		Ph. 1	Ph. 3			
3 A1+1→MIR			Ph. 1	Ph. 3		
4 MW1, IF SAI				Ph. 1	Ph. 3	

Figure 10.3 Timing example.

struction 2), a logic-unit operation of $A1 + B_{001}$ is loaded into the command register (for instruction 3), and instruction 4 is fetched. At clock 5, the MIR is replaced with 2 (for instruction 3), a logic-unit operation of $0 + B_{000}$ is loaded into the command register, and a memory write operation is initiated. All operations in instruction 4 are unconditional, and as a result, instruction 4 has a phase 3. The IF SAI clause in instruction 4 serves to reset the SAI indicator.

The second example combines type I and type II instructions, as follows:

A1 L→A1
COMP 8→SAR
A2 L→A2
A1 R→A1
8→SAR
A2 R→SAR
(type I with logic operations follows)

A timing diagram of this microprogram segment is given in Figure 10.4. At clock 1, instruction 1 is fetched. At clock 2, a logic-unit operation of $A1 + B_{000}$ and a left shift are loaded into the command register, and instruction 2 is fetched. Between clock 2 and clock 3, the adder operation and the left shift are executed. The shift is performed with a residual value that is in the SAR. However, no logic-unit operation is loaded into the command register at clock 3, so the first phase 3 of instruction 1 is changed to a holding phase 2. At clock 3, a COMP 8 is placed in the SAR, and instruction 3 is fetched. Between clocks 3 and 4, the logic-unit command of instruction 1 continues to apply. At clock 4, a

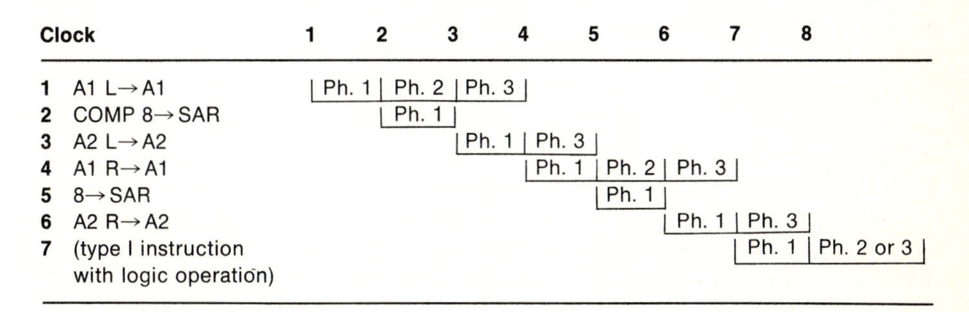

Figure 10.4 Timing example.

logic-unit operation of $A2 + B_{000}$ L (for instruction 3) is loaded into the command register, and the phase 3 cycle of instruction 1 is completed when the output of the barrel switch (that is, the result of the left-shift operation) replaces register A1. Also, instruction 4 is fetched at clock 4. The adder and barrel switch operation from instruction 3 are executed with COMP 8 in the SAR between clocks 4 and 5. At clock 5, instruction 3 is completed at the same time as a logic-unit operation of $A1 + B_{000}$ R is loaded into the command register (for instruction 4). Instruction 5 is also fetched at clock 5. Between clock 5 and clock 6, the adder and a right-shift operation for instruction 4, with a COMP 8 in the SAR which is obviously not desired, are executed. At clock 6, however, no logic-unit operation is loaded into the command register because instruction 5 is a type II instruction. Therefore, the first phase 3 cycle for instruction 4 is turned into a holding phase 2. Two operations performed at clock 6 are that the SAR is loaded with 8 and instruction 6 is fetched. Between clock 6 and clock 7, the adder and right-shift operation of instruction 4 are again executed; this time the SAR contains a correct value of 8. At clock 7, a logic-unit operation of $A2 + B_{000}$ R for instruction 6 is loaded into the command register, and the phase 3 cycle of instruction 4 is completed; A1 is replaced by the right shift of 8 of its previous contents. Also, at clock 7, instruction 8 is fetched. Lastly, the replacement operation of instruction 6 is completed when the logic-unit operation for instruction 7 is loaded into the command register.

The final example combines unconditional and conditional type I instructions, as follows:

```
A2+B→A3
IF MST THEN A3+1→A3, SKIP ELSE STEP
A3+B111+1→A3
(type I instruction with logic operation follows)
```

where MST tests false. A timing diagram of this microprogram segment is given as Figure 10.5. At clock 1, instruction 1 is fetched. At clock 2, a logic-unit operation of $A2 + B$ is moved to the command register, and instruction 2 is fetched. Between clock 2 and clock 3, two events take place: an adder operation of $A2 + B$ is executed and, based on the adder result, the MST condition in instruction 2 tests false. Therefore, the logic-unit operation specified in instruction 2 is not executed, and the first phase 3 cycle for instruction 1 is turned into a holding phase 2. As a result, instruction 2 turns into a one-phase instruction. At clock 3, instruction 3 is fetched. Between clock 3 and clock 4, the logic-unit operation of $A2 + B$ for instruction 1 continues to apply. At clock 4, a logic-unit operation of $A3 + B_{111} + 1$ is moved to the command register, and the phase 3 cycle of instruction 1—that is, A3 is replaced by $A2 + B$—is completed. Also at clock 4, instruction 4 is fetched. Finally, instruction 3 is completed at clock 5 because instruction 4 contains a logic-unit operation, as specified.

The process of turning a phase 3 that has not been completed into a holding phase 2 is determined dynamically and can easily result in several phase 2

Clock		1	2	3	4	5	6
1	A2+B→A3	Ph. 1	Ph. 2	Ph. 3			
2	IF MST THEN A3+1→A3 SKIP ELSE STEP		Ph. 1				
3	A3+B_{111}+1→A3			Ph. 1	Ph. 3		
4	(type I instruction with logic operation)				Ph. 1	Ph. 2 or 3	

Figure 10.5 Timing example.

cycles in succession, as in the following example in which AOV tests false:

```
A1 + LIT R→B                                  (1)
15 LIT, 4→SAR                                 (2)
IF AOV THEN B0TT→MIR, SKIP ELSE STEP          (3)
B→MIR                                         (4)
MW1, IF SAI                                   (5)
```

In this case, a holding phase 2 for instruction (1) is generated for instruction (2) and for instruction (3) because neither instruction has a phase 3 cycle.

10.3 MICROPROGRAMMING SUPERPROBLEMS

The process of doing microprogramming is similar to conventional computer programming in another way, in addition to those already given. Once several microprograms have been written, the challenge is not in writing additional statements but in the design of systems that employ microprogramming technology. Toward that end, five "superproblems" are given that require microprogramming creativity in testing as well as in implementation and that require detailed knowledge of the subject matter.

10.3.1 Dynamic Address Translation

Dynamic address translation is a virtual storage technique that maps a virtual storage address into a real S-memory address. Dynamic address translation is implemented through microprogramming or through a hardware DAT box[1] designed for the same purpose. An overview of dynamic address translation is given in Figure 10.6.

Management of real storage in a virtual storage environment is achieved by structuring both virtual and real storage into pages. A commonly used page size is 4,096 bytes. Pages are moved between real storage and direct-access storage as a storage management technique, and only pages needed to sustain program execution are required to be in main storage during execution of that program.

Each effective address computed by the processing unit is translated into a real main storage address through the dynamic address translation process, which uses segment and page tables to accomplish the translation. Each effec-

[1] DAT is an acronym for dynamic address translation.

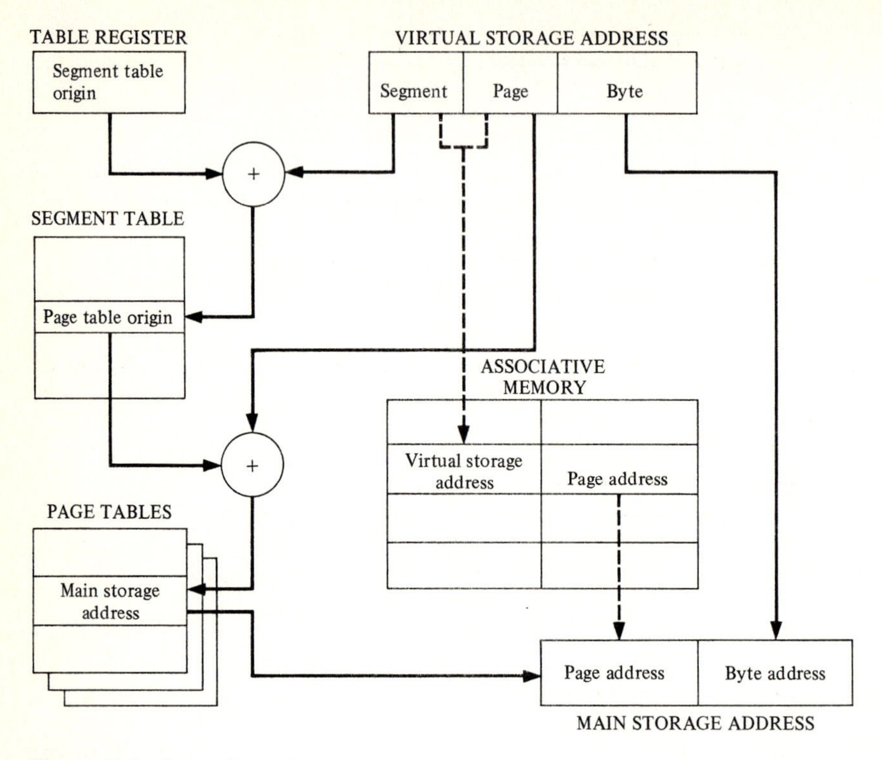

Figure 10.6 Dynamic address translation.

tive virtual address is partitioned into a segment number, page number, and displacement as follows:

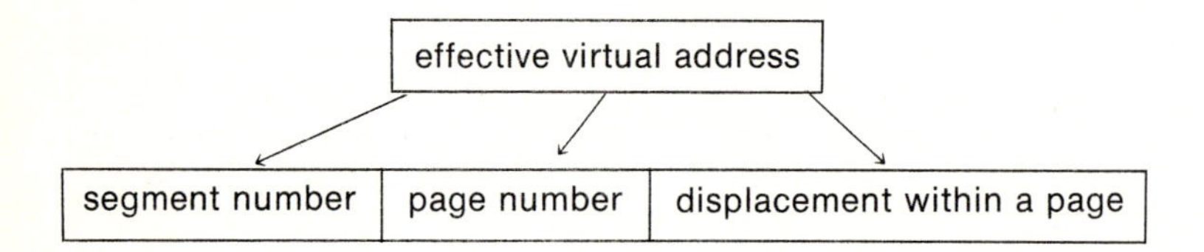

The segment number is used as an index into a segment table, and the page number is used as an index into a page table. Typical field sizes are:

Segment field—4 bits
Page number field—8 bits
Displacement field—12 bits

The 12-bit displacement field corresponds to a 4,096-byte page, so that addresses within a page need not be translated—only the page address.

The table register points to the segment table and has the following format:

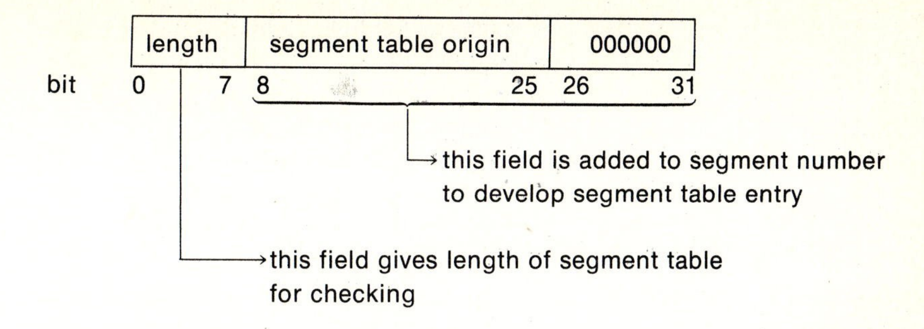

A segment table entry points to the page table and has the following format:

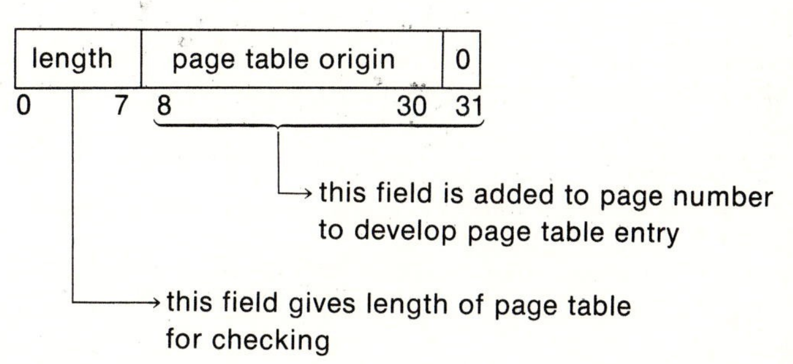

The page table entry gives a real storage address and has the following format:

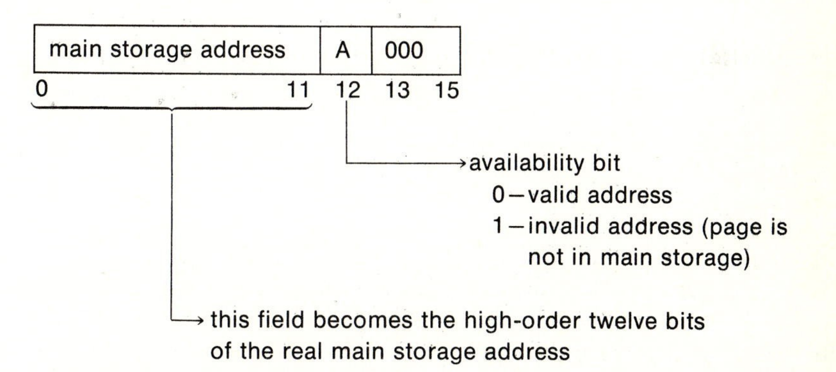

The availability bit is checked during dynamic address translation, and if it indicates an invalid address, which means the needed page is not in main storage, then a program interrupt is generated. The interrupt is fielded by the operating system, which brings the referenced page into the main storage unit and places the main storage address of the page in the corresponding page table entry. The main storage address of the referenced page then replaces the segment and page fields, as indicated in Figure 10.6, and execution of the instruction continues.

Dynamic address translation is time-consuming. Therefore, the process is speeded up with the use of an associative memory that holds the most recently used virtual storage and page addresses.

The problem, of course, is to design, implement, and test a microprogram to do dynamic address translation. Additional information of the various aspects of the problem is given in the references in the footnote.[1]

10.3.2 List Operations

A well-defined computer function is to search a list for an occurrence of a key value. A familiar example is the symbol table of the form (n_i, v_i) where n stands for name and v stands for value. The table is searched with argument name k until $k = n_i$; this process makes the value v_i available for retrieval. A table of this type may hold symbol names and addresses, for a language processor program, or may contain part names and quantity-on-hand for an inventory application. The problem is to construct a single computer instruction to search a list of this type.

10.3.2.1 Form of the Computer Instruction The computer instruction should take the form

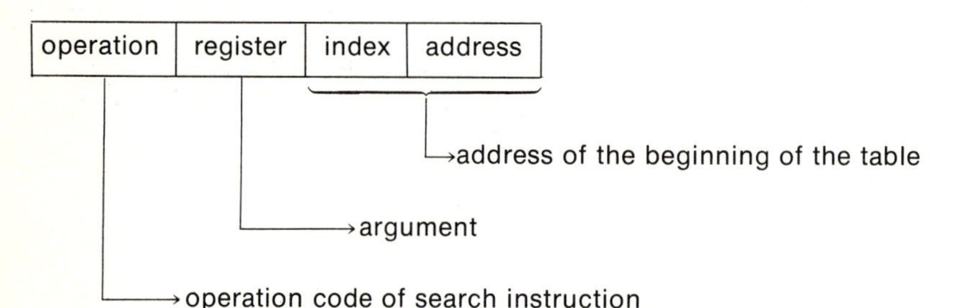

The instruction executes as follows:

1 The effective address, that is, (index) + displacement, is computed, and the search starts there.

2 The argument has been placed in the specified operand register R_i.

3 If the name field of a table entry matches the argument, then the value field is retrieved and placed in register R_{i+1}.

4 After a successful search, the next sequential computer instruction is skipped.

5 If the end of the table is reached and a name field does not match the argument, then an unsuccessful search has taken place. In this case, the next sequential computer instruction is executed.

[1] For additional information on dynamic address translation, see one of the following references: P. Freeman, *Software System Principles: A Survey,* Science Research Associates, Chicago, 1975; H. Katzan, *Operating Systems: A Pragmatic Approach,* Van Nostrand Reinhold Company, New York, 1973; S. E. Madnick and J. J. Donovan, *Operating Systems,* McGraw-Hill, New York, 1974.

Information on table entries is dependent upon the method of storage allocation. Two methods are considered: consecutive allocation and linked allocation.

10.3.2.2 Consecutive Allocation With consecutive allocation, the table is conceptualized as a matrix of the form

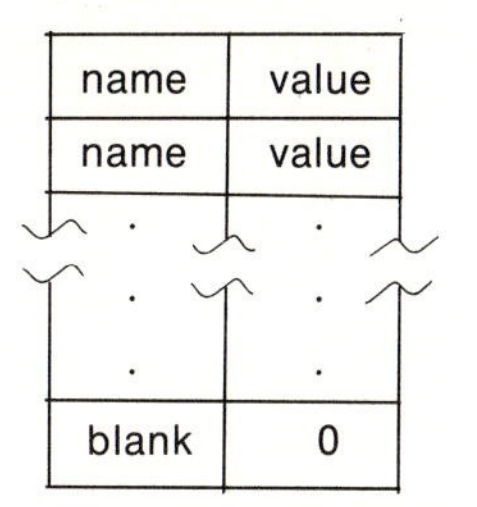

Last entry

that is stored in row order, that is,

$name_1$
$value_1$
$name_2$
$value_2$
. . .
blank
0

Each name and each value data item have a length attribute of one word.

The instruction should be implemented to search the table until a retrieval can be made or the end of the table is reached.

10.3.2.3 Linked Allocation With linked allocation, each table entry has the form:

name
value
pointer

where "pointer" is the address of the next table entry. The last node has a zero pointer field. The fields in a single node are stored consecutively, and each field has a length attribute of one word.

The instruction should be implemented to search the linked list until a retrieval can be made or until the last node is reached.

10.3.3 Matrix Operations

The BASIC language[1] includes matrix operations of the form

$$\text{MAT C} = \text{A} \oplus \text{B}$$

where $\oplus$ is one of the following matrix operations: + (for element-by-element addition), − (for element-by-element subtraction), and * (for matrix multiplication). Assume that a matrix is stored in the following manner:

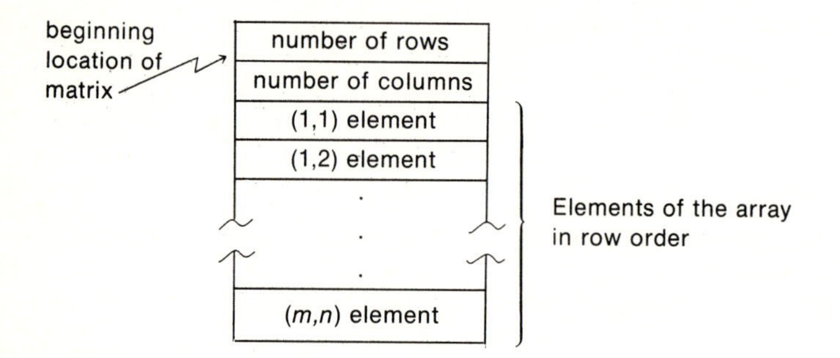

Implement each of the matrix operations through microprogramming. The microprogram should accept any matrix that can be stored in S-memory.

Another aspect of this problem is designing an S-instruction with which the microprogram can be accessed and taking into consideration the fact that each matrix operation requires three operands.

10.3.4 Vector Operations

The APL language includes a rich assortment of vector operations.[2] Some of those that might be considered are:

1 *Element-by-element operations,* such as $+, -, *, /, \wedge, \vee, \sim, >, \geq, <, \leq, =, \neq$, and so forth.

2 *Reduction,* such as

$$\oplus / \text{V}$$

where $\oplus$ is a scalar function and V is a vector. The expression

$$+/\text{A}$$

is defined as $\text{A}[1]+\text{A}[2]+\text{A}[3]+ \cdots +\text{A}[n]$.

[1] A good reference to the BASIC language is J. G. Kemeny and T. C. Kurtz, *BASIC Programming,* Wiley, New York, 1971.

[2] A reference to the APL language is H. Katzan, *APL Users Guide,* Van Nostrand Reinhold Company, New York, 1971.

3 *Reversal,* of the form

$$\phi A$$

which reverses the elements of vector A.

4 *Rotation,* of the form

$$n\phi A$$

which rotates A to the left $|n|$ places if n is positive and rotates A to the right $|n|$ places if n is negative.

5 *Take,* of the form

$$n \uparrow A$$

which selects the first $|n|$ elements of A if n is positive and selects the last $|n|$ elements of A if n is negative.

6 *Drop,* of the form

$$n \downarrow A$$

which eliminates the first $|n|$ elements of A if n is positive and eliminates the last $|n|$ elements of A if n is negative.

Assume that vectors are stored as follows:

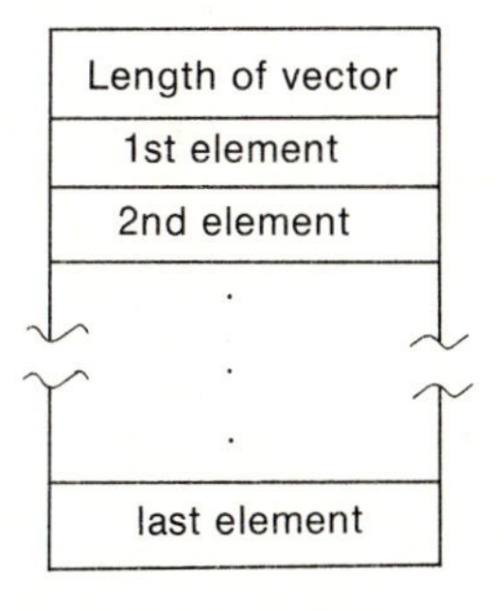

The problem is to implement vector operations through microprogramming. Again, an important aspect of the problem is to design S-instructions with which to reference the microprograms.

10.3.5 Turing-Machine Machine

This superproblem is to develop an emulator for a Turing machine.[1] The tape and Turing machine program should be stored in S-memory, where each tape

[1] A good reference to Turing machines and appropriate algorithms is M. Davis, *Computability and Unsolvability,* McGraw-Hill, New York, 1958.

square could be stored as one word. Any alphabet can be used; however, only B (blank), 0 (zero), and 1 (one) are used in the following example.

10.3.5.1 Brief Description of a Turing Machine The action of a Turing machine is dependent upon the internal state of the machine and the symbol under scan of the read-write head. For simplicity, assume the machine can perform one of the following functions:

1 A new character is written in the tape square under the read-write head.
2 The read-write head is moved right one square.
3 The read-write head is moved left one square.
4 The operation of the machine is halted.

The operation of a Turing machine is governed by a set of rules that specify the action to be taken at each step of a computation. For simplicity, assume that the operation is described by a quadruple that contains the following information:

1 Current state
2 Symbol under scan
3 Action to be taken
4 Next state

The following quadruples are permitted:

1 $s_i \; A_j \; A_k \; s_m$
2 $s_i \; A_j \; R \; s_m$
3 $s_i \; A_j \; L \; s_m$

where s_i is the current state, A_j is the symbol under scan, A_k is the next symbol written, and s_m is the next state. R means move right, and L means move left. Quadruple 1 specifies the replacement of A_j by A_k and an entry into state s_m. Quadruple 2 specifies a move of one tape square to the right and an entry into state s_m. Quadruple 3 specifies a move of one tape square to the left and an entry into state s_m.

An algorithm for a Turing machine, that is, a Turing machine program, is a set of quadruples that contains no two quadruples that contain the same first two symbols. (They are the current state and symbol under scan.) Thus, the current state and the symbol under the read-write head determine the action to be taken, since a unique quadruple is implicitly selected. The machine operates by going from state to state, using the first two symbols of the quadruples to select the next operation. The machine halts when the current state and the symbol under scan do not match any of the quadruples.

10.3.5.2 Sample Algorithm A sample algorithm is given that adds two numbers that are represented on tape by consecutive 1s. A number n is represented as $n + 1$ ones followed by a blank symbol. The two numbers to be added are separated by one blank as follows:

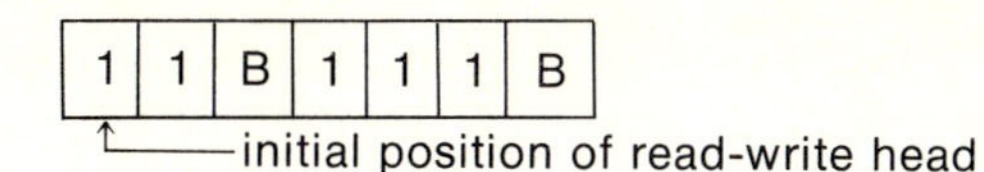

The algorithm for adding the two numbers would operate as follows:

1 Move right along the tape until a blank tape square is reached.
2 Write a 1 in place of the blank character.
3 Move right along the tape until another blank tape square is reached.
4 Move left one tape square.
5 Write a blank character.
6 Move left one tape square.
7 Write a blank character.
8 Halt.

A Turing machine problem for this algorithm would be:

Current state	Symbol scanned	Action	Next state
s_1	1	R	s_1
s_1	B	1	s_2
s_2	1	R	s_2
s_2	B	L	s_3
s_3	1	B	s_3
s_3	B	L	s_4
s_4	1	B	s_4

The machine halts with a blank character under the read-write head when it is in state s_4.

10.3.5.3 Implementation One method of implementation is to store each quadruple as a one-word instruction of the form:

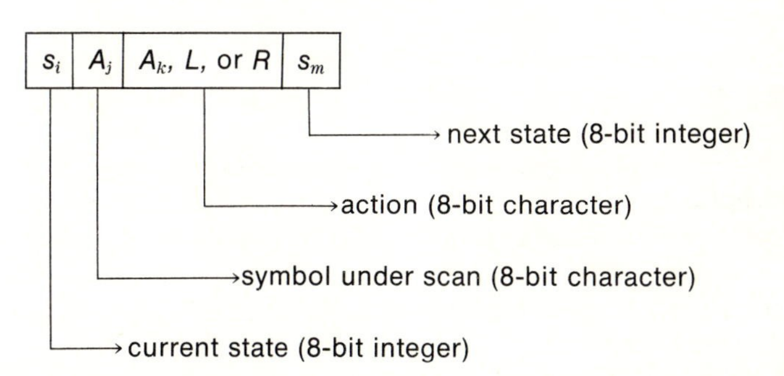

so that the emulator requires a fetch and a decoding routine. Remember, however, that the machine can go to a lower-state number, so that the match of the current state and symbol under scan should, conceptually, start at the beginning of the set of quadruples.

References and Selected Bibliography

Bingham, H. W., R. L. Davis, U. Faber, D. A. Fisher, J. D. McGonagle, E. W. Reigel, and S. Zucker, *Microprogramming Manual for Interpreter Based Systems,* Burroughs Corporation, Paoli, Pa. 1970, TR 70–8.

Casaglia, G. F., Nanoprogramming vs. Microprogramming, *Computer,* vol. 9, no. 1, pp. 54–58 (January 1976).

Chu, Y., *Computer Organization and Microprogramming,* Prentice-Hall, Englewood Cliffs, N.J., 1972.

Husson, S., *Microprogramming: Principles and Practices,* Prentice-Hall, Englewood Cliffs, N.J., 1970.

Jones, L. H., Microinstruction Sequencing and Structured Microprogramming, *Proceedings of the Seventh Annual Workshop on Microprogramming* ($MICRO_7$), 1974, pp. 277–289. (Available from the Association for Computing Machinery, located in New York City.)

Katzan, H., *Computer Organization and the System/370,* Van Nostrand Reinhold Company, New York, 1971.

Reigel, E. W., U. Faber, and D. A. Fisher, The Interpreter—A Microprogrammable Building Block System, AFIPS vol. 40, *Proceedings of the 1972 Spring Joint Computer Conference,* pp. 705–723.

Rosin, R. F., Contemporary Concepts of Microprogramming and Emulation, *Computing Surveys,* vol. 1, no. 4, pp. 197–212 (December 1969).

Wilkes, M. V., The Growth of Interest in Microprogramming—A Literature Survey, *Computing Surveys,* vol. 1, no. 3, pp. 139–145 (September 1969).

Glossary of Key Words

A1 — *A1 register.* Used as an X select operand or a destination operator.

A2 — *A2 register.* Used as an X select operand or a destination operator.

A3 — *A3 register.* Used as an X select operand or a destination operator.

AAD — *And-add logic operator.* X AAD Y is equivalent to $X+(X \wedge Y)$.

ABT — *All-bits-true condition.* Set as a dynamic condition from the logic operation executed during phase 3 of previous type I instruction.

AMPCR — *Alternate microprogram count register.* Used during type II literal assignment statement, as a Y select operand, or as a destination operator from the barrel switch. The 12 least significant bits from the barrel switch are moved to the AMPCR.

AND — *And logical operator.* X AND Y is equivalent to $X \wedge Y$.

AOV — *Adder overflow condition.* Set as a dynamic condition from the logic operation executed during phase 3 of previous type I instruction when adder operation results in an overflow out of the high-order bit.

B — *B-register.* Used as a Y select operand or as a destination operator from the barrel switch. The use of B as a Y select operand is equivalent to B_{TTT}. (The B-register is also used in other commands as a destination register.)

BAD — *B-register from the adder.* Used as a destination operator to route adder output to the B-register.

BBA — *B-register from the adder OR'ed with the barrel switch output.* Used as a destination operator.

BBE — *B-register from the external data bus OR'ed with the barrel switch output.* Used as a destination operator.

BBI — *B-register from prior MIR contents OR'ed with the barrel switch output.* Used as a destination operator.

BEX — *B-register from external data bus.* Used as a destination operator.

BMI — *B-register from prior MIR contents.* Used as a destination operator.

BR1 — *Base register 1.* Destination operator from the barrel switch; takes the second least significant byte of the barrel switch. Used in read and write addressing of external devices.

BR2 — *Base register 2.* Destination operator from the barrel switch; takes the second least significant byte from the barrel switch. Used in read and write accessing of external devices.

C — *Circular right-shift operation.* Specified along with logic-unit operation and takes place in the barrel switch.

CALL — *Successor command.* Branches to the contents of the AMPCR + 1 and places the current MPCR value in the AMPCR for subsequent return.

COMMENT — Key word for *comment line* in program. (COMMNT is used in TRANSLANG.)

COMP — *Complement* operator for literal assignment statement.

COV — *Counter overflow condition.* Set when the CTR is incremented from all 1s to 0.

CSAR — *Destination operator.* Used to complement the contents of the SAR.

CTR — *Counter.* Used as an X or Y select operand or as a destination operator, which takes the least significant 8 bits from the barrel switch output.

ELSE — *Separator word* used to designate the false successor.

END — Key word used to end a microprogram.

EQV — *Equivalent logical operator.* X EQV Y is equivalent to $(X \wedge Y) \vee (\overline{X} \wedge \overline{Y})$.

EXEC — *Successor command.* Used to execute the instruction at (AMPCR) + 1 and continue with normal sequential operation.

F — *False gating out of the B-register.* Used as part of a Y select operand.

IF	Key word denoting the conditional part of a statement.
IMP	*Imply logical operator.* X IMP Y is equivalent to $\overline{X} \vee \overline{Y}$.
INC	*Destination operator.* Used to increment the previous contents of the CTR. May cause the COV condition to be set.
JUMP	*Successor command.* Branches to the contents of the AMPCR + 1, which becomes the contents of the MPCR.
L	*Left-shift operator.* Denotes a left end-off shift in the barrel switch of the adder output, with zero fill on the right.
LC1	*Local condition 1.* Set with the SET LC1 command and reset by testing.
LC2	*Local condition 2.* Set with the SET LC2 command and reset by testing.
LC3	*Local condition 3.* Set with the SET LC3 command and reset by testing.
LCTR	*Destination operator.* Takes the ones complement of LIT contents and places it in the CTR. COV condition is reset.
LIT	*Literal register.* Used as least significant byte of X select or Y select operands, and as a source for LMAR and LCTR commands. Is assigned a value through literal assignment type I instruction.
LMAR	*Destination operator.* Places the contents of the LIT in the MAR.
LST	*Least significant bit condition.* Reflects the rightmost bit position of adder output from the phase 3 of the previous type I instructions. If the bit is 1, the LST condition is set; otherwise, the condition is not set.
MAR	*Destination operator.* Causes the least significant byte of barrel switch output to be moved to the memory address register (MAR).
MAR1	*Destination operator.* Causes the second least significant byte of barrel switch output to be moved to the BR1 register and the least significant byte of barrel switch output to be moved to the MAR register.
MAR2	*Destination operator.* Causes the second least significant byte of barrel switch output to be moved to the BR2 register and the least significant byte of barrel switch output to be moved to the MAR register.
MIR	*Destination operator.* Causes the output of the barrel switch to be moved to the memory information register (MIR).
MR1	*Memory read one command.* Initiates a read from the S-memory location specified in ⟨BR1,MAR⟩.
MR2	*Memory read two command.* Initiates a read from the S-memory location specified in ⟨BR2,MAR⟩.
MST	*Most significant bit condition.* Reflects the leftmost bit position of

the adder output from the phase 3 of the previous type I instruction. If the bit is 1 the MST condition is set; otherwise, the condition is not set.

MW1 — *Memory write one command.* Initiates a write from the MIR to the S-memory location specified in ⟨BR1,MAR⟩.

MW2 — *Memory write two command.* Initiates a write from the MIR to the S-memory location specified in ⟨BR1,MAR⟩.

NAN — *Not-and logical operator.* X NAN Y is equivalent to $\overline{X} \vee \overline{Y}$, which is equivalent to $(\overline{X \wedge Y})$.

NIM — *Not imply logical operator.* X NIM Y is equivalent to $X \wedge \overline{Y}$.

NOR — *Not-or logical operator.* X NOR Y is equivalent to $\overline{X} \wedge \overline{Y}$, which is equivalent to $(\overline{X \vee Y})$.

NOT — *Complement logical operator.* NOT Y is equivalent to $\overline{Y}$.

NRI — *Not reverse imply logical operator.* X NRI Y is equivalent to $\overline{X} \vee Y$.

OAD — *Or-add logical operator.* X OAD Y is equivalent to $X + (X \vee Y)$.

OR — *Or logical operator.* X OR Y is equivalent to $X \vee Y$.

R — *Right-shift operator.* Denotes a right end-off shift in the barrel switch of the adder output, with zero fill on the left.

RDC — *Read complete condition.* Set when external data are ready for input to the B-register. The condition is reset by testing.

RETN — *Successor command.* Branches to the contents of the AMPCR + 2, which becomes the contents of the MPCR. (Can be used as a return from a subroutine.)

RIM — *Reverse imply logical operator.* X RIM Y is equivalent to $X \vee \overline{Y}$.

SAI — *Switch accepts information condition.* Set on a write operation when the operation is complete, as far as the processing unit is concerned, so that the registers used in the operation may be changed. Reset by testing.

SAR — *Shift amount register.* Used to specify the length of a shift operation. The SAR is loaded by literal assignment or as a destination operator in which it receives the least significant byte of the output of the barrel switch.

SAVE — *Successor command.* Places the current contents of the MPCR in the AMPCR and uses the (MPCR) + 1 as the next instruction address.

SET — *Set condition command.* Sets the specified condition indicator.

SKIP — *Successor command.* Skips the next instruction by using (MPCR) + 2 as the next instruction address.

SLIT — *Destination for literal assignment.* Loads the LIT register with a value converted for subsequent movement to the SAR.

STEP	*Successor command.* Steps to the next instruction by using (MPCR) + 1 as the next instruction address.
T	*True gating out of the B-register.* Used as a part of a Y select operand.
THEN	*Separator word* used to designate the true alternative of a conditional statement.
WAIT	*Successor command.* Repeats the current instruction by using (MPCR) as the new instruction address.
WHEN	Key word denoting a conditional statement with an implied ELSE WAIT option.
XOR	*Exclusive-or logical operation.* X XOR Y is equivalent to $(X \wedge \overline{Y}) \vee (\overline{X} \wedge Y)$.

Index